Understanding LIVING TRUSTS®

How You Can Avoid Probate, Keep Control,
Save Taxes, and Enjoy Peace of Mind

Updated Seventh Edition

By Vickie Schumacher

Published by
Schumacher Publishing, LLC
Costa Mesa, CA

Art Direction: Jasmine Murata Clouser
Additional graphic design assistance from TLC Graphics and Hassaan Mahmood

Published by
Schumacher Publishing, LLC

"Understanding Living Trusts" is a registered trademark of Schumacher Publishing, LLC

First edition published March 1988 as *A Will Is Not The Way—The Living Trust Alternative*
and *Avoid Probate—The Living Trust Alternative*
Second edition published May 1990 as *Understanding Living Trusts*®
Third edition published October 1994 as *Understanding Living Trusts*®
Fourth edition published February 1996 as *Understanding Living Trusts*®
Fifth edition published January 1998, May 1999, February 2000, June 2001, May 2002
and January 2003 as *Understanding Living Trusts*®
Sixth edition published May 2015 as *Understanding Living Trusts*®
Seventh edition published May 2016, July 2017, October 2018 and January 2019 as *Understanding Living Trusts*®

This publication is available for bulk purchase. For information:
Schumacher Publishing, LLC
PO Box 2065, Costa Mesa CA 92628-2065
1-800-827-7941
www.SchumacherPublishing.com

ISBN 978-0-945811-28-2

Publisher's Cataloging-in-Publication
(Provided by Quality Books, Inc.)

Schumacher, Vickie, author.
    Understanding living trusts : how you can avoid probate, keep control,
save taxes, and enjoy peace of mind / by Vickie Schumacher. -- Seventh edition.
    pages cm
    Includes index.
    LCCN 2016903879
    ISBN 978-0-945811-28-2
    1. Living trusts--United States. 2. Estate planning--United States.   I. Title.
KF734.S38 2016   343.7305'3
                        QBI16-600076

Printed in the United States of America

What People Have Been Saying About America's Best Book on Living Trusts...

"No investment I'm aware of can remotely approach the return potential your publication provided."—J. Gaier, California

"I couldn't have done it without your book. Thanks so much for providing a necessary and useful tool."—A. B. Platt, Vermont

"I looked at as many books as I could find on trusts and estate planning and, in my opinion, the Schumacher book is by far the best organized, complete, and easy to understand of all the books on living trusts I've looked at."—H. Scheinaus, New Jersey

"After checking our several books on trusts from the library, I was so pleased with the Schumacher book that I purchased a copy for my daughter who is the successor trustee of our trusts."—V. White, Missouri

"This book presents a thorough, non-technical explanation of why and how to create trusts. *Understanding Living Trusts*® is essential reading."—P. Coty, New York

"Easy to read for someone who doesn't like to read. I finished it in two days. That's rare for me."—R. Ferrell, California

"You saved us money and time, and we could read the book in the privacy of our own home."—M. Applegate, Oregon

"Very clear, easy to understand. It's a constant reference."—J. Dolan, Ohio

"I believe your text, *Understanding Living Trusts,*® is the most down to earth text there is. It is simple, all inclusive, written in logical sequence, and the best information an uninformed client can have when interviewing a trust lawyer."—W. Higgins, Georgia

"I am not a reader, usually, but the way in which you wrote your book spurred me on. I sure am glad somebody wrote something we can all understand."—L. Feager, Colorado

"It is by far the best publication available and I tell everyone to read this one first—it may be the only one you read. Even my lawyer was impressed."—J. Cerquoz, Wyoming

"Clearest and most complete discussion I've ever read on the subject."—W. Cary, Texas

"Excellent presentation—you are to be highly commended for an excellent piece of work which is much needed. Everybody should read it."—C. Bruce, Florida

"Amazingly clear and well organized—a beautiful job well done."—M. Hill, California

INTRODUCTION

Congratulations! You are about to read the book that has changed and enhanced the lives of almost 400,000 people, their families and loved ones.

When the first edition was written, the federal estate tax exemption was $600,000 and avoiding estate taxes was a big motivator for people to plan their estates. Now that the exemption is $11.4 million, not very many people need to plan for estate taxes. As a result, some people think they don't need to do *any* estate planning. But nothing could be further from the truth! As you will learn, there are many more reasons to plan your estate than to save estate taxes.

You may be starting to think about how to transfer your assets to your loved ones. But life is complicated today, and you may have concerns that your parents didn't. For example:

■ With people living longer, you may worry what will happen if you become incapacitated.
■ With second and third marriages more common, you may be concerned about how to provide for your surviving spouse without disinheriting your children and other family members.
■ With the high rates of divorce, bankruptcy, and lawsuits, you may be concerned that your assets could end up in the hands of your children's spouses and/or creditors.
■ You may be concerned that your children will not be responsible with assets you worked all your life to accumulate, especially if they are not responsible with their own money.

A living trust can provide the solutions to all of these concerns and more. As you will see in this book, a living trust fits the needs of today's families far better than any other plan.

This is not a "do-it-yourselfer." Generic online forms, books, and kits cannot address the unique needs of families in different states. We believe you need assistance from an experienced attorney, and we'll help you find one. This book is your personal action plan. Inside, you will learn what a living trust is, how it works, and the steps you'll need to take to set up one; what to consider when deciding how you want your loved ones to inherit from you; how to find the right attorney to prepare your documents; how to organize information your family will need; and step-by-step instructions for your family if you become incapacitated and after you die.

This information is presented as a general overview. We have included some variations in state laws as a reminder that you may find some in your state, but usually these will not affect the overall message. Also, some explanations of previous laws have been kept for those of us who like to know how the laws have changed and, perhaps, question our memory.

Our goal in writing this book is to educate and empower you. What you do with this information is up to you. We know the value of a living trust; it has given us great peace of mind. When properly done, it can do the same for you and your loved ones. But if, after reading this book, you decide not to have a living trust, at least you will be making an informed decision.

Meet the Author, Vickie Schumacher

Vickie Schumacher is nationally known for her ability to explain the benefits of living trusts and estate planning in clear, conversational English. She has a unique perspective on what consumers want, what they understand, and what confuses, frustrates, and motivates them when it comes to estate planning—because she is a consumer, too.

"When I first heard about a living trust," says Vickie, "I thought, like many people, that a trust was for the wealthy and estate planning was for seniors." As she learned more, she became convinced that people of all ages need to know this information. She began to ask questions and then to write about living trusts. A former regional head of communications for a major employee benefits consulting firm, Vickie was already an award-winning writer, nationally recognized for her abilities to communicate "legalese" in accurate, understandable English.

In 1988, she proudly finished the first edition of the book—and was promptly rejected by more than 20 publishers, all of whom didn't think there was an audience for this information. The decision was made to self-publish, and the rest has been nothing short of remarkable. The first edition sold more than 50,000 copies. With subsequent editions, that figure is now approaching 400,000, with the book selling well to both consumers *and* professionals.

The success of *Understanding Living Trusts*® led to Vickie being a frequent guest on radio/ TV talk shows and keynote speaker at standing-room-only seminars. She has received praise in *Modern Maturity* and other publications. She is also the creator of a line of brochures, special reports, presentations, and website content used by thousands of attorneys, banks, and financial professionals nationwide. In 2016, she launched all-new brochures and website content for estate planning professionals. (See page 289 for more information.)

For those who have followed Vickie and her family over the years, here is a brief update. Both sons are grown and out of college. James (JJ) is a Captain in the U.S. Army, a Black Hawk helicopter pilot and a Company Commander. He has served two tours in Afghanistan. Charlie is an Investor Relations Analyst with a firm in Newport Beach, CA and a fitness/nutrition coach. In 2008, Vickie married Tom, a contractor, and gained his grown children: Olivia, a city planner, and Bruce, an architect. Olivia added the first granddaughter in 2014 and the second in 2016.

"I am older now and, hopefully, wiser," she says. "I know firsthand about being a business owner, being divorced and a single parent, caring for aging parents, and blended families—life experiences and concerns that I share with many of my readers. It all adds to my perspective and, I think, makes me a better writer."

CONTRIBUTING EDITORS

Over the years, I have been blessed by a number of professionals who have advised and mentored me. Their willingness to share their knowledge and experience has greatly contributed to the balance and content of this book. I thank them for their patience, as I work to keep things accurate *and* understandable.

Here is the current group of contributing editors who have acted as advisors and reviewers for this edition of *Understanding Living Trusts.*® They, too, have been very generous with their time and knowledge. I have learned from them, and I am grateful for their assistance.

Jonathan A. Mintz is a Partner in the national law firm of Evergreen Legacy Planning, LLP, with offices in Newport Beach, California, and Evergreen, Colorado. Jonathan helps both U.S. and non-U.S. families and businesses achieve privacy, protection, and income and estate tax minimization, often for generations.

A former Adjunct Faculty at Chapman University Fowler School of Law (a "Top School" according to the 2018 U.S. News and World Report rankings), Jonathan taught Estate Planning for law and masters in taxation students. He is also past Chair of the Orange County Branch of the Society of Trusts and Estates Practitioners (STEP), where he oversaw the branch's operations, including an Annual Institute in collaboration with UCLA School of Law in Newport Beach.

Previously, Jonathan was a partner in the Orange County firm of Matsen Voorhees Mintz LLP, and before that he served as Chief Operating Officer for WealthCounsel, LLC where he oversaw operations of the nation's premier support organization for thousands of estate and business planning attorneys nationwide. He was also instrumental in the creation of The Advisors Forum, a national interdisciplinary membership organization that helps all disciplines of wealth planning professionals work together more effectively for the benefit of their clients.

Jonathan has served on the editorial board for several treatises, and he has either authored or co-authored articles appearing in the estate planning industry's most prestigious publications, including Estate Planning Journal, the AICPA's The Tax Adviser, and the Journal of Financial Service Professionals, among others. In his 25+ years of practice, Jonathan has taught thousands of professionals, including lawyers, CPAs, financial advisers and fiduciaries, and he is a sought-after national speaker on all areas of sophisticated estate planning.

His family includes his wife, Valerie Peterson (a nationally known elder law and veteran's benefits attorney), and two wonderful daughters. He can be reached at JAM@EvergreenLegacyPlanning.com.

Valerie Peterson is the CEO of ElderCounsel, LLC, a national membership organization that serves elder law, veterans pension and special needs planning attorneys. Prior to joining ElderCounsel, Valerie was a practicing elder law attorney in Ft. Lauderdale and Miami, Florida as the owner of Peterson Law Office, P.A.

She attended Washburn University School of Law in Topeka, Kansas where she received the Order of Barristers award for excellence in courtroom advocacy. A litigator for several years after law school, Valerie decided to focus her practice on elder law after she experienced firsthand the challenges of caring for an elderly loved one.

In her role as CEO, Valerie also sets the curriculum for ElderCounsel's education conferences and serves as instructor in several courses, including the Elder Law Immersion and Practice Building Camp and the VA Pension Planning Immersion Camp. Valerie has also taught for the National Association of Elder Law Attorneys (NAELA), the Academy of Veterans Pension Planners (AVAPP), and for various state bar associations on topics pertaining to Elder Law, Special Needs Planning and Veterans Benefits. As an adjunct professor for Stetson University Law School, Valerie teaches the Veterans Benefits course to Elder Law LL.M. students.

Valerie resides in Evergreen, CO with her husband, Jonathan Mintz.

Dennis Brislawn is a practicing attorney and shareholder in Oseran Hahn, P.S., a multi-attorney firm located in Bellevue, Washington. He is a nationally-recognized speaker, author, and legal systems architect and principal member of the WealthCounsel Companies, comprised of WealthCounsel, LLC, The Advisor's Forum, LLC, and ElderCounsel, LLC. He is the recipient of the Martindale Hubbell AV Peer Review Rating ranking him top in his profession for ethical standards and professional excellence, and he is listed in the Bar Register of Preeminent Lawyers. Seattle Magazine consistently ranked Dennis as a "5 Star Wealth Manager," a list consisting largely of financial professionals and only a few attorneys.

Dennis is admitted to practice in Washington, Oregon, and Alaska, before the Federal Bar and the IRS. His practice is interdisciplinary and counseling-oriented, offering a full range of planning services and mid- to high-end strategies that accomplish client goals. Client representations include estate and gift tax planning, estate and gift tax audits, asset protection, business planning and succession, advanced estate and charitable planning. He regularly co-counsels cases with other attorneys nationwide.

Among the numerous systems Dennis has co-authored or authored are the RLT, Limited Partnership, Limited Liability Company, and SettlementCounsel™ systems, with the latest being GunDocx® all published by WealthCounsel, LLC. He created the GoldDATA® contact management system and co-authored the WealthData™ System distributed by Premier Software. He is the author of a number of print articles and electronic publications through social media.

Dennis married Susan in 1988 and they live in Woodinville. They met while both were serving as active duty US Army officers. Dennis is an Airborne Ranger and French Army Commando among other things as a result of his active duty service.

Today, Dennis is active as a Board member for the Washington State Search & Rescue Advisory Council and in units of the King County Search & Rescue Association as an Operations Leader. His volunteer time often finds him on mountainsides, in the middle of the night, working with his teammates to get somebody who is lost, hurt or both to get home safe.

 **Dennis M. Axman**, CLU, ChFC, AEP, CFP.® A native Kentuckian, Denny attended Bellarmine College in Louisville. He joined The Prudential Insurance Company of America as a representative in Louisville in 1970, and in 1973 he was promoted to management. In 1994, he elected to return to personal production and opened his financial planning practice in Jacksonville, FL. Denny retired from Prudential in 2006 and became an Associate Producer/Financial Planner with Laino & Associates, also in Jacksonville. In 2007, Denny became a Life Product Wholesaler for Prudential. In 2009, Denny re-retired from Prudential and joined Pinnacle Insurance and Financial Services as Director of Advanced Marketing & Vice President of Sales. In 2011, Denny became an Independent Insurance Advisor for Pinnacle. He also co-founded Advanced Market Resources, LLC (AMR) where he was a managing partner. In December 2016, he resigned from Pinnacle, closed AMR and joined Allstate Life and Retirement Advanced Solutions Team.

Throughout his career, Denny has earned sixteen Prudential Presidents' Citations, three Circle of Life Awards, one Court of the Table, and is a Qualifying & Life member with fifteen years of membership in MDRT. Long active in local, state and national Association of Life Underwriters activities, Denny is a member of the Association for Advanced Life Underwriting and has been a member of the Financial Planning Association since 1983. In 1998, he qualified for and was accepted into the Prudential Leaders Council. He has been a member of the Northeast Florida Estate Planning Council for the past 16 years. Denny is also a member of the Jacksonville Society of Financial Service Professionals as well as the Northeast Florida Planned Giving Council. From 2006 to 2008, Denny provided CE workshops for the American College Alumni Association throughout the United States. In November of 2011, Denny was reappointed as an adjunct professor with The American College for the CLU, ChFC and CFP® programs, from which he resigned in December, 2016. He's also held many positions volunteering for the Million Dollar Round Table.

Denny and his wife, Mary Helen, are the parents of three daughters and a son. They have six granddaughters, of which two are twins, and four grandsons. They make their home in Orange Park, Florida.

Michael Ettinger was born and raised in Montreal, Canada, where he graduated from McGill Law School with honors in 1977. In 1978, Mr. Ettinger obtained his Master of Laws degree from The London School of Economics in London, England. Admitted to the New York Bar in 1980, Mr. Ettinger practiced general law in Manhattan and Scarsdale, New York until 1991, when he founded Ettinger Law Firm, devoted exclusively to Elder Law Estate Planning. Today, the firm maintains fourteen New York locations: Albany, Bohemia, Brooklyn, Fishkill, Lake Success, Manhattan, Melville, Middletown, Nyack, Rhinebeck, Saratoga, Southampton, Staten Island and White Plains. Mr. Ettinger was a Founding Member of The American Academy of Estate Planning Attorneys, is Past President of The American Association of Trust, Estate and Elder Law Attorneys, and has been a member of The National Academy of Elder Law Attorneys since 1992. Mr. Ettinger is a contributor to the New York Bar Journal, has published over fifty articles on Elder Law Estate Planning and is the author of "Elder Law Estate Planning" on Amazon.com and Kindle.

Richard Gottlieb and his law firm, Gottlieb & Gottlieb, P.A., have been providing estate planning services for clients throughout central Florida for over 30 years. Holding a B.S. degree from the UCLA School of Public Health, and a J.D. degree from the University of Akron School of Law, he is admitted to practice in Florida and Ohio, before the U.S. Supreme Court, Federal Courts of Appeal for the 6th and 11th Circuits, as well as the Federal District Courts for the Middle District of Florida and the Northern District of Ohio. He is a member of the Florida Bar Association (Real Property, Trust and Probate, Health Law and Elder Law Sections) and the Ohio Bar Association (Probate and Trust Law Section).

Sharon Sides, founder of SidesCPA in West Hills, CA, has been providing strategic financial reporting, business development, operating, tax, and systems support and guidance to US based clients for over thirty years. Passionate about ensuring clients have the information they need to respond to critical business decisions timely and accurately, she and her team provide professional, personalized services to clients across a broad spectrum of industries including digital media, publishing, health care, insurance and manufacturing.

ACKNOWLEDGEMENTS AND THANKS

"Now all glory to God, who is able, through his mighty power at work within us, to accomplish infinitely more than we might ask or think." (Ephesians 3:20, NLT)

Friends and Family

Over the years, my friends and family have learned that this book is always a work in progress. Thank you for your long-suffering with me! Special thanks to my husband Tom, who encourages and supports me; my mom, who thinks I can do anything; my sister Bobbi; my son Charlie, who is my consultant, fitness coach and overall encourager; my son JJ, whose perspective and common sense make me laugh and keep me grounded; and my friends from Community Bible Study.

Other Contributors

Contributions to previous editions by the following individuals are likely still found in these pages. Some have become dear friends; some I have not kept in touch with; and some have passed on. All have made their contributions to this book a part of their legacy.

Roy Adams, Debra Ashton, Louis Austin, Millie Basden, Bill Bedle, Brad Bolinger, Elton Brooks, Shela Camenisch, Natalie Choate, Ted Cranston, Mike Deege, Dick Drummond, Jack Dyer, Donna Fincher, Charles "Skip" Fox IV, Michael Fredlender, Doug Freeman, Adrienne George, Carol Gonnella, Jerry Gottlieb, Ronald Greening, John Hartmann, Carter Howard, Howard Lang, Jim Leese, Marr Leisure, Kenneth Leventhal, Gary McFatridge, Marshal Oldman, Wycliffe "Wyck" Pattishall, Susan Porter, Allen Reid, Steven Rodeman, Jim Schreier, Jim Schumacher, Ed Setzler, Cecil Smith, Dirk Tolle, Steven Trytten, Anita Medina Tyson, Patrick Vaughan, Roy Weitz, Steven Wellner, Michael Whitty, Jerome Wolf

Professional Clients

Thank you for your business, support, loyalty and encouragement over these many years.

Readers

We love that many of you take the time to call, write and visit our website www.Schumacher-Publishing.com/Consumers. While we cannot give you legal advice or answer you individually, please know that your comments, suggestions and questions are carefully considered for future editions. Over the years, our readers have helped make each new edition better than the last!

You can help us reach more families by writing a review on Amazon.com. (See the last page in this book.)

TABLE OF CONTENTS

GOOD PLANS CAN GO WRONG

To avoid probate after she died, Edith, an elderly widow, decided to give her home to her daughter Susan. They had always gotten along very well, and Susan assured her mother she would be able to live in the house for the rest of her life. She even stated so in her will, just in case anything happened to her first. Unfortunately, Susan died in a car accident. Not long after, Edith was shocked when she received an eviction notice. As it turned out, Susan had made her husband joint owner of the house with her, and when Susan died he became sole owner. He had never cared about Edith and decided to sell. Susan's will didn't make any difference, because her share had transferred to her husband immediately upon her death.

Over the years, John and his wife Eleanor had planned carefully, saved, and invested wisely for their retirement. They made sure their wills, which left everything to each other, were always up to date. They even had trusts in their wills for extra protection. Unfortunately, John developed Alzheimer's Disease. As his condition worsened, Eleanor needed to sell some of their investments. But John was no longer able to conduct business and Eleanor soon learned she couldn't sign for him. Only a *court appointee* could sign for him. It was hard enough dealing with John's situation, but now Eleanor also had to deal with the court. She didn't know the court would *stay* involved to "protect" John's share of the proceeds. She had to keep detailed records of everything. The court insisted upon approving all expenses *and* the sale of their jointly owned assets. When John died several years later, Eleanor found herself back in court again, this time to probate his will.

Claire was lonely after Fred, her husband of 40 years, died. To fill her time, she started taking ballroom dancing lessons. Her instructor, a much younger "gentleman," was very quick to provide her with the companionship she was missing. Claire, with a new sense of self-esteem, soon fell head over heels in love. Fred and Claire's children were shocked when their mother announced she had married her instructor. But the real shock came seven months later when Claire died and the children learned their mother had placed everything in joint ownership with her new husband. As the new sole owner, he decided to sell everything and leave town. Because their mother had made her new husband joint owner, the children had been completely disinherited, and everything Fred and Claire had built over the years for their children was gone.

When George and Betty moved to Florida, they gave their home in New York to their daughter Anne, a divorced mother of three. Anne later remarried and, as a wedding present to her new husband, she changed the title on the house from her name to both their names, as husband and wife. Not long after, Anne suddenly became ill and died. Her husband, now the sole owner, promptly booted the children (all teenagers) out of the house. George and Betty will undoubtedly have many sleepless nights—and regrets—over this situation.

Louise had one child, a grown son named David. To make things easier for him when she died, Louise added his name on the title of her house. David was very good to his mother, but he was irresponsible when it came to money. Eventually, he got so far behind in payments to his creditors that they sued him. Louise was shocked when she was forced to sell her home so his debts could be paid.

When Edward and Beth married, they both had children and assets from previous marriages. They had new wills prepared, with each leaving their separate assets to their own children. When Edward died ten years later, Beth's attorney advised her that, as a surviving spouse in that state, she was entitled to a percentage of all of Edward's assets—including the 300-acre farm that had been in his family for generations. Although she knew Edward had wanted the farm to go only to his children, she felt that she and her children had a right to part of it. She decided to claim her share, prompting a bitter battle within the family. Eventually Beth won. But the farm ended up being sold to pay the expenses, and the closeness the family had developed during Edward's lifetime had been destroyed.

Mary was a widow with no children or immediate family. In her will, she left everything in equal shares to three institutions which had been a big part of her life: her husband's university for scholarships in his memory; her neighborhood church; and a children's hospital where their only child had been treated for a terminal illness many years earlier.

When Mary died, her will had to be probated before her assets could be given to the institutions. As required by law, a notice of her death was published in the newspaper and a list of her assets was made public. Some distant relatives Mary barely knew saw the notice in the paper, hired an attorney and contested the will. The institutions had to hire attorneys to try and uphold Mary's will, and Mary's estate also had to be represented by an attorney. A nasty and expensive legal battle began. Finally, more than four years later, the institutions agreed to give Mary's relatives half of her estate just to end the fight. This was obviously not what Mary had wanted.

Betty, recently divorced, had a three-year-old daughter named Sarah. She had heard she should have a will, especially because she had a child, so when she saw an advertisement for a will kit, she ordered one through the mail. In her will, she left everything directly to Sarah. She didn't have that much in assets, so she increased her life insurance and listed Sarah as the beneficiary. She named her sister Linda as Sarah's guardian, thinking Linda would be able to use the insurance money to raise Sarah if something happened to her.

A few years later, Betty died unexpectedly and her will went through probate. Because Sarah was a minor, the court had to establish a guardianship for her. The court did allow Linda to be Sarah's guardian, but the court kept control of the inheritance—everything Betty left Sarah in her will *and* the money from the insurance company. When Sarah turned 18, the legal age in that state, the court guardianship, by law, ended. And Sarah received her entire inheritance in one lump sum, which she quickly spent in just one year of expensive living.

Dorothy, a widow, put all of her property into joint ownership with her married son. She did this thinking that, when she died, her property would automatically go to her son without the need for probate. Several years later, her son and his wife separated, and Dorothy decided to sell her house so she could move in with her son. But she soon discovered she could not sell it without her *daughter-in-law's* signature on the deed.

The daughter-in-law was still legally married to her son and was entitled by law to a "marital interest" in the property. The title company would not insure clear title to the buyer without the daughter-in-law's signature because it wasn't clear what her interest would be. She refused to sign unless she got part of the money when the house was sold. Dorothy was stuck. She didn't know that joint ownership with a married person can include *that person's spouse*. Because Dorothy had placed her house in joint ownership, she lost control of her own home.

On the advice of a neighbor, Frank and Elizabeth, an elderly couple, put everything they owned, including their home and stocks, in their adult daughter's name. They believed this would avoid probate and that all their assets would pass directly to their daughter, their only child, when they were both gone. A year later, Frank died of a heart attack. Several months after that, their daughter died in a car accident.

Elizabeth *never* thought she would survive both her husband and daughter. To add to her distress, Elizabeth now owned nothing in her own name. Everything was in her daughter's name. She was forced to probate her daughter's estate to get back her own property. During this long process she had to rely on the court to grant her living expenses. Sometimes the court would approve them, sometimes not. And during a declining stock market, she helplessly watched the value of her stocks fall to only a fraction of their previous value because the court could not react in time for them to be sold quickly. Elizabeth lost her financial independence plus a substantial portion of her assets to probate while simply trying to get back what was hers in the first place.

John and Ellen had each been married before and had young children from their first marriages. When they married, they considered it a fresh start and one family. They put all of their assets in both their names (joint ownership), with the intention that when they died, all the children would receive an equal share. They didn't have wills because they thought joint ownership would serve the same purpose.

When John died, everything went to Ellen and she continued to raise and care for all the children. When Ellen died many years later, her assets went through probate. But because she did not have a will, under the probate laws of that state Ellen's property could only be distributed to *her surviving blood children*. Because John's children had never been legally adopted by Ellen, they received nothing. Even though John and Ellen thought of all the children as being their own, the probate laws did not. By relying on joint ownership, they unintentionally disinherited John's children.

Doris and Bob owned a family-style restaurant. They had been moderately successful for years and put everything they made back into the business. When Bob died, one of their competitors went to the probate court and looked up his file. In it he found much of Bob and Doris' financial information, a competitor's dream. He also saw in the file that Doris had requested a living allowance from the court, indicating she was short on cash. He offered to buy Doris out—at 50% of what he knew the restaurant was worth. To his amazement, she accepted, without any negotiation. This competitor had inside information, courtesy of the probate court.

Marie, an elderly widow, had a will which left everything in equal shares to her five grown children. When she learned she had cancer, she put everything she owned into joint ownership with her oldest son, thinking this would avoid probate and make things easier for her family when she died. She discussed it with her son and was sure that he would carry out her wishes and divide everything equally among the five children.

When she died, ownership did immediately go to her son. But he died suddenly in a construction accident a few weeks later, *before* the property could be distributed. His wife, only recently married to Marie's son, claimed everything as his surviving spouse, and she decided to keep it all herself! Marie's will (which, remember, left everything in equal shares to her children) could do nothing, because as soon as she died *she no longer owned anything*. Marie's joint ownership plan did avoid probate, but it also disinherited her children!

Stella, recently divorced, added her 12-year-old son as joint owner on the deed to her house, thinking it would automatically become his if something should happen to her. A year later, she needed to sell the house. But she couldn't, because her 13-year-old son (her joint owner) could not legally sign the papers. She had to put her own son in a court guardianship, and the court insisted on approving the sale. By that time, the buyers were long gone—but

A living trust would have prevented these situations

the court was still there. Eventually she was able to find another buyer and this time the sale went through. But the court kept control over her son's share of the proceeds until he turned 18, at which time he promptly spent it all on a sports car, a motorcycle and good times. In the meantime, Stella couldn't afford to buy another house with just her share of the proceeds. She found out the hard way that joint ownership with a minor does not work.

Olivia wanted to make sure her daughter Jill and her new granddaughter would be provided for if something happened to her, so she purchased a new insurance policy and named her daughter Jill as the beneficiary. Not long after, Olivia became ill and died. The insurance proceeds were paid directly to Jill, who deposited the check into her joint checking account. A few days later, Jill's husband withdrew all the money and left town, leaving Jill and her baby with nothing.

....

A living trust would have prevented these good plans from going wrong.

Part One –

WHY GOOD PLANS CAN GO WRONG

Everyone wants to do the right thing for themselves and their families. But, as you've just seen, good intentions often have tragic results. If people could only know what *could* happen, they probably would do things differently.

What we're talking about is *estate planning*. Everyone has an estate. During your lifetime, you accumulate assets and things: a home, car, investments, jewelry, furniture, maybe a business. Some of it is valuable, some of it is not, but most of it means something to you. You can't take it with you when you die so there has to be some way of distributing it to those who are still living. When you die, all of these things you own are called your estate. And how you get them to the people you want to have them is your estate plan.

Estate planning is not just for the wealthy or for old people, whatever those are. It's something we *all* need to do regardless of age, marital status or wealth if we want to keep control of our assets when something happens to us. It's important to plan now, while we can, because with estate planning no one gets a second chance.

In this section, we'll look at five basic ways most people "plan" their estates. You're probably already using at least one of these now, even if you think you haven't done any estate planning. We'll explain how you can easily lose control of your assets if you become incapacitated and after you die when you use one of these plans. Then, in Part Two, we'll explain how one plan—the revocable living trust—gives you far more control than the others.

And we'll explain it all in clear, conversational English *so you can understand it*. Because we want *your* good intentions to have a happy ending.

1 LOSING CONTROL WITH A WILL

A will is probably what first comes to mind when you think about how to plan your estate and transfer your assets to your loved ones. After all, we've been told for years that we should have a will.

In a will, of course, you name whom you want to receive your assets when you die and whom you want to handle your final affairs for you. This person is called an executor (executrix, if a female) or administrator.

But contrary to what you've probably heard and been led to believe, a will may not be the best plan for you and your family. That's because a will:

■ Does not avoid probate when you die;
■ Does not prevent the court from taking control of your assets if you become physically or mentally incapacitated; and
■ Probably does not give you the control you think it does if you have minor children or grandchildren.

Let's see how much control you really do have with a will in each of these situations.

A Will Does Not Avoid Probate When You Die

A will is simply an expression of your wishes—what you want to happen to your assets after you die. All wills must go through some kind of probate court process before they can go into effect. How complicated that process will be will depend on the laws in your state.

You've probably heard of probate, read about it or perhaps even experienced it when a relative died. Let's take a brief look at it now.

What Is Probate?
Probate is the legal process through which the court makes sure that, after you die, your will is legally valid, your debts are paid, and your assets are distributed according to the instructions in your will.

Probate has existed in one form or another for hundreds of years. It was created with the best of intentions to protect your creditors, your assets, and your family by providing an orderly method of paying bills and transferring ownership of your assets after you die—all under direct supervision of the court system.

Why Do We Have To Go Through Probate?

You may be wondering why you can't just appoint someone to pay your bills and distribute your assets after you die *without* involving the probate court. (If you have a living trust, you *can*, as we'll explain in Part Two.)

Well, very simply, if your name is on the title of an asset and you die, probate is the *only legal way* to take your name off the title of an asset and put the new owner's name on.

In most states, a will by itself is not enough authority to retitle assets or release account balances; a court order is required to do this. So, after you die, your family will not be able to change titles on assets that are titled in your name without a court order—and that can only be issued by the probate court.

Also, your will must be validated as being authentic before ownership of your assets can be transferred to your heirs—and only the probate court can do this.

What Assets Go Through Probate?

Not everything you own will automatically go through probate. For example, jointly owned assets that transfer to the surviving owner generally do not go through probate. Nor do assets that have a valid beneficiary designation, like an insurance policy. But there can be some significant problems with both, causing you to lose control of your assets even while you are living. You'll want to finish reading this section if you currently rely on these.

Assets in a trust also avoid probate, as we'll explain in Part Two. However, if you have a trust *in your will* (called a testamentary trust), it does *not* avoid probate. The will has to go through probate *before* the trust can go into effect.

What Happens In Probate?

Probate doesn't happen automatically. Someone, usually a relative or the executor you name in your will, must petition the court for probate proceedings to begin—for example, when checks need to be written or when an asset needs to be sold or transferred to a new owner.

A will does not avoid probate

Probate procedures will vary slightly from state to state, and even from court to court. A traditional "formal" probate will usually include the following general process.

When probate proceedings begin, the probate court takes control of your estate, supervising payment of your debts and distribution of your assets. In most states, the court will require that a notice of your death appear in local newspapers, giving your creditors—and anyone else who feels he/she has a right to part of your estate—a certain length of time (several weeks or months) to present their claims.

At the first hearing, the judge will make sure your will is valid—that it is the correct one (if you had more than one will), that you were competent when you signed it, and that it is properly signed and witnessed. Otherwise, the judge will declare that you died without a will. (See "Losing Control by Doing Nothing" later in this section.) The judge will then officially appoint your executor and open a file on your estate.

You may have named an attorney in your will. If not, your family or executor can usually choose one. Although having an attorney is not always a legal requirement, the paperwork can be complicated. Also, most judges prefer to deal with someone who is already familiar with the process.

Your executor will compile an inventory of your assets, with formal appraisals of valuable assets, and pay your final bills. These are then submitted to the court for approval. Your executor also applies for and collects any death benefits to which your estate is entitled, and has your final tax returns prepared.

A second notice is usually given for a final hearing to settle your estate. At this hearing, the judge will review the paperwork and order your debts paid (including all probate expenses). If there is not enough cash in your estate to pay your expenses, the judge may order some of your assets sold. Your remaining assets will then be distributed according to the terms in your will.

If there are any disputes, the judge will make the final decisions, holding additional hearings if necessary. Finally, your executor will be released from his/her duties and your file will be closed.

Probate

Without a living trust, assets titled in just your name must go through a probate process, and all expenses must be paid, before the assets can be fully distributed to your heirs.

Probate can be expensive

■ Exception—Small Estates

Most states allow very small estates to bypass probate. But few qualify because the limits are typically very low—in some states, as low as $15,000 in assets that are subject to probate.

■ Informal Probate

In an attempt to simplify the probate process, many states now allow informal probate proceedings (also called independent administration). A few states also have special processes for surviving spouses. Generally, these require fewer court appearances and accounting procedures.

However, these are still probate proceedings. Some years ago, The American Association for Retired Persons (AARP) completed a survey of probate files in several states. In its findings, entitled *A Report on Probate*, AARP concluded that informal probate frequently does not save the time and money it was intended to save—because the processes and forms are often still too complicated for most people to handle without substantial attorney involvement.

So, What's Wrong With Probate?

■ It can be expensive.

The same survey by AARP found that probate is big business. AARP estimated that probate costs could top $2 billion a year—$1.5 billion for attorneys and hundreds of millions more for executors, bonding companies, appraisers, and probate courts. (It's very possible those amounts have increased since this survey was taken.)

The costs to probate your estate must be paid before your assets can be fully distributed to your heirs. These costs vary widely from state to state, but usually are estimated at 3-8% of an estate's gross value.

Some states actually do calculate probate fees on the total gross value of an estate, *before* debts are paid. So, for example, if your home is valued at $300,000 when you die, probate fees would be calculated on the full $300,000, even if the mortgage is $250,000.

Some states allow probate fees on the entire value of the estate, including assets (like life insurance) that do not even go through probate!

If someone tells you probate is not expensive where you live, ask for a written estimate of what it would cost to probate your estate if you died today and, if you are married, what it would cost if your spouse died tomorrow. Then you can decide if it's expensive or not.

Who gets most of this money?

The biggest expenses are legal and executor fees. A family member who serves as executor may waive the fee (although AARP estimated in its survey that fully one-third of executors *do* take a fee). Also, in many states, if the attorney who probates your estate is also named as your executor, the attorney is entitled to *both* fees.

Some states have regulated (statutory) fee schedules for attorneys and executors so you can actually look on a chart to determine what it should cost to probate an estate. Some states use hourly fees—$300 to $400 per hour is not an unusual attorney rate. Quite often the executor will be paid at the same rate as the attorney. Other states use what is called a "reasonable" fee system. The problem with "reasonable" fees is there is no way for you to know what the cost will be until the entire process has been completed.

The following chart shows fees in California, Florida and New York for the attorney and executor. (Probate fees in your state may be higher or lower.)

Examples of Probate Fees

Estate Value	Combined Fees For Attorney and Executor*		
	California	*Florida*	*New York*
$100,000	$8,000	$6,000	$10,000
$200,000	$14,000	$12,000	$18,000
$500,000	$26,000	$30,000	$38,000
$1,000,000	$46,000	$60,000	$68,000
$2,000,000	$66,000	$110,000	$118,000
$5,000,000	$126,000	$250,000	$268,000

Statutory fees for California and Florida. New York fees based on attorney's "reasonable" fees being equal to statutory executor fees. Filing, appraisal, and publication fees, bonds and legal fees for "extraordinary" services (will contest, tax advice, tax returns, and real estate transactions, for example) are in addition.

Probate takes time and is a public process

Regardless how fees are initially calculated, a judge usually can and often will allow higher fees, depending on the time and/or circumstances involved. Initial fees often do not include legal fees for real estate transactions, completing tax returns, or if someone contests the will; these are often considered "extraordinary" fees.

Generally speaking, the more time the attorney and executor have to spend probating an estate, the more it will cost.

Why should I care about probate fees in other states?
If you own assets (especially real estate, like a vacation home) in other states, your family will probably face *multiple* probates, each one according to the probate laws and costs of that state. They will also probably need to hire an attorney in each state.

But I don't own that much. Why should I be concerned about probate?
Generally, probate costs take a larger percentage from smaller estates (which can least afford it) than from larger ones.

■ Probate takes time.
It usually takes nine months to two years to complete the process. During part of this time, assets are usually frozen so an accurate inventory can be taken, and nothing can be distributed or sold without the court's and/or executor's approval. If your family needs money to live on, they must request a living allowance, which may or may not be approved. Also, assets could drop in value if the court and/or executor cannot react quickly enough to sell them (for example, if your family wanted to sell stock in a declining market).

Why does it take so long? Keep in mind that probate moves on the court's schedule and the attorney's schedule—not your family's schedule. In most cases, you can't just call the judge and say, "We would like to probate Grandpa's will on Monday." It can take weeks to get a hearing. And, remember, you are not the only client the attorney has. So your family has very little say in how quickly things can happen.

■ Your family has no privacy.
Probate is a public process. Any "interested party" can find out details about your estate, including who the heirs are, what they will receive, their addresses and so on.

It's surprising how easy it is in some states to have access to probate files of *anyone*. Usually all you need to know is the name of the person and the year in which he or she died.

During the writing of an earlier edition of this book, Natalie Wood passed away. As part of our research, we asked to see her file. All the details of her almost $6 million estate were there—her interest in the television series *Charlie's Angels* (valued at $2.3 million); royalties from movies; investments in real estate, oil and gas leases; artwork; a yacht; and at least nine separate bank accounts. Even her half of an $83.31 refund from the telephone company was included in her assets. Also in the file was exactly how much she left her mother, sisters, daughters, and husband, along with their addresses at the time of her death.

Details about Jacqueline Kennedy Onassis's will were published in *The New York Times*, *Money* magazine, *Fortune* magazine, and others. On a trip to New York, we paid a visit to the Surrogate Court and very easily obtained a copy of her probate file. It included her will and John F. Kennedy's will, her death certificate, a list of specific items she gave to certain people, and more. Why are we all able to know such private information about someone who, during her lifetime, kept her personal and financial affairs so carefully guarded? Because of probate, her will is part of the public records—and available for *anyone* to see.

Now, you may not be as wealthy or famous as Natalie Wood or Jackie Onassis. But probate files can make for some pretty interesting reading for the curious/nosy. Do *you* want people you know, or even total strangers, to be able to find out what you owned and to whom you left it?

Some people think, "I won't be around then anyway, so why should I care?" Maybe you don't care about yourself, but think about the ones you leave behind.

It might surprise you to know that there are people who go through probate files and compile lists of new widows/widowers and beneficiaries. These lists are then sold as leads to people who sell investments or want to manage the new inheritances. Some are legitimate, but many are outright scams—unscrupulous solicitors who prey upon bereaved survivors, especially spouses, who are at a particularly vulnerable time in their lives. Many of these surviving spouses

The probate process, not your family, has control

have never had to handle finances before and are not only emotionally upset about the loss of their partners, but are understandably terrified about being alone and on their own. If your estate goes through probate, some of these solicitors may call on your family.

If you are a business owner, the lack of privacy can be devastating to your business. Competitors can get valuable inside information about your financial records and personal family affairs, courtesy of the probate system.

Also, you may have intentionally left one or more heirs out of your will. But the probate process invites them to contest, and *the court*—not you or your family—will decide what, if anything, they will get.

■ You and your family lose control.

The probate process—not you or your family—has ultimate control over how your will is interpreted, how much probate will cost, how long it will take and what information is made public. Families are used to handling their affairs privately and independently. Suddenly losing that control to a legal process, and having to pay for it, can be *very* frustrating.

SUMMARY

Probate is a slow, cumbersome, and public process. It is a product of the horse and carriage days, when it took months to locate and notify relatives (and creditors) of a death in the family. Back then it didn't matter that probate took a long time or was so public. But today it does.

Things move much more quickly today in this age of instant communications. We can contact friends and relatives anywhere in the world in just seconds. Financial decisions must often be made within minutes. And with so much of our financial information in giant databases in the cloud, we often find ourselves struggling to hold onto whatever privacy we have left.

Quite simply, the world in which we live has changed faster than probate. Many people today are more sophisticated and knowledgeable, and they value their privacy. Many are quite capable of handling the responsibilities when a family member dies—perhaps still with professional assistance, but only *as they need it*, not as the court *dictates*.

A properly prepared revocable living trust lets your family—instead of the court—control the process of settling your estate.

Okay, now you know how you can lose control with a will after you die because a will does not avoid probate. Now, let's look at how you can lose control when you have a will—*while you are still living.*

A Will Does Not Prevent Court Control At Incapacity

Many people are surprised to learn that having a will does not prevent the court from taking control of their assets if they become incapacitated. They don't realize that a will only goes into effect *after* you die. A will *cannot* go into effect if you become incapacitated—*because you are still alive.*

Becoming incapacitated and losing control of their financial affairs is a valid concern of millions of older Americans and those who will care for them. With advancements in health care, people are living longer. But this also means that more of us will reach the point where we can no longer take care of ourselves.

Of course, incapacity doesn't just happen to older people. Without warning, any of us at any age could be critically injured in an accident or stricken with a devastating illness.

However, few people plan for this possibility—or they mistakenly think a will is all they need. As a result, many people end up under control of the court *before* they die, and their families must find a way to cope with it.

Why Would The Court Take Control Of Assets At Incapacity?

Think about this for a few moments. If you can't handle your affairs because of mental or physical incapacity (for example, if you have a stroke or a heart attack, develop Alzheimer's Disease, or are injured in an accident), who will conduct business for you?

Sooner or later, your signature will probably be required for something—to withdraw savings, sell or refinance assets to pay your expenses, etc. Of course, you may still be able to physically sign your name but, in the opinion of others, may be unable to make sound decisions.

Your will can't help if you become incapacitated

The person you have named as executor in your will cannot step in and take care of your affairs because your will can't go into effect. And your family or friends can't just take over and sign your name for you. Someone (a relative or friend) will have to petition *the court* to appoint someone to act for you.

What Happens When The Court Gets Involved?

Here again, procedures will vary from court to court, but most will be similar to this explanation. A public hearing will be held to determine your ability to handle your affairs. This is often called a competency hearing. If the court agrees that you need someone to act on your behalf, finding you incompetent, you may lose many of your rights as a citizen—and you and your family will lose control. That's because once the court gets involved, it usually stays involved—to "protect" your interests—until you recover or die.

In some states, this court-controlled process is called a conservatorship. In others, it's called a guardianship. Some people refer to it as a "living probate" because it's similar to probate at death but you're still alive.

The original intent was, of course, honorable. To prevent someone from taking control of your assets and squandering them, the court would step in and take control, make financial decisions for you and look after your welfare.

But there are many things people do not like about this process. It can be *embarrassing* because records and proceedings are open to the public. It can be *expensive* because of court costs, examinations and testimony by qualified physician(s), attorney fees, auditor fees, and bonds. It can be *time consuming* because the person the court appoints to act for you must keep detailed records and submit all expenses to the court for approval.

Also, most people prefer that a family member or friend take care of them. But if the court takes control, the court—not you—will decide who will act for you. The court could appoint someone you would want, like your spouse. But it could also appoint a relative you dislike or one who has only selfish motives, or even a professional guardian or conservator who is a stranger to you. If more than one person wants this position, there could be an expensive court battle, and guess who would pay all the costs? *You* would.

You may remember what happened to Groucho Marx not too many years ago. Toward the end of his life, the court found him incompetent. The woman who lived with him battled members of his family for control over Groucho and his money. Everyone had attorneys, of course, and they were *all* paid with Groucho's money. The hearings were lengthy, expensive, very public, and probably taxing on Groucho who was wheeled in and out of court. (He died soon after the hearings ended.) Like many people, Groucho had a will—but he didn't plan for incapacity.

Sometimes, the court may not have the resources to properly monitor the financial records. In these situations, the assets can (and often do) simply disappear without a trace, with no record of how the money was spent.

If you recover, you must prove to the court that you are now competent and can handle your own affairs, which may be difficult since the court has already found you *in*competent. Finally, this process does not replace probate at death; after you die, your family will still have to go through probate to have your will enforced.

Wouldn't A Power Of Attorney Prevent Court Control Of Assets At Incapacity?

Maybe—but then, maybe not. A power of attorney is a legal document that lets you give someone else authority to conduct business for you. However, most general powers of attorney become invalid at incapacity. So professionals often recommend using a *durable* power of attorney, which does remain valid through incapacity. But even a durable power of attorney may not work when it's needed.

That's because some financial institutions will not accept *any* power of attorney. Others will only accept one if it is on *their* form *and* they know this is what you want. The reason is they have no way of knowing if you have changed your mind, and they don't want to be held liable for giving your assets to someone you may not want to have them. This can be good protection, but it can also be a big problem if you are depending on a durable power of attorney to work for you.

If the durable power of attorney does work, it may work *too well*. In many states, giving someone power of attorney is like giving that person a blank

The court, not the guardian, controls your child's inheritance

check to do whatever he/she wants with your assets. It is possible that you could recover and find you own nothing in your own name.

A durable power of attorney has benefits when used under proper circumstances, but relying on one to prevent the court from taking control of assets at incapacity is risky at best.

If you have a revocable living trust and you become incapacitated, the person you have selected will be able to pay your bills, manage your investments and take care of your financial affairs for as long as necessary—without interference from the court. And, unlike a durable power of attorney, with a living trust this person has more legal responsibilities to you and your loved ones.

Now you know how you can lose control when you have a will after you die and even while you are living. Let's look at one more way you can lose control with a will—when you have minor children or grandchildren.

A Will—And Minor Children (Or Grandchildren)

Many parents and grandparents are very surprised to learn how little control they actually have with a will when it comes to their minor children and grandchildren.

For example, many parents think if they name a guardian for their minor children in their wills and something happens to the parents, that person will automatically be able to use the inheritance to take care of the children. But that's not what happens.

Instead, when the will is probated, the court will set up a guardianship for the child and appoint a guardian to raise the child. Usually this will be the person named in the parent's will, but the court could appoint someone else.

However, *the court, not the guardian, will control the inheritance* until the child reaches legal age (18 or 21). At that time, the child automatically receives the *entire* inheritance. Most parents prefer that their children inherit at a later age, but with a simple will (which is what most parents have) you have no choice.

Note: In some states, the executor can transfer the minor's inheritance to a custodial account under the Uniform Transfer to Minors Act or the Uniform Gifts to Minors Act. These accounts are usually set up at a bank and a custodian is named to manage the funds. Laws will vary from state to state, but generally if the inheritance is more than $10,000, court approval is still required. In any event, the child will still receive the full amount at legal age.

What happens in a court guardianship for a minor is very similar to what happens when the court takes control for an incompetent adult. Things move very slowly and it can be very expensive. Every expense must be documented, audited, and approved by the court. And because the court must do its best to treat everyone equally under the law, it is difficult to make exceptions for each child's special and unique needs.

Note for Divorced or Separated Parents: Courts typically prefer to see a natural parent as guardian whenever possible so, even if you name someone else to be guardian, the court will probably award custody to the child's surviving parent. A disinterested or irresponsible parent may suddenly become *very* interested in the child when he/she learns that an inheritance is involved. Many courts simply do not have the resources to monitor all guardianships carefully, so it's possible your "ex" may have unsupervised access to the child's inheritance.

Can The Court Take Control Of Assets I Leave A Minor Grandchild?

Many grandparents, aunts, uncles and even parents leave money, real estate, stocks, certificates of deposit (CDs), and other investments directly to a minor child. If the child is still a minor when the person dies, the court will usually get involved, especially if the inheritance is substantial.

That's because minor children can be *on* a title, but they cannot *conduct business* in their own names. So as soon as the owner's signature is required to sell, refinance, or transact other business, the court will have to get involved. (Sometimes, depending on the value and type of asset, this happens even before the child can receive the money or be listed on the title.)

The court has to make sure the child's interests are "protected," even if both parents are alive and well. Of course, this protection isn't free, and the child's inheritance (or the parents) will have to pay for it. An attorney will need to represent the child in court and the court will probably insist that a guardian (usually a parent) is added to the titles when they are transferred to the child.

Establishing a guardianship is a relatively simple process, but once it is in place the court will stay involved. Until the child reaches legal age, none of the assets can be sold (or the money spent) without the court's approval. This guardianship could go on indefinitely if the child is physically or mentally incapacitated when he/she reaches legal age.

Wouldn't A Children's Trust In A Will Prevent The Court From Controlling The Assets?

If your will includes a children's trust in it, you can name someone to manage the inheritance after you die instead of the court. But keep in mind that your will must go through probate *first*. The children's trust is funded with your assets after your will is probated. You should also realize that a children's trust in a will *cannot* go into effect if you become incapacitated—because *your will* cannot go into effect until *after* you die.

With a living trust, the person(s) you select—not the court—will control the inheritance for your minor children or grandchildren until they reach the age(s) at which you *want them to inherit—even if you become incapacitated.*

SUMMARY

That was a lot of information, but now you know why a will may not be the best plan for your family. Remember, a will:

■ Does not avoid probate when you die;
■ Does not prevent the court from taking control of your assets if you become physically or mentally incapacitated; and
■ Does not give you as much control as you may have thought when you have minor children or grandchildren.

Now, let's look at how other "plans" can cause you to lose control.

2 LOSING CONTROL BY DOING NOTHING

If you don't have a will, your state has one for you

Doing nothing is another *very* common "plan." Many people procrastinate and don't do anything for any number of reasons. They think they're too busy. Or they don't own enough. Or they're not old enough. Or they're confused and don't know what to do or who can help them.

What happens if you don't do anything? If you own assets in your name and you become incapacitated, the court can take control just as we explained. And when you die, your estate will go through probate.

The only difference is that your assets will be distributed according to state law. Every state has laws for the distribution of assets for those who die without a will. So, if you haven't written a will, or if your will is not accepted by the court, the state in which you live has a will *for* you. The problem is that it probably is *not* what you would have wanted.

For example, in many states if you are married and have children, each will receive a share of your estate. This means your spouse could receive only a fraction of your estate, which may not be enough for him/her to live on. Also, the laws in most states allow for the inheritance of property only by bloodline, so a companion, special friend or charity would not receive anything.

If you have minor children, the court will control their inheritances and it will appoint their guardian(s) *without knowing whom you would have chosen.*

And, finally, it can be expensive and time consuming to look for heirs. All costs, of course, are paid from your assets. And if no heirs are found, the state in which you live will become your heir.

Doing nothing, for whatever reason, is probably the worst possible "plan"— because you have absolutely NO control.

If you have been procrastinating, hopefully the information in this book will motivate you to do something. A living trust does not have to be complicated or expensive. Even a will, with all its issues, lets you have some say in how you want your assets distributed and whom you want to raise your children.

3 LOSING CONTROL WITH JOINT OWNERSHIP

Joint ownership is probably the most commonly used estate "plan," although you may not have thought about estate planning at the time you purchased the asset. If you are married, you and your spouse may own many of your assets jointly. After all, that does seem like the fair thing to do, doesn't it? (The fact that it doesn't cost anything also contributes to its popularity.) Joint ownership is also frequently used between parents and their adult children.

The type of joint ownership most people use, and the one we will be discussing here, is called "joint owners/tenants with right of survivorship."

Many people have come to rely on joint ownership as an alternative to wills and probate. Even some professionals recommend it as a way to avoid probate.

Doesn't Joint Ownership Avoid Probate?

Not really—usually joint ownership just *postpones* probate. When one joint owner dies, ownership *will* transfer to the other owner without probate. (Because that person's name is already on the title, the court does not have to get involved.) But when the surviving owner dies without adding another owner, which often happens, or if both owners die at the same time, the asset *must* be probated before it can go to the heirs.

Are There Other Problems With Joint Ownership?

Joint ownership probably causes more problems than any other estate plan. It can even cause you to unintentionally disinherit your own family, as this illustration shows.

That's because, if you die first, you have no way of controlling what happens to your jointly owned assets. They are not controlled by your will because the transfer of ownership takes place *immediately* upon your death. So, even if your will says you want someone else

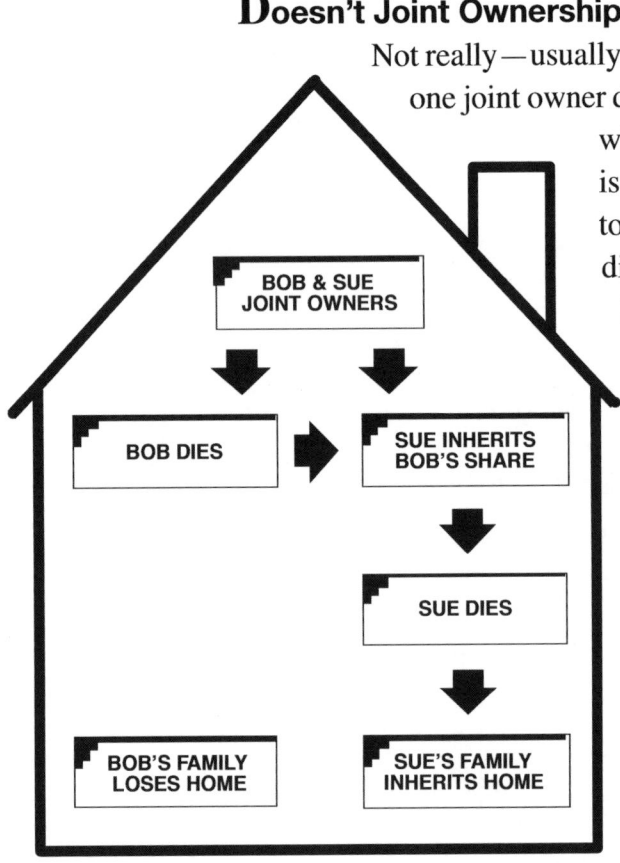

When one joint owner dies, his/her share immediately goes to the other owner. Using joint ownership can cause you to unintentionally disinherit your own family.

to receive your share of a jointly owned asset, it will still go to the surviving owner, who can do whatever he/she wants with it.

If you and your spouse own assets jointly, this would cause you to disinherit any children you have from a previous marriage. Your spouse could include your children in his/her will now, but you still can't be sure they will inherit. Your spouse could always write a *new* will and disinherit your children. Or your spouse could add a new co-owner (like a new spouse), who would then own the asset when your spouse dies.

Disinheriting can be a problem even if you don't have children because if you die first, your co-owner's family (not yours) will eventually inherit your jointly owned assets—even though the assets had once been half yours.

There are other risks when you use joint ownership. For example:
- It's easy to *add* a co-owner. But taking someone's name *off* the title can be very difficult. If your co-owner doesn't agree to be removed, you could end up in court.
- Your assets are exposed to your co-owner's debts and obligations. For example, if you add your adult son on the title of your home and he is successfully sued, you could be forced to sell your home to pay his debts.
- Your co-owner could transfer his/her share to someone else without your knowledge or approval. (This would change the type of joint ownership to "tenants-in-common" which is explained later.)
- If you add a minor as a joint owner of an asset (especially real estate, automobile, boat, stocks, etc.), the only way to sell or refinance the asset later is through a court guardianship, which will not end until the minor becomes an adult.
- There could be gift and/or income tax problems. (We'll explain both of these later—gift taxes in Part Nine, income taxes later in Part One.)
- If your estate is larger, you could be limiting your tax planning options.
- And if your co-owner becomes incapacitated, you could find yourself with a new co-owner—the court!

Why Would The Court Get Involved If My Co-Owner Is Incapacitated?

Many people mistakenly think that joint ownership of all assets is the same as a joint bank account, on which *either* owner can sign checks, make deposits and withdrawals, etc. But on many assets, especially real estate, *all* signatures

Joint ownership causes all kinds of problems

are required to transact business. If you need your co-owner's signature to sell or refinance and he/she is incapacitated, you'll have to ask the court to appoint someone to act for your co-owner—even if the ill owner is your spouse. And, remember, once the court gets involved, it will usually stay involved to protect that owner's interests.

Other Kinds Of Joint Ownership

While joint owners/tenants with right of survivorship is the most commonly used form of joint ownership, there are others.

■ Tenants-in-Common

One kind of joint ownership is called tenants-in-common. Even though it works very differently from joint owners/tenants with right of survivorship, people often confuse them. Under tenants-in-common, when one of the owners dies, that owner's share will be distributed as directed in his/her will (or to the heirs if there is no will). It will not go to the other owner unless the will says so—and it will not avoid probate.

■ Community Property

Ten states—Alaska, Arizona, California, Idaho, Louisiana, Nevada, New Mexico, Texas, Washington, and Wisconsin—have a form of joint ownership between spouses commonly called community property. Community property automatically goes to your surviving spouse unless your will states otherwise. (In Alaska, property is separate unless both parties agree to make it community property by a community property agreement or trust.)

The problem with both tenants-in-common and community property is that you could find yourself with *several* new co-owners when your original co-owner dies and the heirs inherit the property. Sometimes it's hard enough to get two people to agree. Imagine how difficult it could be to get *several* owners to reach an agreement, especially if you are trying to sell real estate. You could also have the same problems we mentioned earlier (incapacity, lawsuits, etc.), but with *several* owners involved, your risks and problems are multiplied.

■ Tenants-by-the-Entirety

Some states have another form of joint ownership between spouses called tenancy-by-the-entirety. Under this kind of ownership, when one spouse dies his/her share *automatically* goes to the surviving spouse, even if the will says otherwise. So you have many of the risks we mentioned earlier, like unintentional disinheriting and court interference if one spouse becomes incapacitated. But, as tenants-by-the-entirety, neither spouse can transfer his/her half to someone else without the other's approval.

Is Joint Ownership Worth The Risks?

Maybe joint ownership will work for you. But then again, maybe it won't. With joint ownership, you're playing a kind of estate planning roulette with your family. Your assets could still end up in probate, your co-owner could become incapacitated, you could be sued, you could even disinherit your own children. If joint ownership is starting to sound complicated, that's because it can be. Just remember that whenever you have a co-owner, you could easily lose control.

With a living trust, you don't have these risks. Even if you die first, you can keep full control of your assets, including who inherits them after you die.

4 LOSING CONTROL BY GIVING AWAY ASSETS

Some people actually re-title assets in their children's names while they are living, thinking it will make things easier for their children when something happens to them. As the owner, you can certainly do this. And it *will* avoid probate of the assets after you die and prevent the court from taking control of them if you become incapacitated. But it can create *all kinds* of problems.

The first problem with giving away an asset is—it's gone. What if you want or need it back? You may think your children would give it back to you. But things change in families, you know. Your children could sell the asset against your wishes, lose it to their creditors, or be influenced by a spouse. If you outlive your children or they divorce, a daughter (or son)-in-law could end up owning the asset. Would he/she give it back to you?

The second problem has to do with taxes. Currently, whenever you give someone other than your spouse more than $15,000 in one year, a *gift tax* may be involved. (We'll explain gift taxes in Part Nine.) And when your children sell the asset, there will probably be a substantial *capital gains tax*.

That's because the asset would not receive a *stepped-up basis*. The *basis* of an asset is the value used to determine gain or loss for income tax purposes—in other words, what you paid for it. If you give an appreciated asset to your children while you are alive, it keeps *your* basis (generally, what you paid for

Giving away assets can cause tax problems

it). But if they receive it as an inheritance through a will or trust, it receives a new *stepped-up* basis and is re-valued as of the date of your death.

Here's what this can mean to your children. Let's say you purchased your home for $50,000 and it's worth $350,000 when you die. If your children receive it as an inheritance after you die, the basis would be $350,000. And if they sell it for $350,000, they would pay no capital gains tax. But if you give it to your children while you are alive, the basis would be $50,000 (what you paid for it). If they then sold the house for $350,000, they would pay $60,000 capital gains tax on the $300,000 gain. (The federal long-term capital gains rate is 20%; 20% of $300,000 = $60,000.)

Gifts Do Not Receive A Stepped-Up Basis

	Transfer By Gift While You're Living (No Stepped-Up Basis)	Transfer By Inheritance Through Your Will Or Trust (Stepped-Up Basis)
Selling Price	$350,000	$350,000
Basis	-50,000	-350,000
Gain	$300,000	$0
Capital Gains Tax (20%)	$60,000	$0

If you give away an appreciated asset while you are living, it keeps your basis. If the asset is transferred by inheritance through your will or trust after you die, it receives a new stepped-up basis and is re-valued as of the date of your death. This can save the new owner a considerable amount in capital gains tax when the asset is eventually sold.

Substantial gifts may also disqualify you from receiving Medicaid and Supplemental Security Income (SSI) benefits for a significant period of time.

You could "sort of" give away an asset—by placing it in joint ownership with your children. But you've just read about the risks of joint ownership. Plus you may have a gift tax liability. (Remember, more about gift taxes in Part Nine.)

Gifting can be a great way to reduce estate taxes if your estate is larger and you can afford to give away an asset. (Estate taxes are explained in Part Three and gifting in Part Nine.) But never give away an asset you may need later, and be sure to get assistance from an experienced professional. Otherwise, there could be serious tax consequences for both you and your children.

A living trust will make things easier for your family when something happens to you without having to give away your assets or lose control of them.

5 LOSING CONTROL WITH BENEFICIARY DESIGNATIONS

Using beneficiary designations to transfer assets is becoming more and more common. That's because many assets today—like insurance policies, IRAs, retirement plans, and some bank accounts (like pay-on-death accounts)—let you name a beneficiary. When you die, these assets will be paid directly to the person(s) you have named as your beneficiary(ies)—without probate. At least that's the way it's *supposed* to work.

Here are some examples of situations you may not have considered:

- If your beneficiary dies before you or you both die at the same time, the proceeds will have to go through probate so they can be distributed with the rest of your assets.

- If your beneficiary is incapacitated when you die, the court will probably take control of the funds through a living probate. That's because most institutions (an insurance company, for example) will not knowingly pay to an incompetent person and will probably insist on court supervision.

- If you list a minor child as a beneficiary, you could be setting up a court guardianship for the child. That's because most institutions (again, like an insurance company) will not knowingly pay these funds directly to a minor—nor will they pay to another person (like a parent) *for* the child. They just do not want the potential legal liabilities and will usually require proof of a court-supervised guardianship.

- If you list "my estate" as the beneficiary, the court must determine who "my estate" is. The funds will go through probate and will be distributed with the rest of your assets.

Even if the funds *are* paid to the beneficiary you have named, things may not work out as you had intended. For example:

■ It's possible the person you name as beneficiary may not be responsible enough to handle such a large sum of money. For example, he/she could be too easily influenced by a spouse or others, make bad investment decisions, or could lose the funds to a creditor.

■ If you name someone as a beneficiary *with the understanding* that the funds will be used to care for another or will be held for that person until a later time, you have no guarantee your wishes will be followed. For example, if you name the parent of a minor grandchild as beneficiary with the understanding that the money is for the child, you cannot be sure the child will ever see the money.

■ If your estate is larger, you could be limiting your tax planning options. This could cause serious tax consequences later for your family.

Using beneficiary designations to transfer assets directly to your loved ones after you die may seem simple. But you can easily lose control.

With your living trust as the beneficiary, you—not the courts or Uncle Sam—will keep control over the full proceeds, even if your loved one is irresponsible, a minor, incapacitated or has died before you.

Summary

Now you know about the five plans most people use...

1 **Wills**
2 **Doing Nothing**
3 **Joint Ownership**
4 **Giving Away Assets**
5 **Beneficiary Designations**

...and you know how you can lose control when you use them. We could go on about potential problems, but you've probably got the general idea by now.

Let's move on to the sixth plan—the revocable living trust—and see why it gives you far more control over your assets than any of these other plans.

Part Two—

KEEPING CONTROL WITH A REVOCABLE LIVING TRUST

Now that you know how you can lose control with other plans, let's look at how you can *keep* control with a revocable living trust.

In this section, you will learn what a living trust is and how it works. You'll learn about the many benefits of a living trust—which go far beyond avoiding probate. We'll even tell you what a living trust does *not* do and if there are any disadvantages of having one.

And, finally, we'll tell you why living trusts have become so popular and why you may not have been told about them before.

WHAT IS A REVOCABLE LIVING TRUST?

A revocable living trust is a legal document that, to many of us, looks much like a will. And, like a will, it includes your instructions for whom you want to handle your final affairs and whom you want to receive your assets after you die.

But, *unlike* a will, a living trust:

- Does not go through probate.
- Prevents the court from controlling your assets at incapacity.
- Gives *you*—not the courts—control over the assets you leave to your minor children or grandchildren.

And it does *much* more, as you will soon see.

	Will	Revocable Living Trust
Compare a Will and a Revocable Living Trust		
Used 100s of Years	✔	✔
Names Someone To Handle Final Affairs	✔	✔
Names Whom You Want To Receive Assets	✔	✔
Avoids Probate		✔
Prevents "Living Probate"		✔

Before we go much farther, let's be clear that there are different *kinds* of trusts. For example, an *irrevocable trust* is frequently used in tax planning. Usually, after an irrevocable trust has been set up, you cannot change it or remove assets that have been transferred into it. Some of these are explained in Part Nine.

A *testamentary trust* is created after you die by a provision in your will. It can be used in tax planning or to manage assets for minors or other beneficiaries. However, a testamentary trust does *not* avoid probate and it provides *no* protection if you become incapacitated—because it is part of your will. Also, in some states, a testamentary trust is subject to ongoing court supervision.

The kind of trust discussed in this book is a *revocable living trust*. The actual legal name is a *revocable inter vivos trust*. *Inter vivos* means that it is created while you are living. *Revocable*, of course, means that it can be revoked (changed or discontinued). To keep this book easy to read, we often refer to it as a living trust, and sometimes just "the trust" or "your trust."

Why Does A Living Trust Avoid Probate And Prevent Court Control At Incapacity?

When you set up a living trust, you transfer ownership of your titled assets (home, other real estate, bank accounts, stocks, etc.) from your individual name to the name of your living trust—which *you* control.

For example, you would change the titles on your assets from "John and Mary Smith, husband and wife" to "John and Mary Smith, Trustees of the Smith Family Trust dated (insert date the trust was created)."

Technically, *you* no longer own anything—everything is now in the name of your trust. So there is nothing for the courts to control when you die or if you become incapacitated. The concept is very simple, but *this* is what keeps you and your family out of the courts.

Do I Lose Control Of The Assets I Put In My Living Trust?

No. You keep full control. You can continue to do everything you could do before, including buying and selling assets. You can make changes or even cancel your trust. Remember, it's a *revocable* living trust. In fact, the Internal Revenue Service considers putting assets into a revocable living trust to be a non-event because you can take them out at any time. *Nothing changes but the names on the titles*.

As you'll see in the next few pages, not only do you *not* lose control, you'll actually have *more* control over your assets when they are in a revocable living trust than you do now.

Are Living Trusts New?

No, living trusts are not new, and they are not tax shelters or gimmicks. They have been used successfully, in one form or another, for hundreds of years and, in fact, go back at least to the Middle Ages.

The concept was used by knights and other nobility who received land in exchange for providing services to the king. For the knight, this usually meant going off to fight wars. To keep the land, the knight had to keep providing his services. After years of fighting the King's wars—and with the increasing availability of money taking the place of the barter system—the weary knight started paying the king a fee instead. And the king would then hire a mercenary to fight in the knight's place.

Eventually the knights got pretty smart and figured out they could transfer the title of their land to individuals (like clergymen and church members) who were exempt from paying fees to the king—but the knights retained the use of the land for their lifetimes or for several generations to come.

With a living trust, you'll have more control over your assets

Putting Your Assets into a Living Trust Avoids Probate

ASSETS TITLED IN YOUR NAME	ASSETS TITLED IN YOUR TRUST'S NAME (NO PROBATE)

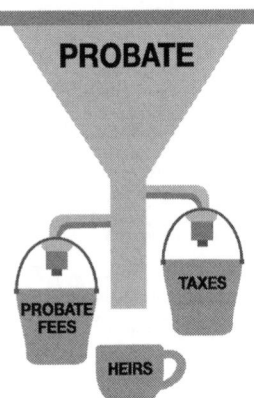

CHANGE TITLES
(Nothing left to probate)

PROBATE

PROBATE FEES

TAXES

HEIRS

LIVING TRUST

TAXES

BENEFICIARIES

Assets titled in just your name must go through a probate process before they can go to your beneficiaries. But assets that you re-title in the name of your trust completely avoid probate and can go straight to your beneficiaries. Final income taxes will still have to be paid, but a living trust (like a properly prepared will) can reduce or eliminate estate taxes.

This became known as a trust, because the knight trusted the clergymen to allow him to continue using the land. So the knight kept the use of his land, the clergymen got title to it—and the king didn't get his fees. This was the beginning of the living trust concept as we know it today. (Now, wasn't that interesting?)

Only you can make changes to your trust

HOW A LIVING TRUST WORKS

Your Living Trust Team
To understand how a living trust works, you need to understand the roles of the people involved with your trust and their legal names. The accompanying *Living Trust Team* chart will also be helpful.

■ The Grantor
When you set up your trust, you become what is called in legal terms the *grantor* (also called creator, settlor, trustor, or trustmaker). This is the person *whose trust it is.* If you are married, you and your spouse can be co-grantors of one living trust, or you can be grantors of your own separate trusts. Only the grantor (you) can make changes to your trust. That's the key. That is how you keep control.

■ The Trustee
You will name a *trustee* to manage the assets in your trust. This can be anyone you wish, including yourself. If you are your own trustee (as many people are), you will continue to handle your affairs for as long as you are able. If you are married, you and your spouse can be *co-trustees*. This way, either of you can automatically act for the other (just like a joint checking account) and, if one of you becomes incompetent or dies, the other instantly has control of all trust assets—with no court involvement.

You don't have to be your own trustee if you don't want to or don't feel you are capable. There are many qualified institutions that manage trusts professionally (these are called corporate trustees), or you can name another individual like an adult son or daughter. In Part Four, we'll discuss your options in detail.

Even if you name someone else as trustee, *you're still in control.* As long as you are competent, you can replace your trustee at any time—because you are the *grantor* of your trust.

Your successor trustee steps in when needed— with no court interference

■ The Successor Trustee

You need to name someone you know and trust as your *successor trustee* to step in and manage your trust if the trustee becomes incapacitated, dies or decides he/she no longer wants to be trustee.

For example, if you are the only trustee, someone will need to step in and manage your trust if you become incapacitated and when you die. Even if you and your spouse are co-trustees, eventually you will both die and you may both become incapacitated before then. So you need to have a "back-up," someone you trust who can step in and take over for you.

Successor trustees can be individuals (trusted friends, adult children, other relatives) and/or a corporate trustee.

■ The Beneficiaries

In a living trust, the people and/or organizations who will receive your assets and possessions when you die are called your *beneficiaries*. Most people leave their assets to relatives, but you can leave them to anyone or to any organization(s) you wish. Many people like to include a favorite charity, foundation, religious group, or fraternal organization.

Now, let's look at the roles these people have when you die and if you become incapacitated.

What Happens When You Die?

Your successor trustee (or co-trustee) will have the same responsibilities an executor would if you had a will. But because he/she does not have to report to the court, everything can be done more efficiently and privately.

Your successor (or co-trustee) collects any income, pays your final bills, sees that tax returns are filed, and then follows your instructions for distributing your assets. Your successor can even sell assets, if that's what you wanted. Because all of your assets are titled in the name of your trust, it's very easy for your successor trustee to conduct business.

What Happens If You Become Incapacitated?

Your successor trustee (or co-trustee) automatically steps in and handles your financial affairs for you for as long as necessary. He/she can write checks, make deposits, apply for disability benefits, pay bills, even sell assets.

Your Living Trust Team

Grantor(s): Person(s) creating the trust—you (and your spouse). Also called creator, settlor, trustor, or trustmaker.

Trustee(s): Manages the trust now. Usually you (and your spouse) and/or another individual or a corporate trustee (bank or trust company).

Successor Trustee(s): Will step in and manage the trust for as long as necessary if you (and your spouse) become incapacitated. At your death(s), your successor will distribute your assets according to your instructions. Successor trustees can be adult children, trusted friends and/or a corporate trustee. You should name more than one, in order of your preference, in case your first choice is unable to act.

Beneficiaries: Persons and/or organizations who will ultimately receive the assets in your trust when you (and your spouse) die.

Children's Trust: If you have minor children, you will want a children's trust set up within your living trust. If you (and your spouse) become incapacitated or die, your assets can then be used to care for your children without court interference.

```
          ┌──────────────────┐
          │   GRANTOR(s)     │
          └──────────────────┘
                   │
          ┌──────────────────┐
          │   TRUSTEES(s)    │
          └──────────────────┘
                   │
          ┌──────────────────┐
          │   SUCCESSOR      │
          │   TRUSTEE(s)     │
          └──────────────────┘
           │               │
    ┌────────────┐   ┌────────────┐
    │BENEFICIARIES│  │ CHILDREN'S │
    └────────────┘   │   TRUST    │
                     └────────────┘
           │               │
    ┌────────────┐   ┌────────────┐
    │ CHILDREN'S │   │ CHILDREN'S │
    │  GUARDIAN  │   │  TRUSTEE   │
    └────────────┘   └────────────┘
               │
          ┌──────────────────┐
          │    CHILDREN      │
          └──────────────────┘
```

Guardian: Person you have named to raise your children if you (and your spouse) are unable to because of incapacity or death. Must be an adult.

Children's Trustee: Manages the assets in your children's trust until the children reach the age(s) you specify they will inherit. Provides for education, maintenance, and support of your children from the assets in the trust. Can be the same person you name as guardian, another adult, and/or a corporate trustee.

Your successor trustee must follow your instructions

No courts or attorneys are required, and everything is done privately. If you recover, you simply start handling your affairs again and your successor trustee returns to being your successor. There is no complicated paperwork or procedure to regain control. Plus, you have peace of mind knowing that, if this should ever happen to you or your spouse, you will be taken care of by someone *you* have selected, someone you know and trust—not someone a court appoints to take care of you.

■ Who Decides If You Are Incapacitated?

Actually, *you* can. Your living trust can include a provision that lets you specify who has the authority to determine your ability to manage your affairs. You can include how many and what kinds of doctors you want to examine you. You can even name certain doctors if you wish. (Just try to choose ones you think will be around longer than you.) This will prevent a conspiracy by relatives to have you declared incompetent.

Why You Can Be Sure Your Successor Trustee Will Follow Your Instructions

Many living trusts state that when someone steps in for you and becomes your acting trustee, he/she must keep the beneficiaries (and sometimes, the other successor trustees) informed of all actions. So there can be a lot of checks on your acting trustee's decisions.

In addition, a trust is a binding legal contract when it is signed (unlike a will, which becomes binding only after you die and it is accepted by the court). Trustees are fiduciaries; by law they have a legal duty to follow your trust instructions and to act in a prudent (conservative) manner at all times for the benefit of the trust beneficiaries. Of course, anyone you name as a trustee, co-trustee or successor trustee should be someone you can trust. But if an acting trustee were to abuse his/her fiduciary duties (for example, by failing to follow the instructions in your trust document), he/she could be held legally liable.

If you are still concerned, you can name a *trust protector* to oversee, and even remove and replace, your acting trustee. More about this in Part Four.

What Happens If You Have Minor Children/Grandchildren

If you have minor children or grandchildren, you will need to set up a children's trust within your living trust to prevent the court from taking control of the inheritance. Here's why.

When you (and your spouse) die, your acting trustee, following your instructions, will probably distribute your assets and dissolve your trust. If you have minor children or grandchildren, your trust needs to specify that their inheritance goes immediately from your trust into one for the children. The children's trust inherits *for* the minor children; they do not directly receive the inheritance in their own names.

As long as the inheritance stays in a trust—first in yours, then in one for the children—you will prevent the court from taking control of the inheritance.

You will name a trustee to manage the inheritance and provide for the children according to your instructions until each reaches the age(s) you specify. If you are a parent (or legal guardian), you will name a guardian to raise your children. The trustee and guardian can be the same person or different people. The trustee can also be a corporate trustee. The court must still appoint the guardian, but this is only a minor formality when compared to a court guardianship in which the court also controls the inheritance.

With a children's trust in your living trust, there does not have to be a court guardianship or any delays involved with your children's inheritance—even if you become incapacitated. So the trustee and guardian will have much more flexibility, and will be able to respond more quickly, to meet your children's changing needs. And with your hand-picked trustee controlling the money, there may be no real incentive for an irresponsible "ex" or other relative to oppose your choice for guardian.

Having a children's trust in your living trust is better than having one in a will because:

1.   With a living trust, the assets can go into the children's trust without the delays or expenses of probate. But if the children's trust is part of your will, the assets must go through probate *before* they can go into the children's trust.

2.   A living trust can be written so that the children's trust can go into effect at your incapacity. But if the children's trust is part of your will, the children's trust *cannot* go into effect if you become incapacitated—because *your will* can only go into effect *after* you die.

Your trust is prepared from your decisions

How a Living Trust is Set Up

The attorney you select prepares your living trust from your decisions about what you want to happen if you become incapacitated and when you die. *You* make the basic planning decisions: decide who will manage your assets now (trustee), who will handle your financial affairs if you become incapacitated and when you die (co-trustee or successor trustee) and who will eventually receive your assets after you die (beneficiaries).

Trust documents are usually prepared from standardized trust forms. Many commercial banks, trust companies, and financial advisers have sample trust forms if you want to look at some basic trust provisions. Your attorney will probably not need to create something completely new and customized for you. Many people only need one basic trust document to handle all of their needs and assets.

This may sound pretty simple and it is—as long as you use an estate planning attorney who is experienced in preparing living trusts and can make the necessary modifications to handle your family's situation. It is very important that your living trust is prepared properly.

After your attorney has prepared your living trust document and you have read and approved it, you sign the trust, and it is notarized. Titles and account names for your assets (home, other real estate, bank accounts, investments, etc.)—and many beneficiary designations—will then need to be changed from your name to the name of your trust. This is called "funding" your trust.

Now, don't worry; we'll help you with all of this. In Part Four, we give you information to help you decide who will be your trustee, successor trustee(s) and how to provide for your beneficiaries. There is also an Organizer in Part Ten to help you organize your assets. In Part Five, we'll help you find the right attorney to prepare your trust for you. And in Part Six, we explain—asset by asset—how titles and beneficiary designations are changed to your trust.

Don't Leave Your Living Trust Unfunded

Your living trust is unfunded if you have signed your trust document but haven't changed titles or beneficiary designations. You do not want to leave your living trust unfunded, because anything you leave out of your trust will probably have to go through probate when you die and would be subject to court control if you become incapacitated. *The only way to completely avoid probate at death and court control at incapacity is to put everything you own into your trust.*

You should be suspicious if someone tells you that you only need to place one asset (or maybe one dollar) into your living trust to fund it.

Why It's Important To Change Beneficiary Designations

As explained earlier, beneficiary proceeds (for example, from a life insurance policy) are intended to be available immediately upon death and paid directly to the beneficiary outside of the probate process.

You now know that doesn't always happen. And even when the proceeds are paid directly to your beneficiary, what happens then is not always what you intended. Remember, this person may be easily influenced by others, could make bad investments, or could lose the money to a creditor (or spouse).

Making your living trust the beneficiary will prevent the possibility of the court taking control of the proceeds and will give you maximum control over the proceeds, even after you die. For example:

■ If a loved one is incapacitated when you die, your successor trustee will be able to use the funds to care for him/her *without* court involvement.

■ If you wish to provide for minor children or grandchildren, the funds will flow through your living trust into a children's trust. The trustee *you* select (not the court) will manage the assets until each child reaches the age(s) *you* want him/her to inherit.

■ You can keep the funds in trust to provide for an adult beneficiary and protect the money from irresponsible spending, bad investments, creditors, a spouse (or ex-spouse), and those with undue influence.

Also, having all of your assets—including beneficiary proceeds—flow through your living trust is a very convenient way to coordinate your total estate plan through one document.

■ **Possible Exception**

There may be valid tax reasons to name your spouse as first beneficiary (and your living trust as second beneficiary) on tax-deferred savings plans like your IRA, 401(k), pension plan, and Keogh. A discussion of your options is included in Part Six.

THE BENEFITS OF A LIVING TRUST FOR YOU AND YOUR FAMILY

One of the main reasons people initially set up a living trust is to avoid probate. But as they soon find out, and as you'll see in the following pages, avoiding probate is only *one* of the many benefits of a living trust.

Avoids Probate When You Die

Saves Money. By avoiding probate, you can potentially save thousands of dollars. This means more of your hard-earned and carefully-managed assets can go to your loved ones instead of unnecessary legal fees and court costs.

Takes Less Time. Without court interference, your successor trustee will be able to move more efficiently to wrap up your final affairs. With smaller estates, where no estate tax returns are required (explained in Part Three), beneficiaries may be able to receive their inheritances in just weeks instead of months or years.

Maximum Privacy. A living trust is more private than probate. In most states, no announcements have to be placed in the paper (so no one is "invited" to contest your trust) and your trust is not part of the public court records.

If you live in Florida, your trustee must file a Notice of Trust with the probate court after you die to let creditors and any other "interested parties" know that your trust exists and that its assets will be available to satisfy any claims they may have. But no information about your assets is required—just your name, when you died, the name and date of your trust, and the trustee's name and address.

If you live in California, your trustee must notify your beneficiaries after you die. However, nothing is required to be published or filed with the probate court.

If your state has an inheritance tax, an inventory or summary of assets may be required to be filed with the tax return. But otherwise, no information about your assets, beneficiaries or trustees will ever have to be made public. In fact, a living trust is usually so private that disgruntled heirs or opportunity seekers who might have contested your will may not even know you have died.

So, while a living trust cannot guarantee *complete* privacy, it gives you the *maximum privacy possible*. And that is much more than you get with a will, which is guaranteed to be made public through probate.

Minimizes Emotional Stress. With court restrictions removed, your family can continue its normal daily routines. Your affairs can be handled more efficiently. Your family will be able to mourn your passing privately and move on with their own lives without the frustration of prolonged court proceedings.

Avoids Multiple Probates
One living trust can control all of your assets, even real estate you may own in other states. So there will be no need for additional probates in other states.

Prevents Court Control Of Assets At Incapacity
Your hand-picked successor trustee (or co-trustee) can immediately step in for you. There are no court delays or interferences, you save countless dollars in unnecessary attorney fees and court costs, and your situation stays private.

Prevents Court Control Of A Minor's Inheritance
Your trustee can automatically step in at your death or incapacity and use your assets to provide for your minor children or grandchildren. Because the court cannot control the inheritance, there are no court delays or interferences.

Your trustee can react more quickly to provide funds to meet the individual needs of each child. The money you save in attorney fees and court costs can go to provide for the children. No information about the inheritance will be made public. And with your hand-picked trustee controlling the money, relatives (or an "ex") who might only be interested in the inheritance will be discouraged from competing to be named as guardian.

You Control When Your Beneficiaries Inherit
Maybe you can't take it with you, but with a living trust you can sure *keep control* of it after you're gone!

A living trust avoids probate and more

With a trust, you control when your beneficiaries inherit

One of the most powerful benefits of a trust, unlike a simple will, is that *you* control when your beneficiaries will receive their inheritances. Assets can be distributed right away, or they can stay in the trust until your beneficiaries reach the age(s) you want them to inherit.

For example, you could give children or grandchildren their inheritances in installments so they don't blow through it all at one time. You can provide for a loved one with special needs. You can even keep assets in the trust to protect them from creditors and predators or for future generations. (More about this in Part Four.)

More Equitable (Fair) Distributions

Most parents want to treat their children fairly. This may mean giving each an equal share or it may mean giving more to one child than another. For example, you may want to leave more to your son who is a teacher than to your daughter who is a doctor. Or you may want to compensate a daughter who takes care of you during your last years.

This is often much easier to do with a living trust than with a will. That's because many people who have a will also own some assets that transfer outside the will, such as jointly owned assets that transfer automatically to the surviving owner and assets that will be paid directly to named beneficiaries. The problem is that the values of many assets (home, stocks, savings, retirement plans, a business) can fluctuate greatly over time. So how can you be sure your children will receive the amount you want each one to have?

For example, let's say you add your daughter as a joint owner on some stocks and you name your son as the beneficiary of an insurance policy. At the time you decide to do this, the values are approximately what you want each to receive. But when you die, the value of the stocks has decreased while the insurance proceeds have stayed the same. Your son receives what you intended, but your daughter receives much less.

If you want your son and daughter to receive equal shares, you could put both their names on all your assets. But what if one wanted to sell and the other didn't? Or you could have all your assets titled in just your name or paid to your estate, and then specify in your will how much you want each one to receive. But then everything would have to go through probate.

When you change titles and beneficiary designations to your living trust and have all your assets in one "pot," your successor trustee can look at their values when you die and make sure each beneficiary receives the amount you intended, all without probate.

Prevents Unintentional Disinheriting

With a living trust, you don't have to worry about unintentionally disinheriting a loved one. Remember how easily you can unintentionally disinherit your own family when you use joint ownership? But joint ownership isn't the only culprit.

Unintentional disinheriting can happen anytime you give an asset to someone—through joint ownership, a beneficiary designation, or outright—with the understanding that the asset is really for someone else. You can't be sure your intended receiver will ever see the asset, because you have no control over what the messenger will do with it. He/she could sell the asset, spend the proceeds, give it to someone else, or even lose it to a creditor or spouse.

By contrast, when your assets go through your living trust, *you have complete control* over what *your trust* will do with them. The instructions in your trust must be followed, so there is no risk of unintentional disinheriting.

More Difficult To Contest

A living trust *can* be contested, but not nearly as easily as a will. With a will, anyone can come forward and claim to have a right to part of your estate, without having to hire an attorney. It's very easy to find out about your estate when notices of the probate proceedings appear in the papers and the entire process is public.

By contrast, because a living trust is more private and the assets are not frozen as they usually are for some time with a will, the trustee may have already made distributions to the beneficiaries by the time a disgruntled "heir" finds out about the trust. The contesting "heir" must then hire an attorney and sue each beneficiary and/or the trustee individually. This complicated, expensive and time-consuming process often discourages frivolous claims.

This could also be a valuable benefit if you want to provide for someone who is not related to you (a special friend or companion) or a charitable organization, and you think someone might try to contest your wishes.

You can change your trust at any time

Effective Pre-Nuptial Protection

A living trust can even provide effective pre-nuptial protection. That's because any assets you put into your living trust before you marry remain the property of that trust and stay separate from property accumulated during your marriage, even in community property states. You just have to be careful not to commingle assets acquired before and after the marriage.

It is not uncommon to see three living trusts in one family. Each spouse has a separate living trust for property acquired before the marriage (usually giving it to his/her respective children from a previous marriage or to other relatives), and they have one common living trust for assets acquired during the marriage.

No Special Government Forms Required

As long as you are living, you continue to use your social security number and file the same personal income tax returns as you do now. No special forms are required if you become incapacitated or if you decide not to be a trustee of your trust while you are living. However, after you die, your successor trustee will need to apply for a separate tax identification number and file a separate tax return for the trust. An attorney, CPA or a corporate trustee can provide assistance if needed.

Flexible—Can Be Changed Or Cancelled At Any Time

Your living trust can change with you throughout your lifetime as your family situation and goals change.

For example, as minor children become adults, and as family members are born, marry, divorce, become ill and die, you will probably find you need to change something in your trust. You may want to change the trustee or successor trustee, or add a beneficiary. You may decide to disinherit (or "re-inherit") someone. You may want to change how your beneficiaries will inherit. You do not need to have your trust completely redone to make these changes—your attorney will simply prepare an amendment for a nominal cost.

You can take assets out of your living trust and put new ones in. You could even cancel your trust, because it's revocable. And because *all* of your assets (home, other real estate, bank accounts, investments, business interests, stocks, insurance) can be controlled by *one* set of instructions, when you want to make a change to your estate plan it's easy. You only have to change your *one* trust document.

Easier For Your Family

When you set up a living trust, you're doing much of the work that will need to be done after you die. In effect, you are "pre-probating" your own estate.

The process makes you organize your assets, locate documents, and make sure everything is in order now, instead of paying for the courts and attorneys to help your family do it *for* you when you can't.

Taking the time now to get organized and having all of your assets flow through your living trust with one set of instructions will make things much easier for your family at what will be an emotional and potentially vulnerable time. And you'll feel very good now about having done it.

Also, if it turns out that you uncover a problem with an account or a title, think how much better it will be for you to straighten it out now instead of your family, attorney, and the court trying to sort it out without you.

Professional Asset Management

With a living trust, you have the option of having a corporate trustee (bank or trust company) manage your assets for you. This can be especially valuable now if you don't have the time, ability, or desire to manage your assets. It can also be valuable later on, if you become unable to manage your assets or if you decide to keep assets in trust for your beneficiaries.

A corporate trustee has the experience, time, and resources to help you achieve your investment goals without you losing control. In Part Four, we'll give you more information so you can decide if you should have a one involved with your trust.

Reduces Or Eliminates Estate Taxes

A living trust can include provisions to reduce or even eliminate estate taxes. So can a will, if it includes a testamentary trust. But, remember, with a will you have probate and court control of assets if you become incapacitated.

We'll explain all about estate taxes—what they are, who has to pay them, how much they are—and how a living trust can reduce them in Part Three, which comes next.

Benefits of a Revocable Living Trust

- Avoids time and expense of probate when you die

- Avoids multiple probates if you own real estate in more than one state

- Provides easier, more efficient administration of your estate

- Prevents court control of assets at physical or mental incapacity

- Gives you maximum privacy

- Minimizes emotional stress on your family

- Often allows quicker distribution of assets to beneficiaries (especially with smaller estates)

- Lets you keep assets in trust until beneficiaries reach age(s) you want them to inherit

- Easier to provide equitable/fair distributions to beneficiaries

- Prevents court from controlling assets when minor children inherit

- Can protect dependents with special needs

- Prevents unintentional disinheriting

- More difficult than a will to contest

- Provides effective pre-nuptial protection

- Inexpensive, easy to set up and maintain

- Can be changed or cancelled at any time

- Professional asset management if you use a corporate trustee

- Can reduce or eliminate estate taxes

- Lets you keep maximum control while you are living—even if you become incapacitated—and after you die

- Peace of mind

Gives You Maximum Control

The reason a living trust gives you all these benefits is simple.

Anytime a *person* is on the title of an asset or is named as a beneficiary, things can happen over which you have no control. People, including you, can become ill, they become injured, they die, they get divorced, they remarry, they go bankrupt—and they can be influenced by others.

This is why many good plans go wrong and why assets end up in probate, conservatorships, and guardianships. It's why loved ones are unintentionally disinherited. It's why assets end up with children's ex-spouses, creditors, and other unintended heirs. It's why the court can take control of your assets if a beneficiary is a minor, incapacitated, or dies before you. And it's why you can end up paying too much in taxes.

When you transfer your assets to your living trust, you don't have these problems. *A trust is not a person.* It doesn't become ill or injured, die, marry, or divorce. Regardless of what happens to the *people* you care about, you can keep control over what happens to the *assets* in your trust.

A revocable living trust may not be perfect. Few things are. But no other plan can give you all these benefits and this much control.

Peace Of Mind

Once you set up your living trust, you get the best benefit of all—peace of mind. We all know that this is something we *should* do. And once you've finally taken the time to put your plan in place, you can relax with your family and friends, knowing you've done the best you can do for yourself and those you love.

WHAT A LIVING TRUST DOES NOT DO

As much as a living trust does, it does not do *everything* you might want. For example, a revocable living trust:

Does Not Control Medical Decisions

Many people confuse a living trust with a living will. Although the names are similar and they are both legal documents, they do very different things.

With a living trust, you have peace of mind

A living trust, which we are discussing in this book, is for keeping control of your *assets*. A living will is for keeping control over *medical* decisions. It lets others know how you feel about life support in case of terminal illness. In Part Five, we discuss living wills and the durable power of attorney for health care, another health care document.

Does Not Protect Assets From Creditors While You Are Living

Because a living trust is revocable, you still have control of your assets and have access to them at all times. Remember, even the IRS considers a revocable living trust to be a non-event because you can put assets in your trust and take them out at any time. So, a living trust does not shield your assets from creditors while you are living.

However, after you die, creditors only have a certain length of time to file claims so there is some protection then. (More about the creditor claims period later in this section.)

If you are concerned about protecting your assets from creditors while you are living, your attorney will be able to suggest some options for you to consider. (Some of these are explained in Part Nine.)

Does Not Affect Your Income Taxes

A revocable living trust has no effect on your income taxes while you are living. You still must report any income you earn each year and any taxes owed must be paid. Remember, as long as you are living, you continue to file the same income tax returns as you do now and use your own social security number. (A separate tax identification number and separate tax return for your trust are required only after you die.)

Does Not Help You Qualify For Medicaid

Medicaid is a federally funded health care program that was created primarily to provide health care services for the poor. It also pays for an unlimited number of days of nursing home care, which makes it appealing to many who are *not* poor.

To qualify for Medicaid, you can only have a limited amount of assets and receive a certain amount of income. People who want to qualify have two choices: 1) spend down their assets, or 2) give them away which, depending on the values and when the assets are transferred, could cause them to be ineligible for benefits for some time.

Some people have thought that putting their assets in a revocable living trust would help them qualify for Medicaid because the assets would no longer be titled in their individual names. But, because a living trust is revocable, you still have full control and access to your assets at all times, so you haven't really "given them away." The assets in your living trust will be considered "available" when either spouse applies for Medicaid. To be clear, putting your assets in a revocable living trust will not qualify you for Medicaid.

> **Note:** Under current law, if you give away assets directly from your living trust, it could take longer to become eligible for Medicaid benefits. If you find you need to give away some assets in order to qualify for Medicaid after you have put them in your living trust, you will probably need to transfer those assets back into your own name first.

However, before you do *anything* about trying to qualify for Medicaid, consult with an attorney who specializes in Elder Law. Two good sources are ElderCounsel (www.eldercounsel.com) and The National Academy of Elder Law Attorneys (www.naela.org).

One alternative to Medicaid is long term care insurance, which was specifically created to help pay for the costs of long term care. Having this insurance would let you keep your independence because you would not have to spend or give away your assets to receive benefits. Another possibility is an irrevocable trust for which, again, you should consult an Elder Law attorney.

ARE THERE ANY "DISADVANTAGES" OF A LIVING TRUST?

You may be thinking that a living trust sounds too good to be true. Surely, there must be *something* wrong with it.

You will, undoubtedly, hear some negative things about living trusts. When you do, consider the source. Does this person have something to gain by my not using a living trust? Is this person trying to sell me something? Could this person simply be misinformed?

What some people may think is a disadvantage usually turns out to be either bad or outdated information or, at the most, only a minor inconvenience that pales when compared to the many benefits a living trust can provide. Let's take a look at some objections and "disadvantages" you may encounter.

"Probate Isn't Expensive Here, So There's No Reason To Have A Living Trust."

If someone tells you probate is not expensive, ask this person to help you understand how inexpensive it is. After all, what is not expensive to a $300 (or more)-per-hour attorney may be very expensive to you.

Ask this person to give you a written estimate of what it would cost to probate your estate, including attorney and executor fees, if you died today. If you are married, ask him/her to write down what the probate would cost if your spouse dies tomorrow.

If you live in a state that has statutory fees (a set fee schedule), this will be fairly easy. The person will be able to determine what the costs will be, depending on the value of your assets. (Make sure you know if the attorney and executor fees apply to assets that do not go through probate.)

However, if you live in a state that has "reasonable" fees, this will be more difficult, if not impossible. There will be no way to know how much the probate will cost until the entire process is over. And when was the last time you bought something without knowing what it would cost?

Next, ask this person to write down what the attorney and court costs would be if you became incapacitated today and, if you are married, what they would be if your spouse becomes incapacitated tomorrow. No one should be able to give you a good estimate because no one can predict how long an incapacity will last and what complications might arise.

Keep in mind that avoiding the cost of probate is only one reason to have a living trust. Don't forget about the other benefits, which include maximum privacy and control. For many people, the fact that a living trust prevents court control of assets if you (and your spouse) become incapacitated is, in itself, worth the entire cost of the trust.

"A Living Trust Is More Expensive Than A Will."

It will probably cost more *initially* to set up a well-drafted living trust than to have a will prepared. One reason is that a living trust usually has more provisions than a will because it deals with issues while you are living as well as after you die. A will, of course, only deals with issues after you die.

There may also be some costs to transfer assets into your living trust when you set it up, and from your trust to your beneficiaries after you die. However, these will be minimal if you and your successor trustee do much of the work yourselves. By contrast, with a will, you will be paying the courts and attorneys to do this *for* you *after* you die. (Which do you think will cost less?)

Of course, with both a living trust and a will, final income tax returns (and estate tax returns, if required) must be prepared.

When comparing costs, don't forget that the true cost of a will must include the costs of probate when you (and your spouse) die, the potential costs of a conservatorship if you (or your spouse) become incapacitated, and the costs of a guardianship if you leave assets to minor children. When you make a true comparison, a living trust is really quite a bargain.

"With A Living Trust, You Have To Pay Management Fees."

Trustees are entitled to receive a reasonable fee for their services. However, if you are your own trustee (which is what most people choose to do), you will pay no management fees while you are able to manage your trust yourself. Your successor trustee is entitled to receive a fee when he/she actually steps in for you, but many family members do not accept a fee.

If you name a corporate trustee as your trustee or successor trustee, they will charge a management fee only when they start to act for you. Usually this fee is quite reasonable when compared to the services they provide and the experience they have, and often their fee is offset by their investment performance. In other words, the earnings they are able to generate on your assets are often considerably more than the fee they charge.

"It Takes Time To Change Titles And Beneficiary Designations."

Yes, it does take some time to change titles and beneficiary designations to your living trust. But, remember, you can either do it now or you can pay the courts and attorneys to do it for you later.

Most "disadvantages" are just incorrect or outdated information

It's best to just make this process a priority and don't stop until everything has been changed to your trust. If you only do a few assets now and then, it could take you a long time. Or worse, you may never get it done. Stay positive and focused. Remember, you'll probably only have to do this once. Remind yourself why you are doing it. Think how much easier things will be for your family. And look forward to the peace of mind you'll have when you're done!

"Refinancing Real Estate Can Be Difficult."

As living trusts have become more popular, this isn't the problem that it used to be. However, depending on where you live, you still may encounter some difficulty if you want to refinance property that is in your trust. Here's why.

Local banks, and savings and loans, often re-sell their mortgages to institutions in the secondary lending market. They have been reluctant to refinance property in the name of a living trust because these secondary lenders did not have any guidelines for whether or not a revocable living trust would be considered an "eligible borrower."

However, because living trusts have become so widely accepted across the country, the major secondary lenders (Fannie Mae, Freddie Mac and Ginnie Mae) have published guidelines under which they will accept a revocable living trust as an eligible borrower.

If you find refinancing becoming a problem, you can transfer the title back to your name temporarily, just until the loan has been approved and closed. Then transfer the property back into your trust as soon as possible. This entire process can often be done when you sign the new loan. Or you may want to find another, more trust-friendly, lender.

"It's Better To Have The Probate Court's Supervision."

Many people who set up a living trust name a family member as successor trustee. But some forget to inform this person about his/her responsibilities. As a result, their successor trustees don't know what they are supposed to do when the person dies. Some simply do nothing, which can eventually cause some problems and unnecessary expenses. For example, there can be penalties if tax returns are not filed when they are due.

Probate advocates argue that people *need* the supervision of the probate court in order to do things correctly. But the solution is not probate. *It's education.*

Your successor trustee needs to know that, even with a living trust, some things *do* need to be done after you die—and *you* need to choose your successor with care. Remember, your successor trustee has the same responsibilities as an executor—paying final bills, having tax returns prepared, getting appraisals if needed, distributing assets. The only difference is that your successor trustee does these things without court interference.

In Part Seven, we have included step-by-step instructions for what your successor trustee needs to do if you become incapacitated and when you die.

"A Living Trust Is A Waste Of Time And Money Because Most People End Up Going Through Probate Anyway."

If your living trust is properly prepared and funded, your assets will *not* go through probate. There are only three reasons your assets would go through probate if you have a living trust:

1. *Your trust is not fully funded.* This can happen if you procrastinate and don't finish changing titles and beneficiary designations, or if you simply forget an asset. It can also happen if you acquire additional assets and don't title them in the name of your trust.

2. *Your trust is not properly written.* This can happen if you use a do-it-yourself kit or software program. It can happen if your trust is prepared by an out-of-state attorney who is not familiar with your state's laws. It can also happen if you use an attorney who is not experienced specifically in living trusts. (If you need help finding an attorney, see Part Five.)

3. *You do not have a revocable living trust.* Some attorneys write testamentary trusts (in a will) even when the client asks for a living trust. Some attorneys have even written living trusts that make all the assets go through probate before they go to the beneficiaries.

   How can you know what you have? If you have a trust but did not change titles, you either have a testamentary trust or a living trust that is not funded. If you have any questions about your trust, read your document.

If you can't understand it, it might be worth it to have it reviewed by another attorney. A trust officer at your local bank or trust company may also be able to provide some assistance.

If your revocable living trust has been properly prepared and funded, your assets will avoid probate. It is very important that your living trust is prepared by an attorney who has experience in living trusts. And your living trust must be funded because it can only control the assets that you put in it.

Now, having said all that, in a few states there may be some procedures your beneficiaries will want or need to have done through the probate court, like getting a shorter time limit on creditors' claims or a homestead determination in Florida. (Both are explained below.) Even so, your assets will not have to go through probate if they are in your living trust.

"Creditors Have Less Time In Probate To Submit Claims."

Probate proponents have long argued that one of the disadvantages of a living trust is that creditors have a much longer time during which they can present claims (including lawsuits) after you die than in probate.

With probate, creditors usually have only a few months to present their claims. After this time, they are "forever barred" and the executor can distribute the assets without fear of any future claims. In some states, the normal statute of limitations is the only time limit that applies if you have a living trust.

Because of this, you may have heard that professionals and business owners who are concerned about the risk of a lawsuit after they die should have wills instead of living trusts.

Well, times and the laws are changing. Several states now allow a living trust to have the same time limit for creditors' claims as probate. But even if you live in a state that doesn't have this, there is no reason for all of your assets to go through probate. You can still have a living trust *and* get the shorter time limit on creditor claims that probate provides. Here's how.

You set up a living trust just as we have explained and transfer your assets into it. Then, after you die, a probate can be opened to see if any creditors have claims to present. If they do, then *just enough assets to satisfy the claim(s)* can be transferred out of your living trust; the rest are protected from probate. And all of your assets are protected from any future claims from creditors.

A good example is Florida. When there is no probate (because all of your assets are in your trust), creditors have up to two years to file their claims. But, with probate, they can be limited to just three months. So, if your beneficiaries are concerned about creditors and don't want to wait for two years, they can open a probate proceeding and start the creditor clock running. No assets have to go through probate, but all creditor claims can be cut off within three months.

"You'll Lose Your Homestead Exemption."
Most states have laws that protect a certain amount of homestead property (house, other buildings and surrounding land used as your residence) from creditors. You might also get a deduction on your property taxes.

There is usually a limit on the value of property that can be claimed as a homestead. But in some states, including Florida and Texas, there is no dollar limit; there is only a limit on the number of acres you can own.

For example, in Florida, homestead property can be up to one-half acre within a municipality or up to 160 acres outside a municipality. In Texas, a homestead can be up to ten acres in an urban area and up to 100 acres in a rural area. So you can see that homestead exemptions can be very valuable. In both Florida and Texas, putting your home in a living trust will not cause you to lose your homestead exemption, and it should not in other states.

"You Can Lose Bankruptcy Protection On Your Home."
In some states, a portion or all of your home is automatically protected from creditors if you file for bankruptcy. In a few states, putting your home in a living trust can cause you to lose this exemption. But the amount of protection you forfeit (which varies, depending on the state in which you live) may be so insignificant that it doesn't matter. For example, in Missouri, only the first $15,000 of a personal residence can be protected from bankruptcy, certainly not enough to warrant leaving your home (the most valuable asset most people own) out of your living trust.

If you are considering filing for bankruptcy, you will want to find out if your state has a homeowner's exemption, how much it is worth, and if you will

Any inconvenience usually pales when compared to all the benefits

lose any of it by putting your home in your living trust. A bankruptcy attorney in your state can advise you of options you may have.

"ATM Withdrawals Can Be Inconvenient."

If you use a credit card to withdraw cash from your personal checking account through an automatic teller machine (ATM), you may run into a problem. Most banks will not issue a credit card in the name of a trust, and for the ATM to work, the names on the account and the credit card must match. So if your personal checking account is in the name of your trust and your credit card is in your name, the ATM won't work. If this turns out to be a problem for you, you can make the withdrawal as a cash advance against the credit card itself instead of against your checking account.

If your bank issues a separate ATM withdrawal card, you'll probably be okay, especially if you are your own trustee. However, some banks may still be hesitant to issue an ATM card to a trust account if they're not sure who is authorized to use it. So they may ask to see your trust document before approving it. (A certificate of trust, explained in Part Five, will probably satisfy this requirement.) Of course, if you have a good relationship with your bank, you probably won't have a problem.

"A Trustee Has More Personal Liability Than An Executor."

Your successor trustee, just like an executor, is not personally liable for any debts you owe when you die. In other words, their personal assets cannot be seized to pay your debts.

If the trustee distributes all of the assets to the beneficiaries and Uncle Sam says more taxes are due, the trustee will be liable for the payment of those taxes if the beneficiaries will not give the money back to the trustee. The trustee can go ahead and distribute assets, but to protect themselves from this potential liability, most trustees will hold back a reserve amount until the IRS sends written confirmation that the taxes have been paid in full. An executor does not have this liability, but only because the probate court *will not allow* all of the assets to be distributed until the confirmation has been received from the IRS.

A trustee also has certain legal responsibilities. If a trustee abuses his/her powers (for example, if your successor trustee does not follow the instructions in your trust or uses your assets for his/her own benefit), he/she can be sued by the beneficiaries and held personally liable. This, remember, is for your protection. Usually this is not a problem because most trustees, even family members, take their responsibilities seriously.

"A Trustee Is Liable For Clean Up Of Contaminated Property."

In 1980, Congress passed a law that defined who is liable for the clean up of hazardous substances. This law is known as CERCLA: the Comprehensive Environmental Response, Compensation and Liability Act of 1980. Responsible parties include past, and current, owners and operators of contaminated property. Other federal and state laws place similar liabilities on those responsible for clean up of petroleum products and other pollutants.

This means a trustee can be personally liable for the clean up of any pollutant found on property that is in your trust. If you are your own trustee, this won't impact you because, as the owner of the property, you are already liable. However, your successor trustee(s) and your beneficiaries could also be liable if the clean up has not been completed and paid for by the time of your death, and the contamination continues after they begin to manage the property.

Be sure to tell your attorney if there is a possibility that property you own is contaminated. For example, a gas station with underground tanks, or a printing facility or other business that used chemicals, may have been on property you now own. It's best to find out the extent of the contamination and estimated cost of clean up before transferring the property to your trust. Your attorney can then help you with your planning options, which may include:

- Compensating your successor trustee for the liability. (Life insurance on your life is one possibility.) Your successor trustee should also be fully informed of the situation before agreeing to serve.

- Leaving this property out of your trust and letting it go through probate. Under existing law, there is a possibility that letting the property go through probate may reduce the risk of liability for the executor and heirs.

- If the cost to clean up the property exceeds its value, you could give it to the U.S. government or to an ex-spouse. (Just kidding!)

"Congress Will Probably Eliminate Living Trusts."

Anything's possible, but this is highly unlikely. Remember, living trusts have been around, in one form or another, for hundreds of years. Besides, neither the state nor federal government receives income from probate, so there's no incentive for them to eliminate living trusts and make people go through probate. In fact, the states have every reason to *encourage* living trusts as a way to reduce the already overcrowded court system.

"Probate Has Better Income Tax Planning Options After You Die."

There used to be some *differences* (not necessarily advantages) in how federal income taxes were determined, after you die, when an estate goes through probate and when you have a living trust.

Most families were not affected by these differences. However, attorneys (especially pro-probate attorneys) loved to debate the importance of these differences and, in some cases, they actually persuaded people *not* to set up a living trust because of them.

Over the years, pro-trust attorneys pushed to make the taxation of trusts and probate estates equal. In *The Taxpayer Relief Act of 1997,* the last remaining differences were all but eliminated.

We have included an explanation of these issues in Part Eight, including how they used to be different and how they are now the same, just in case you run into someone who is not current with the law.

SUMMARY

As mentioned earlier, many of these "disadvantages" simply turn out to be incorrect or outdated information. For most people, any real disadvantages either never come up or can easily be planned around. However, if you are concerned about any of these, be sure to mention them to your attorney.

WHY HAVEN'T LIVING TRUSTS BEEN USED MORE IN THE PAST?

Probate is big business

If a living trust is so wonderful, why did so many of us get a will?

"It's The Way We've Always Done It."
We inherited wills and probate from the English and after several hundred years, this was a system that worked. Probate laws and procedures are pretty much set, and there are plenty of tested and proven cases to rely upon.

Many law firms have developed entire departments that do nothing but handle probate estates. And as new attorneys are brought into a firm, they are taught how things are done by the more experienced attorneys. So the traditional way of doing things (probate) has been handed down through generations.

"Trusts Are Only For The Wealthy."
Trusts have been around for hundreds of years, too. But they were mainly being done by the larger firms for wealthy clients who needed special tax planning. As a result, trusts became associated with well-to-do families, like the Rockefellers and the Morgans, who used trusts to transfer enormous amounts of wealth from one generation to the next.

Some corporate trustees, who only managed trust assets of substantial value, also helped encourage the myth. Because it generally wasn't cost effective for them to handle smaller accounts, they often told people of moderate means they didn't need a trust.

So, it's easy to see how the public, and many professionals, came to believe that trusts are only for the wealthy.

Probate Is Big Business
Wills and probate have been, and still are, a lucrative business. Remember, AARP's report estimated that probate was generating as much as $1.5 billion a year for attorneys and hundreds of millions more for bonding companies, appraisers, and the probate courts.

Building a "will practice" was pretty simple and profitable. Some attorneys would draft your will for a nominal charge because they knew they had an excellent chance of probating your will when you died and your spouse's will when your spouse died. Frequently, the attorney would even be named in the will to represent your estate(s) in probate.

And if you and/or your spouse became incapacitated, or died leaving minor children, the same attorney would also probably represent you or your children in the court proceedings (yet another source of attorney fees).

You Get What You Ask For

The public didn't know there was another way. And if all you know about is a will, and you ask for a will, then you'll probably get...a will.

Resistance To Change

So, no wonder the legal profession had been reluctant to make changes. With wills and probate, attorneys had a well established and lucrative business doing something clients asked for. They were comfortable. Why should they take the time to learn a different way? You know the old saying: "If it ain't broke, why fix it?"

So WHY ARE LIVING TRUSTS SO POPULAR NOW?

One simple reason: consumer demand.

With more than 65 million Americans over the age of 50, more people than ever before are starting to think about how to transfer their assets and provide for their loved ones after they're gone.

They all want to do the right thing. What parent or grandparent doesn't? But things are so much more complicated today. This generation has concerns that most of their parents didn't have to face. For example:

■ With people living longer, they worry about what will happen if they become incapacitated.
■ With second (and even third) marriages so common, many worry about how to provide for their surviving spouses without disinheriting their children and grandchildren.

- With the high rate of divorce and lawsuits, they worry that their assets will end up in the hands of their children's spouses or creditors.
- With today's "spend now, save later" attitude and values so different from their own, many worry that their children will not be responsible with the assets they worked all their lives to accumulate.
- With our personal information available to others through giant computer databases, they worry about how to protect their privacy.
- Concerns about taxes, legal fees, and other costs cause them to worry about how much of their assets their loved ones will actually receive.

In their research (through reading earlier editions of this book and other publications), people began to find out what can happen when they use wills, joint ownership, and beneficiary designations to transfer assets. They learned that, without proper planning, much of their assets can be lost *unnecessarily* to court costs, legal fees, unintended heirs, and taxes.

They also began to find out about revocable living trusts, and they liked what they learned. The living trust met their needs far better than any other plan. Here, finally, was a way that not only avoids probate and saves taxes, but also gave them more flexibility, control, and maximum privacy.

Armed with this knowledge, this generation—one of the largest, and most powerful and influential we have ever had—started asking for living trusts instead of wills. And the legal profession scrambled to meet the demand.

The progress in just the last few years has been nothing short of amazing. Instead of being on the fringes, the living trust is now embraced by professionals and consumers alike, and is preferred over a will as the primary estate planning document.

Thanks, in large part, to the efforts of this generation, it is now much easier than ever before to find an attorney who will offer you the choice of a living trust and can prepare one for you.

A Comparison At A Glance

	With No Will	**With A Will**	**With A Living Trust**
At Incapacity* (inability to handle your financial affairs)	*Court Control:* Court appointee oversees your care, must keep detailed records, reports to court, and usually must post bond (even if appointee is your spouse). Court oversees financial affairs, approves all expenses.	*Court Control:* Same as with no will.	*No Court Control:* Co-trustee or successor trustee manages your financial affairs according to instructions in your trust for as long as necessary. If you recover, you can resume control with no court interference.
Court Costs & Legal Fees	Impossible to estimate. Court and attorney usually involved until you recover or die.	Same as with no will.	No court costs. Minimal legal fees if attorney assistance is desired.
At Death	*Probate:* Court orders your debts paid and assets distributed according to state law.	*Probate:* Court orders debts paid and assets distributed according to your will (if valid and no successful contests).	*No probate:* Debts are paid and assets distributed to beneficiaries by successor trustee according to your trust's instructions.
Court Costs & Legal Fees	Your estate pays all court costs, legal, and executor fees (often estimated at 3-8% or more of an estate's value).	Same as with no will. Costs and fees can increase if will is contested.	Minimal or no court costs. Reduced legal fees (minimal for small estates; larger/complex estates require more). Trustee entitled to reasonable fee.
Time	Usually 9 months to 2 years before heirs can inherit.	Same as with no will.	Can be just weeks. Larger estates may take longer for estate tax filings.
Flexibility and Control	*None:* Court processes, not your family, have control at incapacity and death. When you die, assets are distributed according to state law (probably not what you would have wanted).	*Limited:* Same as no will, except assets are distributed when you die per your will (if valid and no contests are successful). Will can be changed until your incapacity.	*Maximum:* You can change/discontinue trust until incapacity. Assets stay under control of your trust, even at incapacity and after your death. More difficult to contest than a will.
Privacy	*None:* Court proceedings are public record. Family can be exposed to disgruntled heirs, unscrupulous solicitors.	*None:* Same as with no will.	*Maximum:* Living trusts are not public record. Your family can take care of your financial affairs privately.
Minor Child	*Court Control:* Court controls inheritance, appoints guardian. All decisions and financial transactions require court approval. Child receives full inheritance at legal age.	*Court Control:* Same as with no will. Children's trust in a will provides limited protection, but the will must be probated first and cannot go into effect at your incapacity.	*Minimal Court Control:* Trustee you select manages inheritance and provides funds for expenses until child reaches age(s) you specify. Court approves guardian, but cannot overrule your choice of trustee and has no control over inheritance.
Court Costs & Legal Fees	Impossible to estimate. Court and attorney usually involved until child reaches legal age. All costs paid from child's inheritance.	Same as with no will. Costs may be less with children's trust in will.	Minimal.

*Durable Power of Attorney for Health Care/Health Care Proxy can prevent court interference in medical decisions.

Part Three—

THE ABCs OF A LIVING TRUST

How to Reduce/Eliminate Estate Taxes, Provide for Your Spouse Without Disinheriting Your Children, and More

By now, you know about the many benefits a living trust offers you and your family. But so far we haven't talked much about estate taxes that may have to be paid when you die—and how your living trust can reduce or even eliminate them.

In this section, we'll explain what estate taxes are, who has to pay them, and how much they can be. We'll explain how additional provisions in your living trust can give you powerful tax planning and other benefits—including how you can provide for your surviving spouse for as long as he/she lives, yet keep control over who will eventually receive your assets. This can be especially important if you have children from a previous marriage. So even if you don't have to worry about estate taxes, this section may contain valuable information for you.

EXPENSES THAT CAN REDUCE YOUR ESTATE

When you die, there are basically three ways your estate can be reduced before it can go to your beneficiaries. One is probate which, as you know by now, can be avoided with a living trust. There are also income and estate taxes. Both of these are different from—and in addition to—probate costs. Let's first look at the income taxes.

Regardless of whether or not you have a living trust, your estate must file a federal income tax return for the year in which you die—just as you do now every year. (Depending on the state in which you live, state income taxes may also need to be paid.) Any income you receive in the year you die must be

Expenses That Reduce Your Estate

When you die, your estate can be substantially reduced in three ways:

1) **Probate**, which can be avoided with a living trust;

2) **Income Taxes**, which must be paid on any income you receive in the year you die; and

3) **Estate Taxes**, which can be reduced or even eliminated with a living trust and other planning options.

reported and any taxes due on that income must be paid. A living trust has *no* effect on your income taxes. However, additional planning can help reduce income taxes while you are living and after you die.

Income tax planning areas may include IRAs and other tax-deferred retirement plans, capital gains tax and stepped-up basis, Medicare surtax on investment income, and others. Income tax issues are discussed in Parts Eight and Nine, and there is a discussion about IRAs and other tax-deferred plans in Part Six. During the estate planning process, your attorney will also be able to review your income tax situation and recommend specific planning strategies, many of which are introduced in Part Nine.

The federal estate tax is part of the transfer tax system, which was designed to tax assets whenever you transfer them to another person during your lifetime and after your death. (The other parts of the transfer tax system are the gift tax and generation-skipping transfer tax. A discussion of these taxes is delayed until Part Nine.)

Fortunately, as you will see, most families are no longer affected by the federal estate tax. However, many states have their own death/inheritance tax that affects even modest estates. By planning ahead, you can reduce or even eliminate state and federal estate taxes. If you are married, one easy way to do this is through your living trust. In Part Nine, we explain other ways to reduce taxes that can be used by both married and single people.

UNDERSTANDING ESTATE TAXES

What Are Estate Taxes?

The federal estate tax is a tax on the net value of your estate (your assets less your debts) at the time of your death. Some people call this the death tax.

What makes the estate tax so egregious to many taxpayers is that it is, in effect, a double tax. Over the years, you've already paid income taxes on the money and assets that now make up your estate. When you die, your estate may have to pay taxes on these assets again.

Estate taxes must be paid in cash, usually within nine months of your death. As a result, assets often must be sold quickly, at depressed prices. Many family farms and businesses have not survived for the next generation because families have been forced to sell in order to pay estate taxes. (There is one exception to the nine-month deadline. If you are a business owner and your business is at least 35% of your taxable estate, you may be able to pay the estate taxes in installments.)

Who Has To Pay Estate Taxes And How Much Are They?

Your estate will have to pay estate taxes if its net value (assets minus debts) when you die is more than the exempt amount set by Congress at that time.

In 2019, the federal estate tax exemption is $11.4 million and the estate tax rate is 40%. This means if you die in 2019 and your net estate is less than this, your estate will pay no federal estate tax. If you die in 2019 and your net estate is more than this, every dollar over this amount will be taxed at 40%.

The good news is, with the exemption this high, most people are currently not subject to the federal estate tax. This means they are free to plan their estates the way they want without having to plan around federal estate taxes. However, some states have their own death/inheritance tax, usually starting at a lower threshold. So it is possible that your estate could be exempt from federal tax and still have to pay state tax.

If your net estate is less than $11.4 million, you *could* skip the rest of this chapter. But, remember, if you have children from a previous marriage, you will probably want to learn how you can provide for your surviving spouse without disinheriting your children. Also, it is possible that your assets could appreciate

Your estate could be exempt from the federal estate tax but have to pay a state tax

and make your estate subject to estate taxes when you die. It is also possible that the federal estate tax exemption could change. Finally, you may live in or own assets in a state that has a death and/or inheritance tax. So learning about the ABCs of a living trust might still be worth your time. But, first, a little history.

Federal Estate Tax History Is Important

During the American Civil War and the Spanish-American War, a temporary federal estate tax was imposed to raise money to fund these wars. After the latter tax was repealed in 1902, a few American businessmen and entrepreneurs built huge fortunes. Fearing that such concentrated wealth and power would lead to control of the government by these few families, the new Progressive movement advocated for an inheritance tax and graduated income tax as a way to address income and wealth inequality. The 16th Amendment to the Constitution was passed, and the federal income tax was born. In 1916, as World War I approached, Congress enacted the federal estate tax.

Ever since, the estate tax has been a political football. Generally speaking, Democrats favor higher taxes as a way to redistribute wealth and Republicans favor lower taxes as a way to help small businesses and grow the economy. As you can see from the following chart, keeping up with the federal estate tax in recent years has been a real challenge. This may give you some empathy for professionals who must plan without knowing what the exemptions and tax rates will be when their clients eventually die.

During George W. Bush's presidency, Republicans pushed for a total repeal of the estate tax, but they did not have the additional votes they needed from Democrats to make it permanent. They reached a compromise, resulting in an increase in the exemption and a decrease in the top tax rate over several years (which effectively lowered the tax) and a one-year repeal in 2010. The Republicans had hoped to have control of Congress before 2011 and make the repeal permanent, but that did not happen.

After the one-year repeal in 2010, the estate tax was scheduled to revert to a $1 million exemption and 55% top tax rate. The estate planning community was surprised when President Obama agreed to a two-year $5 million exemption, tied to inflation, with a 35% tax rate. With only a two-year law in place, uncertainty again seemed the norm. But in *The American Taxpayer Relief Act of 2012*, the $5 million exemption, tied to inflation, was made *permanent*, along with a 40% tax rate. (That means it's the law until Congress decides to change it.)

Recent Historical Federal Estate Tax Exemption and Top Tax Rate

Year of Death	Exemption	Top Tax Rate
1987-1997	$600,000	55%
1998	$625,000	55%
1999	$650,000	55%
2000 and 2001	$675,000	55%
2002	$1,000,000	50%
2003	$1,000,000	49%
2004	$1,500,000	48%
2005	$1,500,000	47%
2006	$2,000,000	46%
2007 and 2008	$2,000,000	45%
2009	$3,500,000	45%
2010	N/A (repealed)	0%
2011	$5,000,000	35%
2012	$5,120,000	35%
2013	$5,250,000	40%
2014	$5,340,000	40%
2015	$5,430,000	40%
2016	$5,450,000	40%
2017	$5,490,000	40%
2018	$11,200,000	40%
2019	$11,400,000	40%

President Trump wanted to eliminate the federal estate tax entirely. While that did not happen, *The Tax Cuts and Jobs Act (TCJA)*, passed in December 2017, increased the exemption from $5,490,000 to $11.2 million. With an adjustment for inflation, the exemption increased in 2019 to $11.4 million.

The Tax Policy Center estimates that in 2018, only about 1700 estates (less than 0.1 percent of all deaths) were subject to the federal estate tax, compared to 52,000 in 2000 when the exemption was $675,000. But because the law passed under budget reconciliation with a simple majority in the Senate (no Democrats), the increase could not be made permanent. In 2025, it is scheduled to revert to a $5 million exemption, indexed for inflation.

So, the history lesson is this: Anything is possible when it comes to the federal estate tax. Because we cannot know when we will die and what the laws will be at that time, the smart move is to plan your estate based on the laws currently in effect, then review your plan with your attorney whenever the tax laws (and/or your circumstances) change.

Assets can appreciate greatly over time

Planning For Appreciation

Before you assume your estate isn't large enough to be affected by estate taxes, you may want to do some math. Some assets, especially real estate and stocks, may have appreciated greatly since you bought them, and you may find you are worth more than you think.

Remember that estate taxes are based on the value of your estate *when you die*. Many of your assets will continue to appreciate between now and then. As the following chart shows, even a moderate estate can appreciate significantly over time. Also, the laws can change at any time. So, while you may not have an estate tax problem now, you could have one by the time you die.

How An Estate Can Appreciate Over Time*			
Today	*In 5 Years*	*In 10 Years*	*In 15 Years*
$1,000,000	$1,276,282	$1,628,895	$2,078,928
$2,000,000	$2,552,563	$3,257,789	$4,157,856
$3,000,000	$3,828,845	$4,886,684	$6,236,785
$4,000,000	$5,105,126	$6,515,579	$8,315,713
$5,000,000	$6,381,408	$8,144,473	$10,394,641

Assumes 5% growth

Determining Your Taxable Estate

To determine the current size of your taxable estate, add the current market value of everything you own and subtract any debts and mortgages. (The Organizer in the back of this book will help you do this easily.) Be sure to include assets you own outright and *your share* of any jointly owned assets.

Assets include real estate, checking and savings accounts, investments (including CDs, stocks, bonds and mutual funds), profit sharing balances, IRAs, pensions, investments in partnerships and/or businesses, notes payable to you, any personal property you own, automobiles, boats, campers, and any benefits to which your estate will be entitled when you die.

Your assets also include—this one may surprise you—the death benefits from *all* life insurance policies on your life for which you have any "incidents of ownership" as defined by the IRS. This would include policies you can borrow

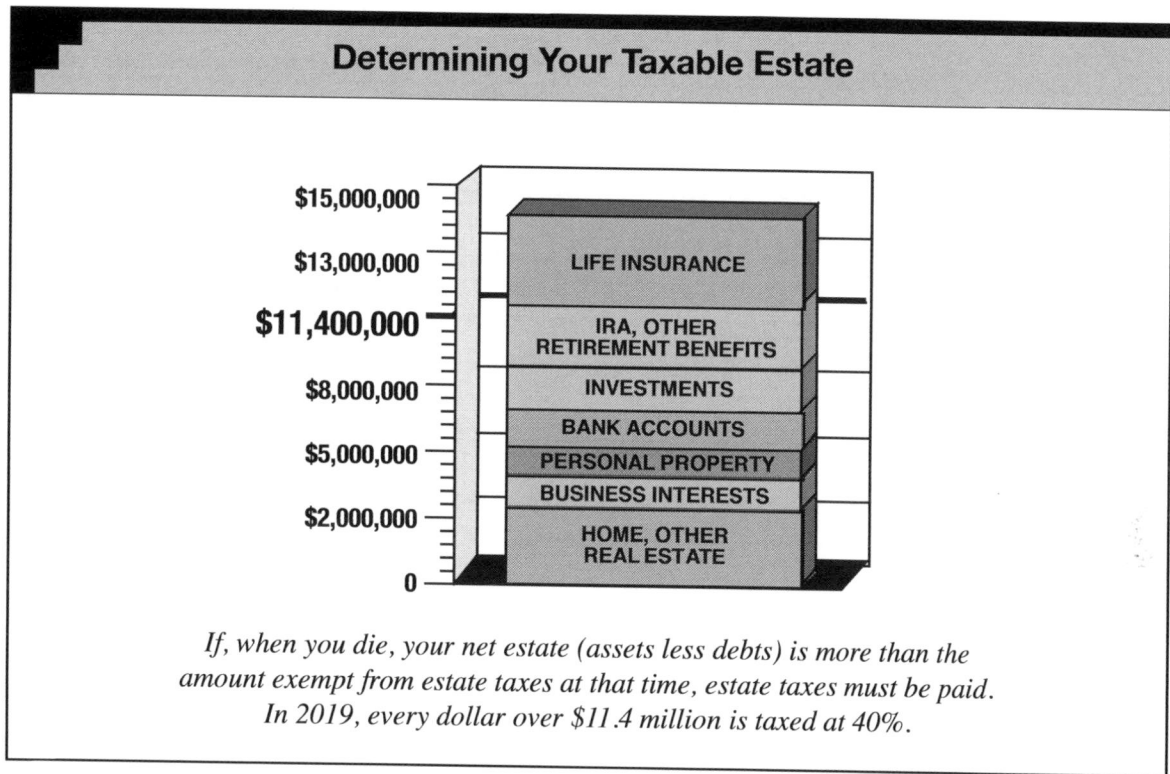

Determining Your Taxable Estate

$15,000,000

$13,000,000 — LIFE INSURANCE

$11,400,000 — IRA, OTHER RETIREMENT BENEFITS

$8,000,000 — INVESTMENTS

BANK ACCOUNTS

$5,000,000 — PERSONAL PROPERTY

BUSINESS INTERESTS

$2,000,000 — HOME, OTHER REAL ESTATE

0

If, when you die, your net estate (assets less debts) is more than the amount exempt from estate taxes at that time, estate taxes must be paid. In 2019, every dollar over $11.4 million is taxed at 40%.

against, assign, or cancel, for which you can revoke an assignment, or for which you can name or change the beneficiary—regardless of who actually *owns* the policy. For example, insurance provided by your employer would be included if you can name and/or change the beneficiary. (This is why you may want your life insurance to be owned by an irrevocable life insurance trust, as discussed in Part Nine.)

■ Add Taxable Gifts

There is one more thing you may need to do before calculating estate taxes: add back in taxable gifts you have made since 1976. What is a taxable gift?

This is easier to explain by starting with *non*taxable gifts. Each year, you can make as many tax-free gifts to as many recipients as you wish, as long as each gift is within the limit set by Congress. Currently, the amount for annual tax-free gifts is $15,000; it is tied to inflation, and increases from time to time. If you are married, you and your spouse can each make annual tax-free gifts and double the amount you give.

Generally, anytime you give anyone other than your spouse *more* than the annual tax-free limit, you have made a taxable gift. The gift does not have to be in cash. For example, if you give your son some stocks, or make your daughter a joint owner on your home, these are gifts. And if the value of the gift exceeds the annual tax-free limit, the excess is a taxable gift—and Uncle Sam wants to know about it. That's because Uncle Sam wants to make sure you don't give away some or *all* of your assets without paying *any* estate taxes. Otherwise, you could give everything away and have a taxable estate of "0." (In Part Nine we explain more about making gifts and gift taxes.)

How Much Will Your Estate Have To Pay In Estate Taxes?

As explained earlier, if you die in 2019 and the net value of your estate is more than $11.4 million, every dollar over this exempt amount will be taxed at 40%. The following chart shows various size estates and what the estate taxes would be in 2019. Find one close to your net estate for an idea of how much your estate would have to pay.

Federal Estate Taxes in 2019*	
Taxable Estate	**Estate Tax**
$11,400,000 and below	$0
$12,000,000	$240,000
$13,000,000	$640,000
$14,000,000	$1,040,000
$15,000,000	$1,440,000
$18,000,000	$1,840,000
$20,000,000	$3,440,000

* In 2019, every dollar over $11.4 million is taxed at 40%.

Now, what can you do about these estate taxes?

How To Reduce Or Eliminate Estate Taxes

If you plan ahead, you can reduce or even eliminate estate taxes. In the simplest terms, there are three ways to do this:

■ **Reduce the size of your estate *before* you die.** If you reduce the *size* of your taxable estate now (by spending or giving away some of it), you will reduce your estate tax *bill*. But you have to make gifts correctly— otherwise, you will end up paying too much in gift/estate taxes or income taxes. In Part Nine, we explain some of the best ways to do this.

■ **Buy life insurance to pay estate taxes.** Depending on your age and health, buying life insurance can be an inexpensive way to pay any remaining estate taxes. However, if you are the owner of the policy, that will just increase the size of your taxable estate and the amount of estate taxes that must be paid. In Part Nine, we explain how to purchase insurance and keep it out of your taxable estate.

■ **But first, if you are married, include a special tax-planning provision in your living trust.** In the rest of this section, we'll explain how this works.

By planning ahead, you can reduce or even eliminate estate taxes

Leaving everything to your spouse

The Unlimited Marital Deduction: Uncle Sam's Plan #1

You may not know it, but if you are married and your spouse is a U.S. citizen, you already have a plan to reduce estate taxes when you die. But you didn't sit down and plan it—your dear old Uncle Sam did it for you.

Currently, when you die you can leave *any* amount of assets to your spouse and there will be *no* estate taxes at that time. This is called the *unlimited marital deduction* for two reasons: 1) there is *no limit* on the value of assets one spouse can leave to the other, estate tax-free, and 2) the assets you leave to your spouse are *deducted* from your taxable estate. So, if you leave everything to your spouse, *your* taxable estate will be zero.

That sounds pretty good—so far. But when your surviving spouse dies, everything your spouse owns, including the assets you leave to your spouse when you die, will be subject to estate taxes before the assets can be distributed to the beneficiaries. Of course, your spouse's estate will be entitled to your spouse's estate tax exemption. So, in 2019, there will be no estate taxes on the first $11,400,000 your spouse owns.

But guess what? *Both* you and your spouse are entitled to an exemption. And if you leave everything to your spouse, you will potentially *waste* yours. This could cause your family to pay too much in estate taxes. Uncle Sam is patient—he'll wait until the second spouse dies to collect estate taxes.

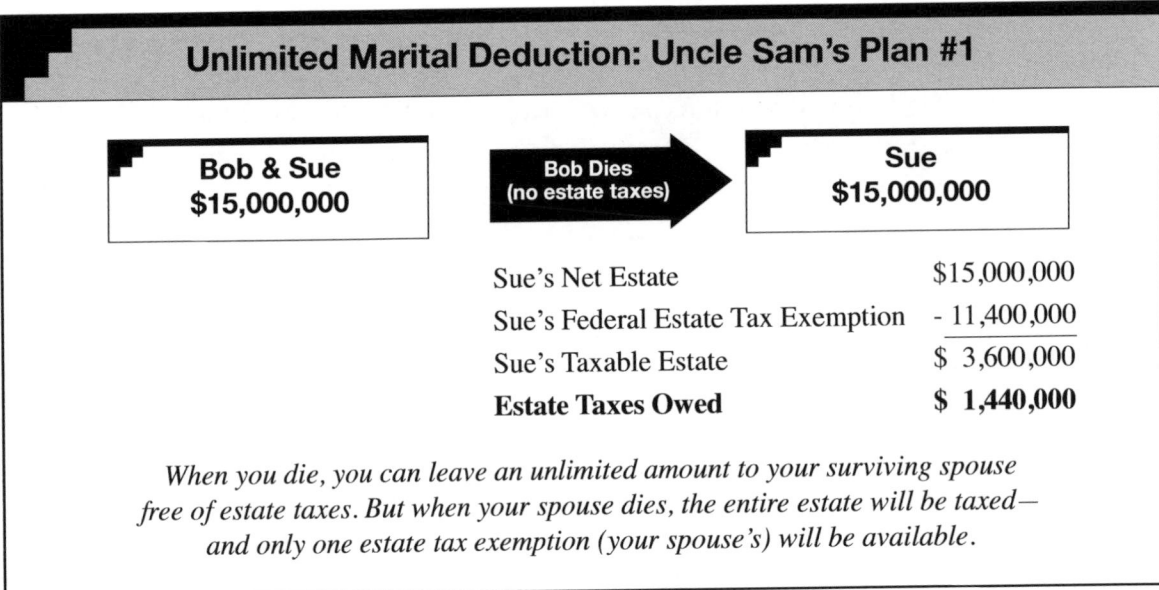

Unlimited Marital Deduction: Uncle Sam's Plan #1

Bob & Sue	Bob Dies	Sue
$15,000,000	(no estate taxes)	$15,000,000

Sue's Net Estate	$15,000,000
Sue's Federal Estate Tax Exemption	- 11,400,000
Sue's Taxable Estate	$ 3,600,000
Estate Taxes Owed	**$ 1,440,000**

When you die, you can leave an unlimited amount to your surviving spouse free of estate taxes. But when your spouse dies, the entire estate will be taxed—and only one estate tax exemption (your spouse's) will be available.

Portability: Uncle Sam's Plan #2

In 2010, Congress tried to fix this problem by introducing a provision called portability. (It was made permanent in *The Taxpayer Relief Act of 2012*.) Portability, which allows the surviving spouse to use the deceased spouse's unused exemption (DSUE), is considered a back-up plan for married couples who neglect to do their estate planning while both are living.

Portability is not automatic. An estate tax return (Form 706) must be filed within nine months after the death of the first spouse, unless an extension is granted. If this is not done within the allowed time frame, portability and the deceased spouse's unused exemption are forever lost, resulting in only the surviving spouse's single exemption being available.

Remarriage does not change the identity of the most recently deceased spouse, and a surviving spouse can use multiple DSUEs. Here's an example:

> When Bob died, Sue's attorney filed an estate tax return for his estate, making portability available. A few years later, Sue married Tom. Sue decided to use Bob's unused exemption and made gifts to their children. When Tom died a few years later, Sue's attorney filed an estate tax return for Tom's estate, making portability available for *his* unused exemption. When Sue died, her estate was able to use both her exemption and Tom's unused exemption. Had Sue not used Bob's DSUE before Tom died, it would have been wasted, as Tom would be her most recently deceased spouse.

Leaving Everything to Your Spouse Means You Lose Control

With the estate tax exemption as high as it is now, you may not be as concerned about using both exemptions to save estate taxes. The bigger problem for many families is that leaving everything to your spouse gives one spouse complete control over all of the assets. After you die, your spouse can leave those assets to whomever he/she wants. That may be okay with you if there are no children outside this marriage. But if you have children from a previous relationship or want some say about who receives your share of the assets (especially if your spouse remarries), you probably want to keep some control.

Most couples want to make sure the surviving spouse is provided for, and they want to avoid estate taxes when the first spouse dies so the entire estate will be available to care for the spouse who is living. They think they're doing the right thing by leaving everything to each other through their "sweetheart" wills, joint ownership, beneficiary designations, even their living trusts. Plus, it's easy—you don't have to plan ahead to use the unlimited marital deduction. And you can wait until after one spouse dies to elect portability.

But planning ahead can be easy, too. With your living trust, you can avoid probate, provide for your surviving spouse without disinheriting your children, keep control over your share of the assets if your spouse remarries, and reduce or even eliminate estate taxes by using both exemptions.

The unlimited marital deduction and portability are not bad planning tools. In fact, your attorney may incorporate one or both of them in your estate plan and for some couples, especially those with one long-term marriage, they can be very helpful. But you will have the best results when you plan ahead with all available options, instead of being limited because you neglected to plan.

Now, let's get into the ABCs of a living trust.

> **Note:** The following pages are intentionally written in a general manner to help you understand the basics of how these provisions work. Even though most Americans currently are not subject to the federal estate tax, these provisions can still be beneficial for many families. Your attorney may suggest some variations not presented here.

Portability is not automatic

THE A-B LIVING TRUST SOLUTION

You and your spouse together can set up one common living trust (just like we've been discussing), of which each of you owns half. For as long as you are both living, you have *one* living trust with all of your assets in it. Then, when one of you dies, this trust will automatically split into two *separate* trusts.

This is called an A-B living trust because the two separate trusts are often referred to as Trust A (for the surviving spouse) and Trust B (for the deceased spouse). To help keep these straight, think of Trust A as the one "**A**bove the ground" (for the living person) and Trust B as "**B**elow the ground" (for the deceased person). It is a bit direct but, as a word association trick, it works.

You and your spouse can also start out with separate trusts instead of one common trust. While you and your spouse are living, both of these trusts are considered "A" trusts. (Remember, you're both **A**bove the ground.) Then, when one of you dies, the deceased spouse's trust becomes Trust B, and the surviving spouse's trust remains Trust A. (More on separate trusts later in this section.)

If you live in a community property state, you and your spouse will probably have a common A-B trust. If you live in a noncommunity property state, you and your spouse will likely have separate trusts. Either way works. They are only different while you and your spouse are both living. After one spouse dies, they are exactly the same.

> **Note:** Your attorney may refer to this as a living trust with an A-B provision. He/she may also use different names for the separate trusts. For example, Trust A is often called a *survivor's trust* or *marital trust*, because it's for the surviving spouse. Trust B is often called a *bypass trust* because it "bypasses" estate taxes, or a *credit shelter trust* because it "shelters" the estate tax "credit." (The estate tax credit is the amount of estate taxes that would be due if there were no exemption. In 2019, an estate of $11,400,000 with no exemption would pay $4,560,000 in taxes, so $4,560,000 is the estate tax credit.) We prefer to call them Trust A and Trust B—we just think it's easier to understand.

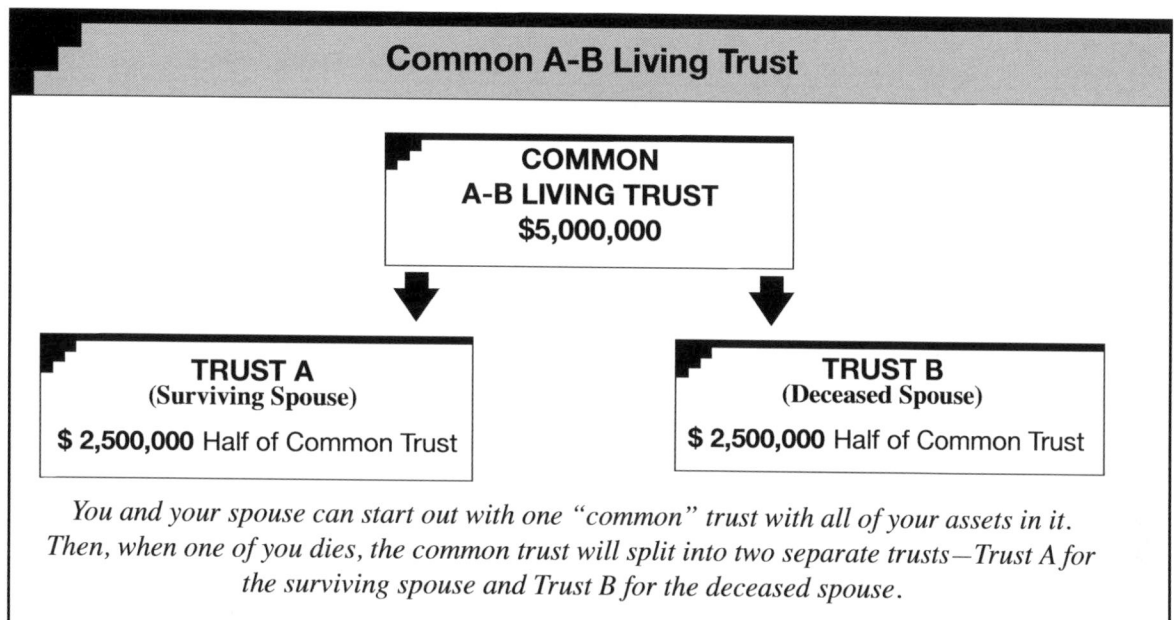

Common A-B Living Trust

COMMON A-B LIVING TRUST
$5,000,000

TRUST A
(Surviving Spouse)
$ 2,500,000 Half of Common Trust

TRUST B
(Deceased Spouse)
$ 2,500,000 Half of Common Trust

You and your spouse can start out with one "common" trust with all of your assets in it. Then, when one of you dies, the common trust will split into two separate trusts—Trust A for the surviving spouse and Trust B for the deceased spouse.

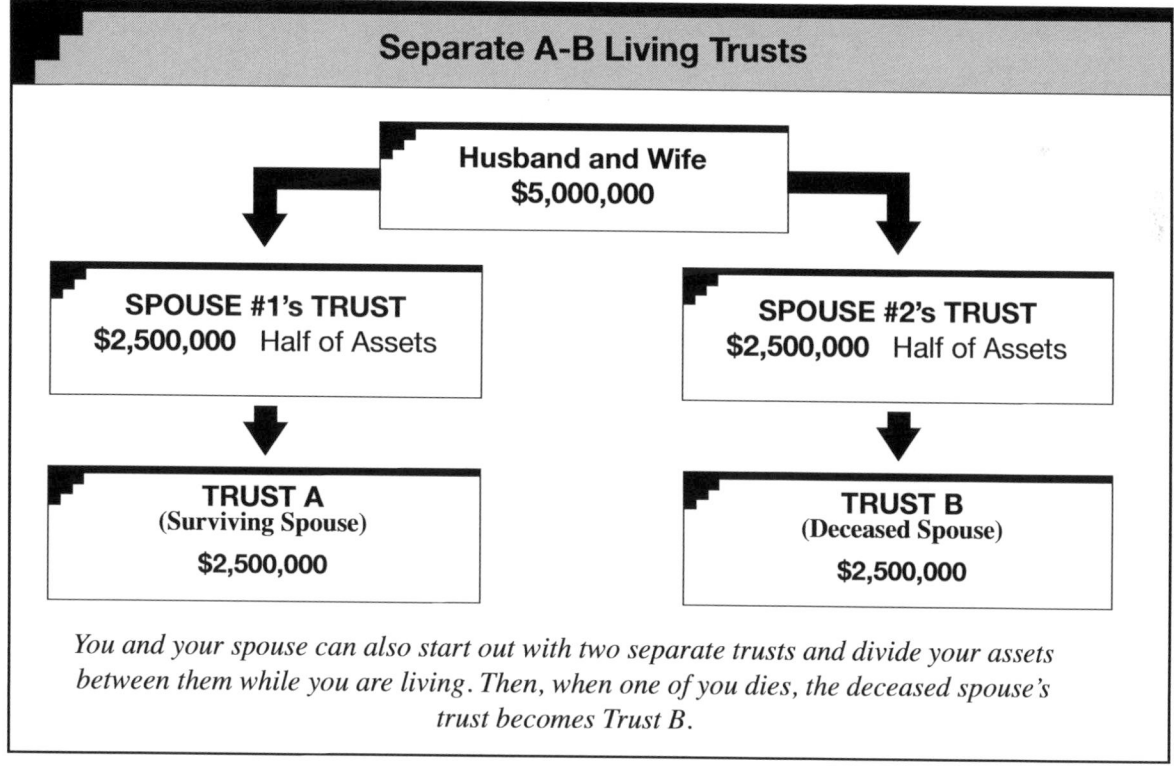

Separate A-B Living Trusts

Husband and Wife
$5,000,000

SPOUSE #1's TRUST
$2,500,000   Half of Assets

SPOUSE #2's TRUST
$2,500,000   Half of Assets

TRUST A
(Surviving Spouse)
$2,500,000

TRUST B
(Deceased Spouse)
$2,500,000

You and your spouse can also start out with two separate trusts and divide your assets between them while you are living. Then, when one of you dies, the deceased spouse's trust becomes Trust B.

How An A-B Living Trust Saves Estate Taxes

This is best explained with some examples. With the federal exemption currently so high, some of these examples may be well beyond the size of your estate. That's okay, though, because they illustrate the power of an A-B living trust, *especially* with a high exemption. You can substitute the size of your estate to see how these examples might work for you. These concepts also work for state taxes. We assume that no assets have been left out of your trust(s).

■ If Your Net Estate Is The Amount Of Two Exemptions Or Less

If you have a common trust and its value is *not more than* two exemptions when the first spouse dies, usually half of the value of the assets is placed in Trust A and half is placed in Trust B. If you start out with separate trusts, you divide your assets between the two trusts while you are living, so the assets are already divided when one spouse dies.

Each trust will be entitled to an estate tax exemption—Trust B uses the deceased's exemption and Trust A will use the surviving spouse's exemption when he/she dies. As the chart below shows, in 2019, this simple strategy will shield up to *$22.8 million* from federal estate taxes, saving up to $4,560,000.

This is not a tax shelter or some tricky way to avoid paying taxes. The estates *are* being taxed when both spouses die—*you are both simply using the exemptions to which you are entitled.*

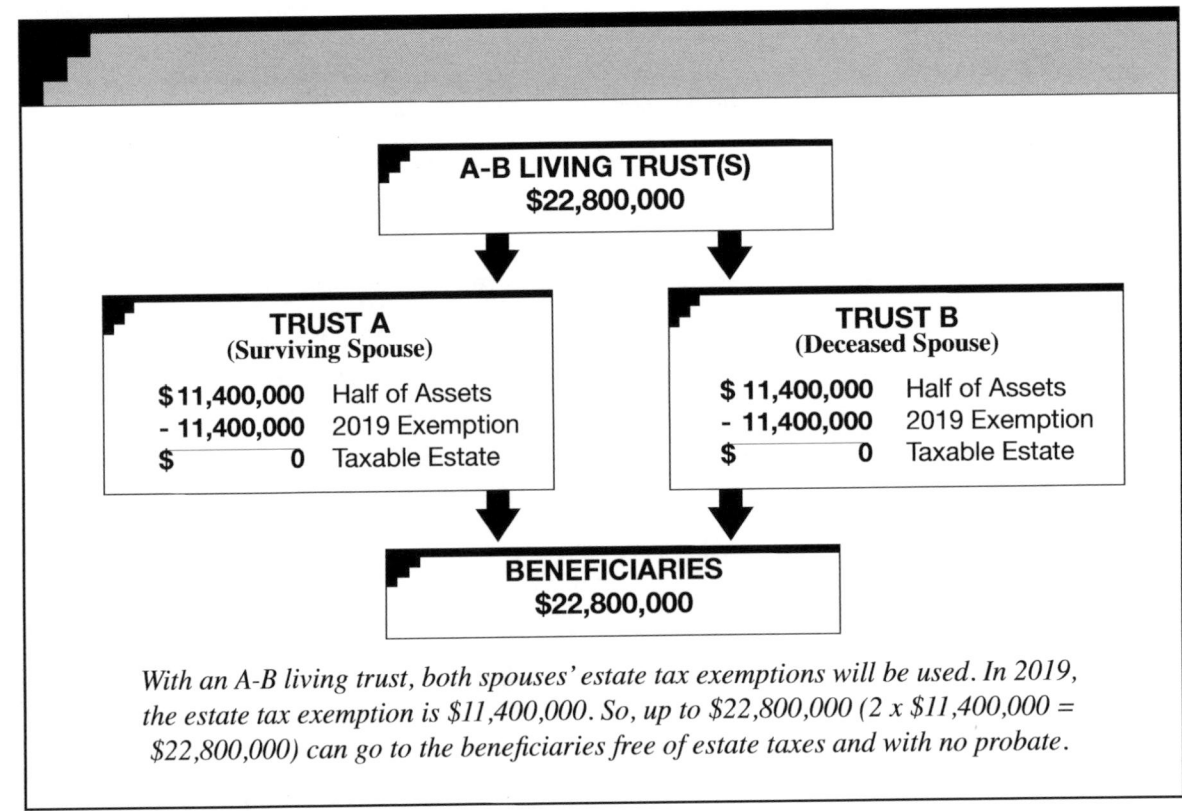

With an A-B living trust, both spouses' estate tax exemptions will be used. In 2019, the estate tax exemption is $11,400,000. So, up to $22,800,000 (2 x $11,400,000 = $22,800,000) can go to the beneficiaries free of estate taxes and with no probate.

■ If Your Net Estate Is More Than The Amount Of Two Exemptions

If the value of the common trust is *more* than two exemptions when the first spouse dies, usually only the amount of one exemption is placed in Trust B. The rest, as shown below, is added to Trust A (the surviving spouse's trust). If you already have separate trusts and the deceased spouse's trust (Trust B) is more than one exemption, the excess is usually transferred to the surviving spouse's Trust A.

If you leave more than one exemption in Trust B, estate taxes would have to be paid on the excess. So by not having more than one exemption in Trust B, there are no estate taxes on Trust B. And there are none due now on the rest of the deceased spouse's assets because they are transferred to Trust A using the marital deduction. So no estate taxes will be due until the surviving spouse dies. Then, his/her exemption will be used on the assets in Trust A.

Based on current law, the estate tax exemption is tied to inflation and is scheduled to increase annually. With that in mind, how much should go into each trust will depend on the total value of the estate and the amount of the exemption when the first spouse dies.

In 2019, an A-B living trust will let you leave up to $22.8 million to your loved ones, estate tax-free and with no probate

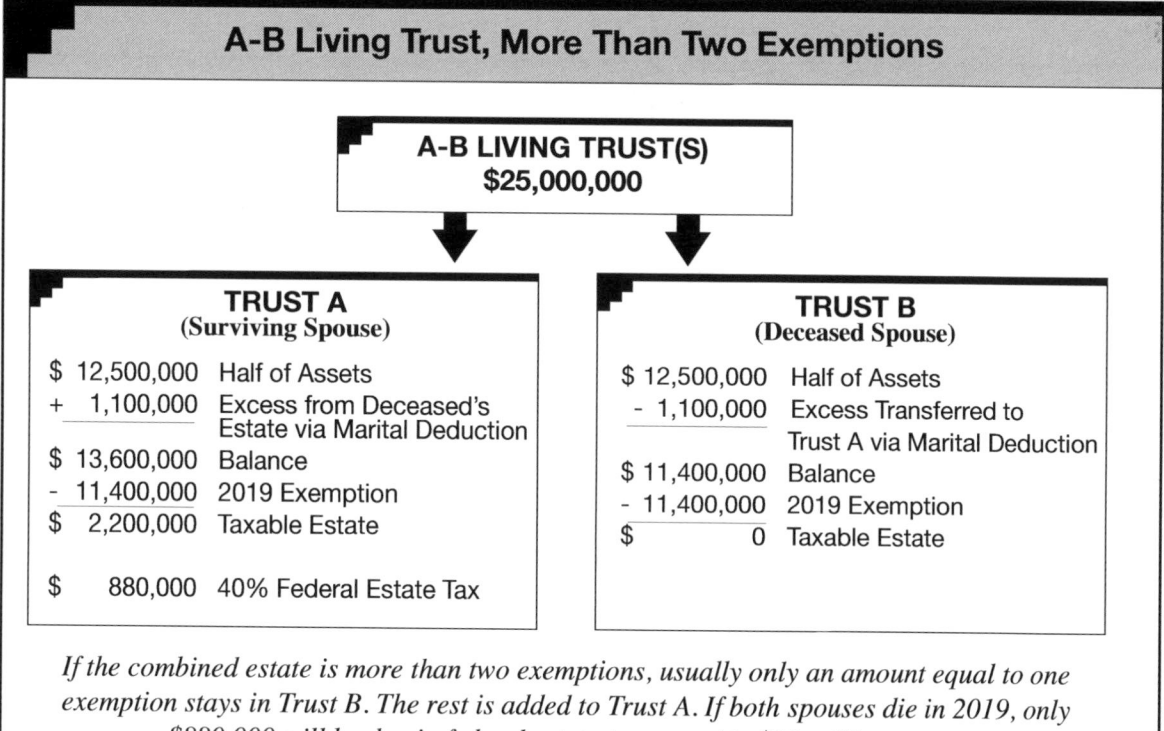

A-B Living Trust, More Than Two Exemptions

A-B LIVING TRUST(S)
$25,000,000

TRUST A (Surviving Spouse)		TRUST B (Deceased Spouse)	
$ 12,500,000	Half of Assets	$ 12,500,000	Half of Assets
+ 1,100,000	Excess from Deceased's Estate via Marital Deduction	- 1,100,000	Excess Transferred to Trust A via Marital Deduction
$ 13,600,000	Balance	$ 11,400,000	Balance
- 11,400,000	2019 Exemption	- 11,400,000	2019 Exemption
$ 2,200,000	Taxable Estate	$ 0	Taxable Estate
$ 880,000	40% Federal Estate Tax		

If the combined estate is more than two exemptions, usually only an amount equal to one exemption stays in Trust B. The rest is added to Trust A. If both spouses die in 2019, only $880,000 will be due in federal estate taxes on this $25 million estate.

Provide for your spouse and keep control

Provide For Your Surviving Spouse

You may be thinking, "If our assets are divided and in separate trusts, what happens if my spouse doesn't have enough in his/her trust? Will my spouse be able to get money from my trust after I die?"

Yes—and that's another reason why many couples find an A-B living trust so appealing. Even after you have died and the assets are in two separate trusts, you can still provide for your surviving spouse *for as long as he/she lives.*

Let's assume, for ease of explanation, that the husband dies first. When the assets are divided into Trust A and Trust B (as shown in the chart on the next page), his wife now has complete control over Trust A and can do whatever she wants with its assets. (Remember, this is now her trust.) In addition, she can receive any income generated by Trust B for as long as she lives and can even withdraw from the principal if needed for health, education, maintenance, and support. If she is trustee of Trust B, she could also change its investments.

There are some restrictions if she receives money from Trust B for other reasons, but these areas cover anything she would need for normal living expenses. She cannot have 100% control over the assets in Trust B because that would legally give her ownership of them, causing them to be taxed when she dies. (Because of this, if you want your surviving spouse to be trustee of Trust B, your attorney may want a co-trustee named to act with your spouse.)

The surviving spouse, then, has complete control over her own trust (Trust A) plus, for the rest of her life, she can receive all the income from Trust B and principal from it when needed for the purposes explained above. Then, when she dies, the assets in both trusts will go to the beneficiaries without probate. Assets in Trust B will also be estate tax-free, as will the assets in Trust A up to the amount of the estate tax exemption at that time.

Keep Control

There is something else the A-B living trust does that a lot of people, even those who *don't* have an estate tax problem, like very much. It lets you keep control of your share of the assets—even if you die first.

As this chart shows, when the first spouse dies, Trust B becomes *irrevocable.* So, even if you die first, you can be sure your share of the assets will go to

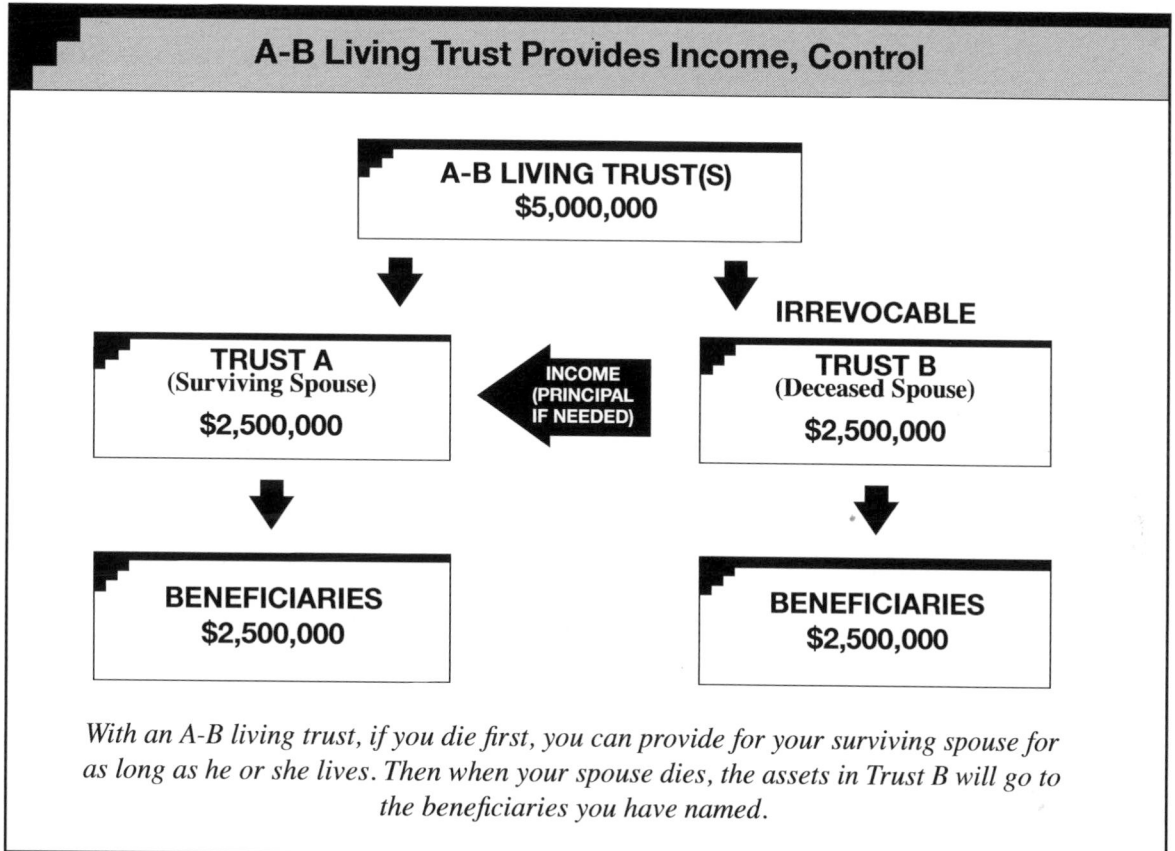

A-B Living Trust Provides Income, Control

A-B LIVING TRUST(S)
$5,000,000

TRUST A
(Surviving Spouse)
$2,500,000

INCOME
(PRINCIPAL
IF NEEDED)

IRREVOCABLE

TRUST B
(Deceased Spouse)
$2,500,000

BENEFICIARIES
$2,500,000

BENEFICIARIES
$2,500,000

With an A-B living trust, if you die first, you can provide for your surviving spouse for as long as he or she lives. Then when your spouse dies, the assets in Trust B will go to the beneficiaries you have named.

whomever *you* have named as beneficiary(ies). *Your* beneficiaries could be the same as your spouse's or, as the chart shows, they could be different.

This could be important if either of you has children from a previous marriage and you want to provide for them or if you want to make sure that, if your spouse later remarries, your part of the estate doesn't end up going to your spouse's new husband or wife.

If you wish, your spouse can continue to enjoy your assets while he/she is living. For example, if you die first, you may want your spouse to continue to live in the home you have owned together. Then, when your spouse dies and the house is sold, your share of the proceeds will go to whomever you have named as beneficiary(ies)—your children from your first marriage, other relatives, a nonprofit organization, etc.

You can give your spouse limited ability to change beneficiaries of your trust (Trust B) if, for some reason, you want to do that. But unless this provision (called a limited power of appointment) is specifically included in the trust document, your surviving spouse will only be able to make changes to Trust A (his/her trust).

Of course, there is no way for you to know now if your trust will be Trust A or Trust B because you don't know which of you will die first. It doesn't matter—you simply specify in the trust document that, if you die first, certain instructions will apply to Trust B. Your spouse will do the same.

So an A-B living trust lets you reduce or even eliminate federal and state estate taxes, provide for the surviving spouse for as long as he/she lives, *and* keep control over your share of the assets—even if you die first.

Dividing Assets Between Trust A And Trust B

Remember, if you have a common A-B living trust, when one spouse dies the trust will split into two separate trusts. At this time, the trustee (often the surviving spouse) will need to decide which assets to put in Trust B and which ones to put in Trust A.

If you have separate trusts, your assets will already have been divided. But, depending on how your document is written, you may be able to "swap" assets between Trust A and Trust B.

How do you know which assets to place into which trust? From an estate tax perspective, it would be smart to place into Trust B assets that will appreciate the most in value over the next few years. That's because the assets in Trust B are only valued and taxed *when the first spouse dies*. They are *not* re-valued later when the second spouse dies and they may be worth much more.

For example, let's say you die in 2019 and you own some assets that are worth $10 million. They are placed in Trust B. No estate taxes will be due at this time because the value of Trust B does not exceed your exemption. Now, let's say that by the time your spouse dies, these assets have appreciated in value to $15 million. *The full $15 million* will go to your beneficiaries *estate tax free*—because the value of Trust B was "locked in" for estate tax purposes at the time of your death.

The assets that are placed in Trust A (the surviving spouse's trust) will not be valued and taxed until his/her death, which could be many years later.

So it would be smart, if possible, to place into Trust A those assets that will appreciate more slowly. (However, if your beneficiaries intend to sell assets in the future, the timing of the sale may impact whether assets are placed in Trust A or Trust B.)

Under current law, the amount of the estate tax exemption is tied to inflation and is scheduled to increase each year (until 2025 when, under current law, it is set to revert back to $5 million plus inflation). So you *could* gamble that the surviving spouse will live long enough to have a larger exemption, and put appreciating assets in Trust A. But you can't know for sure how much longer the surviving spouse will live. Plus, remember, Congress can change the law any time it wants. In either case, the assets could appreciate to more than the surviving spouse's estate tax exemption, triggering estate taxes. That won't happen when appreciating assets are in Trust B.

Sometimes, with a common trust, the division of assets between Trust A and Trust B is done on paper through bookkeeping. However, some attorneys prefer to actually change titles from the old common trust to the new separate trusts. They feel this more clearly defines which assets are in which trust, in case they ever need to show the records to the IRS.

The surviving spouse doesn't have to worry about *how* to do this. Your attorney, CPA, or trust officer can help make sure everything is done properly and that your best tax planning options are used.

However, it *is* important that you and your spouse *both* realize what needs to happen when one of you dies so you don't lose the benefits. In Part Seven, we'll give you step-by-step instructions for what needs to be done, when it needs to be done, and who needs to do it.

One Common Trust vs. Separate Trusts

As mentioned earlier, regardless of whether you start out with one common trust or two separate trusts, the end results and benefits are the same.

Common A-B living trusts are routinely used in community property states. If you live in a non-community property state, your attorney may use separate trusts. But, common trusts are becoming more "common," even in non-community property states. For example, the Bar Association in Missouri, a non-community state, has published a model common A-B living trust document that attorneys can use.

Careful thought will be given as to which assets are placed in Trust B

For many long-married couples, having one common trust makes a lot of sense. Those who have built their estates together over the years and are used to owning their assets together like the idea of having one trust. It's easy for them to understand because it's similar to joint ownership (but without the risks). And one trust is easier to manage than two trusts—there is only one document and the assets do not have to be divided until one spouse dies.

However, there may be valid reasons why you may *not* want a common trust. For example, you may not want to put all your assets in one trust with your spouse's assets, especially if this is a new marriage and you have substantial assets of your own, or if you are expecting to receive a large inheritance. (Some couples have *three* trusts—separate ones for property acquired before a marriage or for inheritances, and a common trust for assets they want to own together or acquire during the marriage.)

If you live in a non-community property state and find the idea of a common trust appealing, look for an experienced attorney who is familiar with the drafting and funding of common trusts. (See Part Four for help in finding an attorney.) Be prepared; your search may not be easy. And it simply may not be worth the time or trouble.

Remember, ultimately it makes little difference whether you start out with one trust or two. What's more important is that your trust is done *correctly*. It is far better to have separate trusts that are well drafted and properly funded than to have a common trust that is not—or no trust at all!

> **Note:** The tax benefits are the same for both separate and common A-B living trusts. Some aggressive attorneys in non-community property states have attempted to use the common trust as a way to get a stepped-up basis for both spouses' interests in trust assets when one spouse dies, which is what happens in a community property state. But this is a benefit of community property *ownership*, not of a common trust. In a non-community property state, only the deceased spouse's interest will receive a step-up in basis when one spouse dies.
>
> A notable exception is Alaska. Its community property "opt in" law lets property owners receive the full step-up of community property. Even if you live in a separate property state, you can have this benefit by placing property in an Alaska Community Property Trust.

Couldn't This Same Planning Be Done In A Will?

Yes, but only if the will includes a trust in it. Remember, this is called a testamentary trust—and it does *not* avoid probate. A testamentary trust cannot go into effect until *after* the will has been probated. With an A-B living trust, you save estate taxes *and* avoid probate.

Do You Have To Have An A-B Trust To Use Both Exemptions?

No. Any assets you leave to someone other than your spouse (say, directly to your children) can be used to satisfy your exemption. But, unless they have a sizeable estate, most married couples want all the money to be available to provide for the surviving spouse. Then, whatever is left after he/she dies will go to the kids. Usually, the best way to provide for your spouse, use both exemptions, and not disinherit your children is with an A-B trust. However, your attorney may recommend other strategies for you.

If Your Spouse Is Incapacitated

An A-B living trust must be set up while you are both alive and healthy. But if your spouse is incapacitated, you may still have some options.

In some states, you can place your spouse in a conservatorship and request permission from the court to sign estate planning documents for your spouse. (In California, the *doctrine of substituted judgment* is used to do this.) This would allow you to do estate planning for your spouse, including setting up a living trust for him/her, or even a common A-B living trust for both of you.

You can then transfer your spouse's assets (his/her share of any jointly owned assets and any separately owned assets) *out* of the conservatorship and *into* the trust, and request that the conservatorship file be closed. The judge will often agree in order to reduce the court's work load and if he/she believes the trustee will do a good job. (Having a corporate trustee involved, especially one the judge knows and has confidence in, will often help.)

Of course, you run the risk of the court not closing the file and staying involved; that decision will vary from judge to judge and from state to state. And you may run into some other problems. For example, if your spouse already has a will, you would have to convince the court that if your spouse were competent today, he/she would now want a living trust instead.

This same planning can be done in a will, but you won't avoid probate

Check with your attorney to see if this is possible in your state. But even if your state doesn't allow this, *you should still set up your own living trust* for your share of the estate.

Depending on the size of your estate, it may be worthwhile to include an A-B provision. If you die first, Trust B (your trust) would use your exemption. The remaining assets would go to your spouse's trust using the marital deduction. So no estate taxes would be paid when you die. Your spouse's exemption would be used later when your spouse dies.

But if your spouse doesn't have a trust and dies first (which may happen, since your spouse is already ill), and everything is left to you, you would only be able to use *one* exemption (yours) through the A-B planning. If someone else (like your children) inherits some of your spouse's assets, some or all of your spouse's exemption could be used. This would also be an excellent time to use the portability provision, which would allow you to use your deceased spouse's unused exemption.

Of course, these options should *not* take the place of planning your estate while you and your spouse are both healthy. But if your spouse is *already* incapacitated, they may be worth investigating.

Will The Assets In Trust B Have To Be "Spent Down" If My Surviving Spouse Needs To Qualify For Medicaid?

The answer used to be "No." One of the benefits of an A-B living trust *was* that the assets in Trust B could be protected if the surviving spouse needed to qualify for Medicaid after the first spouse died.

To do this, the trust document had to give the trustee *discretion* over whether or not to distribute income and principal from Trust B to the surviving spouse. Then, if the surviving spouse needed to qualify for Medicaid, the trustee would simply decide *not* to provide any income or principal to him/her. So the assets in Trust B would be considered "unavailable" to the ill spouse and could be preserved for the beneficiaries of the deceased spouse.

However, the 1993 tax laws changed this. Medicaid now considers any assets that *could* be available to the surviving spouse *are* available. This means that if assets in Trust B *could* be used to provide for the surviving spouse, Medicaid says they *must* be used (spent down) before benefits will be available.

If you already have an A-B living trust and you are relying on this provision for Medicaid planning, you should contact an attorney immediately to find out about other options. Your best source for current information is an attorney who specializes in Elder Law. (See Part Two for sources.)

If You Are Married And Your Spouse Is Not A U.S. Citizen

If your spouse is not a U.S. citizen, he/she is not entitled to the marital deduction. So, if you die first and don't plan ahead, everything in your estate over the amount of the estate tax exemption at that time will be taxed. To prevent this, your attorney will use a *qualified domestic trust* as part of your A-B living trust plan. (For an explanation of the qualified domestic trust, see Part Nine.) If your spouse is not a U.S. citizen, make sure you tell your attorney at your first meeting, before any documents are prepared.

If You Are Not Married

If you are not legally married now (and that includes if you are divorced, widowed, or have never been married) you cannot use the A-B living trust to save estate taxes. It is designed to use both *spouses'* estate tax exemptions. As a single person, you are entitled to just one.

You should still have a living trust for all the non-tax reasons explained earlier. Then, if your estate is large enough to pay estate taxes, there are strategies you can use *in addition to* your living trust. Some of these are explained in Part Nine.

If Your A-B Living Trust Was Prepared Before 2012

Many older trust documents contain language stating that when the first spouse dies, an amount equal to the federal estate tax exemption is to be placed in Trust B and the excess in the surviving spouse's Trust A. This was done to maximize the federal estate exemption of the first spouse to die.

When the exemption was $600,000 to $1 million, this was common planning. But now that the exemption is $11.4 million, this wording could cause all of the assets to be placed in Trust B, leaving nothing for the surviving spouse's Trust A. If you are concerned about this, contact your attorney and see if your trust needs to be revised.

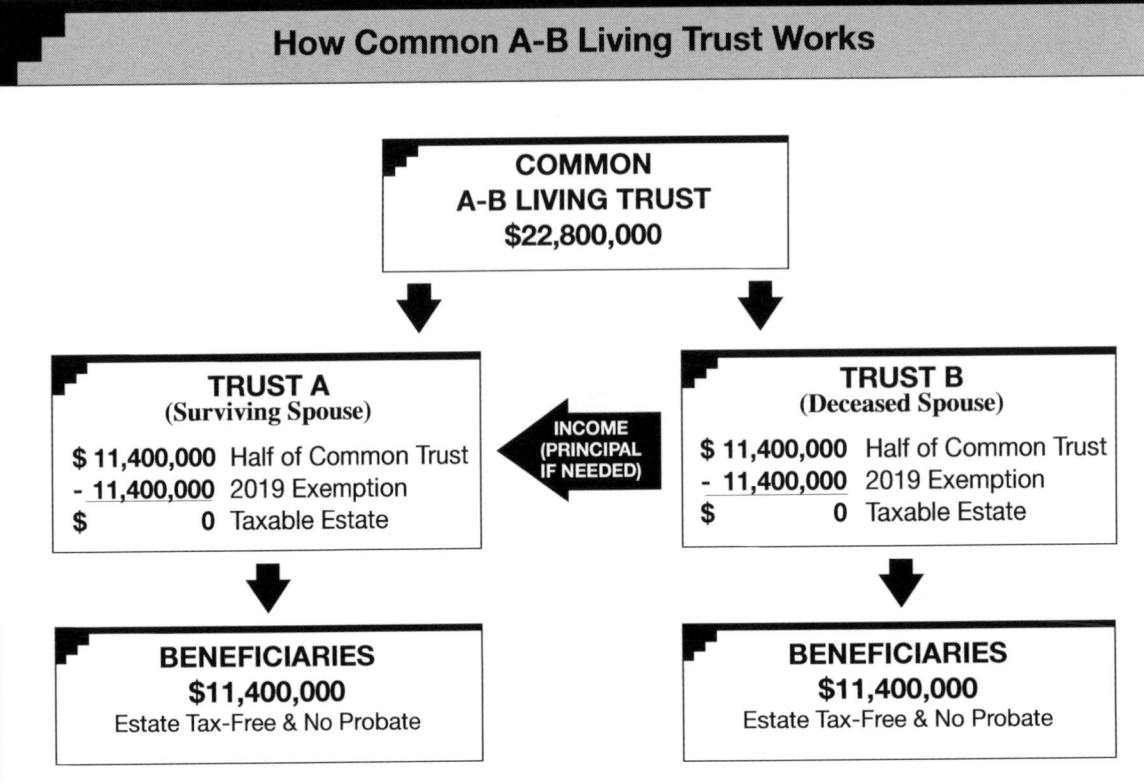

How Common A-B Living Trust Works

**COMMON
A-B LIVING TRUST
$22,800,000**

TRUST A
(Surviving Spouse)

$ 11,400,000	Half of Common Trust
- 11,400,000	2019 Exemption
$ 0	Taxable Estate

**INCOME
(PRINCIPAL
IF NEEDED)**

TRUST B
(Deceased Spouse)

$ 11,400,000	Half of Common Trust
- 11,400,000	2019 Exemption
$ 0	Taxable Estate

**BENEFICIARIES
$11,400,000**
Estate Tax-Free & No Probate

**BENEFICIARIES
$11,400,000**
Estate Tax-Free & No Probate

How It Works

1. While you are both living, you transfer your assets into one common living trust. Upon the death of one spouse, this common living trust automatically divides into two separate trusts—Trust A for the surviving spouse and Trust B for the deceased spouse.

2. If the value of the common trust is less than two federal estate tax exemptions, usually half of the assets are placed in Trust A and half in Trust B. If the value of the common trust is more than two exemptions, usually only an amount equal to one exemption ($11,400,000 in 2019) is placed in Trust B—the rest is transferred to Trust A using the marital deduction.

3. Trust B is taxed when the first spouse dies, but because its value usually does not exceed the amount of the estate tax exemption, no estate taxes are due. Trust A is taxed when the surviving spouse dies. In the meantime, the surviving spouse has complete control over Trust A, and can receive the income (and principal if needed for certain living expenses) from Trust B.

(2019 estate tax exemption used.)

How Common A-B Living Trust Works

4. When the surviving spouse dies, the assets in both trusts are distributed to the beneficiaries, which may be the same or different.

Benefits

■ **Reduce/Eliminate Estate Taxes**—With an A-B living trust, you and your spouse can both use your federal estate tax exemptions. In 2019, this lets you leave your beneficiaries up to $22,800,000 estate tax-free and with no probate—saving up to $4,560,000 in federal estate taxes, plus probate fees.

■ **Provide for Surviving Spouse**—The surviving spouse has complete control over Trust A. In addition, he/she can receive the income (and principal, if needed for certain living expenses) from Trust B.

■ **Control for First to Die**—After the first spouse dies and the common trust has been divided into Trust A and Trust B, no changes can be made to the provisions of Trust B—giving the first spouse to die complete control over who will eventually receive the assets in Trust B.

■ **Estate Tax-Free Appreciation of Trust B**—The assets placed in Trust B are valued and taxed only when the first spouse dies. There will be no re-valuation or estate taxes paid on any appreciation of these assets later when the surviving spouse dies and the assets in Trust B are distributed to the beneficiaries.

■ **Estate Taxes Delayed Until Surviving Spouse Dies**—Usually only an amount equal to the estate tax exemption is placed in Trust B, so there are no estate taxes on Trust B when the first spouse dies. The rest of the assets are transferred to Trust A using the unlimited marital deduction. So no estate taxes will be due until after the surviving spouse dies. This leaves the estate intact until then, so the full amount is available to provide for the surviving spouse.

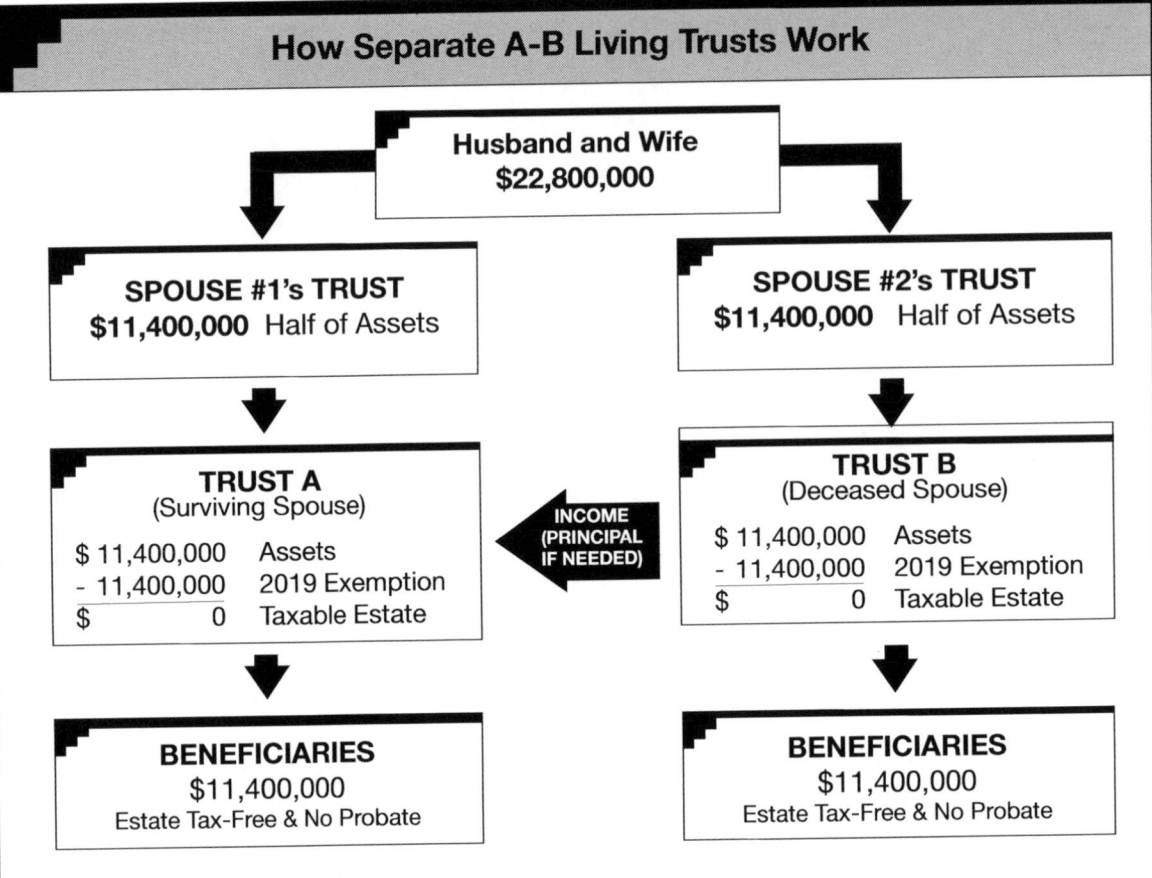

How Separate A-B Living Trusts Work

Husband and Wife
$22,800,000

SPOUSE #1's TRUST
$11,400,000 Half of Assets

SPOUSE #2's TRUST
$11,400,000 Half of Assets

TRUST A
(Surviving Spouse)

$ 11,400,000	Assets
- 11,400,000	2019 Exemption
$ 0	Taxable Estate

INCOME
(PRINCIPAL
IF NEEDED)

TRUST B
(Deceased Spouse)

$ 11,400,000	Assets
- 11,400,000	2019 Exemption
$ 0	Taxable Estate

BENEFICIARIES
$11,400,000
Estate Tax-Free & No Probate

BENEFICIARIES
$11,400,000
Estate Tax-Free & No Probate

How It Works

1. While you are living, you and your spouse divide your assets and transfer them into two separate trusts. Periodically, you review the values of the assets in both trusts and move assets between the trusts to take full advantage of both exemptions.

2. When the first spouse dies, the deceased spouse's trust becomes Trust B. If Trust B is more than the federal estate tax exemption at that time, the excess is usually transferred to the surviving spouse's trust (Trust A) using the marital deduction.

3. Trust B is taxed when the first spouse dies, but because its value usually does not exceed the amount of the estate tax exemption, no estate taxes are due. Trust A is taxed when the surviving spouse dies. In the meantime, the surviving spouse has complete control over Trust A, and can receive the income (and principal if needed for certain living expenses) from Trust B.

(2019 estate tax exemption used.)

How Separate A-B Living Trusts Work

4. When the surviving spouse dies, the assets in both trusts are distributed to the beneficiaries, which may be the same or different.

Benefits

■ **Reduce/Eliminate Estate Taxes**—With separate A-B living trusts, you and your spouse can both use your federal estate tax exemptions. In 2019, this lets you leave your beneficiaries up to $22,800,000 estate tax-free and with no probate—saving up to $4,560,000 in federal estate taxes, plus probate fees.

■ **Provide for Surviving Spouse**—The surviving spouse has complete control over his/her trust (Trust A). In addition, he/she can receive the income (and principal, if needed for certain living expenses) from the deceased spouse's trust (Trust B).

■ **Control for First to Die**—After the first spouse dies, no changes can be made to the provisions of Trust B, giving the first spouse to die complete control over who will eventually receive the assets in Trust B.

■ **Estate Tax-Free Appreciation of Trust B**—The assets in Trust B are valued and taxed only when the first spouse dies. There will be no re-valuation or estate taxes paid on any appreciation of these assets later when the surviving spouse dies and the assets in Trust B are distributed to the beneficiaries.

■ **Estate Taxes Delayed Until Surviving Spouse Dies**—Usually only an amount equal to the estate tax exemption is placed in Trust B, so there are no estate taxes on Trust B when the first spouse dies. The rest of the assets are transferred to Trust A using the unlimited marital deduction. So no estate taxes will be due until after the surviving spouse dies. This leaves the estate intact until then, so the full amount is available to provide for the surviving spouse.

THE A-B...AND NOW C

If you are married and your combined net estate is *more* than two exemptions, you should know about the A-B-C living trust. It works basically the same as the A-B living trust, but it adds another trust—the "C" trust.

This is *not* a way to avoid paying estate taxes if your estate is more than two exemptions. You are already using your two estate tax exemptions through the A-B part of your living trust.

Like the A-B living trust, the A-B-C living trust lets you *delay* payment of any estate taxes until the surviving spouse dies, so more will be available to provide for this spouse while he/she is living. It also lets the spouse who dies first keep control of more of the estate. Let's look at how it works.

Keep Control Over More Of Your Estate

This, too, is best explained with an example. Let's again say you both die in 2019 when the estate tax exemption is $11,400,000.

If your estate is more than two exemptions and you use an A-B living trust, the spouse who dies first will probably end up controlling only an amount equal to one estate tax exemption. Usually that's all that is put in Trust B—the rest goes to the surviving spouse's trust (Trust A) through the marital deduction to avoid paying any estate taxes when the first spouse dies.

So, for example, as the chart on the top of the next page shows, if your total estate is worth $25 million and you die first, you would probably only control $11,400,000 while your surviving spouse would control $13,600,000.

Maybe that's okay with you. But let's say you want things to be more equal. This could be important, as mentioned before, if you have children from a previous marriage. Or you may be concerned that if your spouse remarries, his/her new spouse could end up with everything except what's in Trust B.

Of course, *more* than the exempt amount can be placed in Trust B—giving you control over more of the estate. But then estate taxes would have to be paid on the excess when you die. And that would leave less to support your spouse.

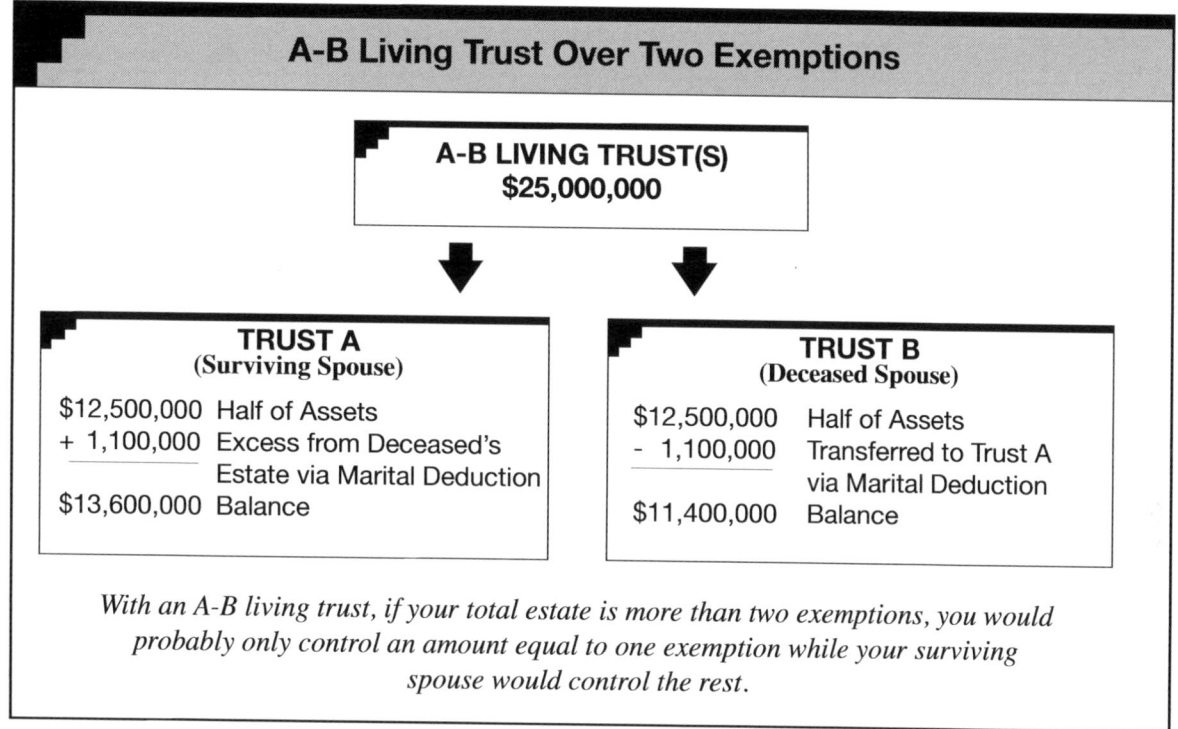

A-B Living Trust Over Two Exemptions

A-B LIVING TRUST(S)
$25,000,000

TRUST A (Surviving Spouse)	**TRUST B** (Deceased Spouse)

$12,500,000 Half of Assets
+ 1,100,000 Excess from Deceased's
               Estate via Marital Deduction
$13,600,000 Balance
	$12,500,000 Half of Assets
	- 1,100,000 Transferred to Trust A
	               via Marital Deduction
	$11,400,000 Balance

With an A-B living trust, if your total estate is more than two exemptions, you would probably only control an amount equal to one exemption while your surviving spouse would control the rest.

An A-B-C living trust would let you control more of the estate—*without* having to pay estate taxes when you die. Let's again say that your total estate is worth $25 million and you die first in 2019.

As the chart on the next page shows, the estate is split *equally*. $12,500,000 goes into Trust A (your spouse's trust). $12,500,000 is divided between Trust B and Trust C (your trusts). Usually, an amount equal to the federal estate tax exemption ($11,400,000 in 2019) goes into Trust B and the rest ($1,100,000) goes into Trust C.

Your surviving spouse controls Trust A, and you control Trust B *and* Trust C. When your spouse dies, the assets in all three trusts will be distributed to the beneficiaries you have each named; they could be the same or they could be different. So you each keep control over *half* of the estate.

Now, let's look at the benefits of not having to pay any estate taxes when the first spouse dies.

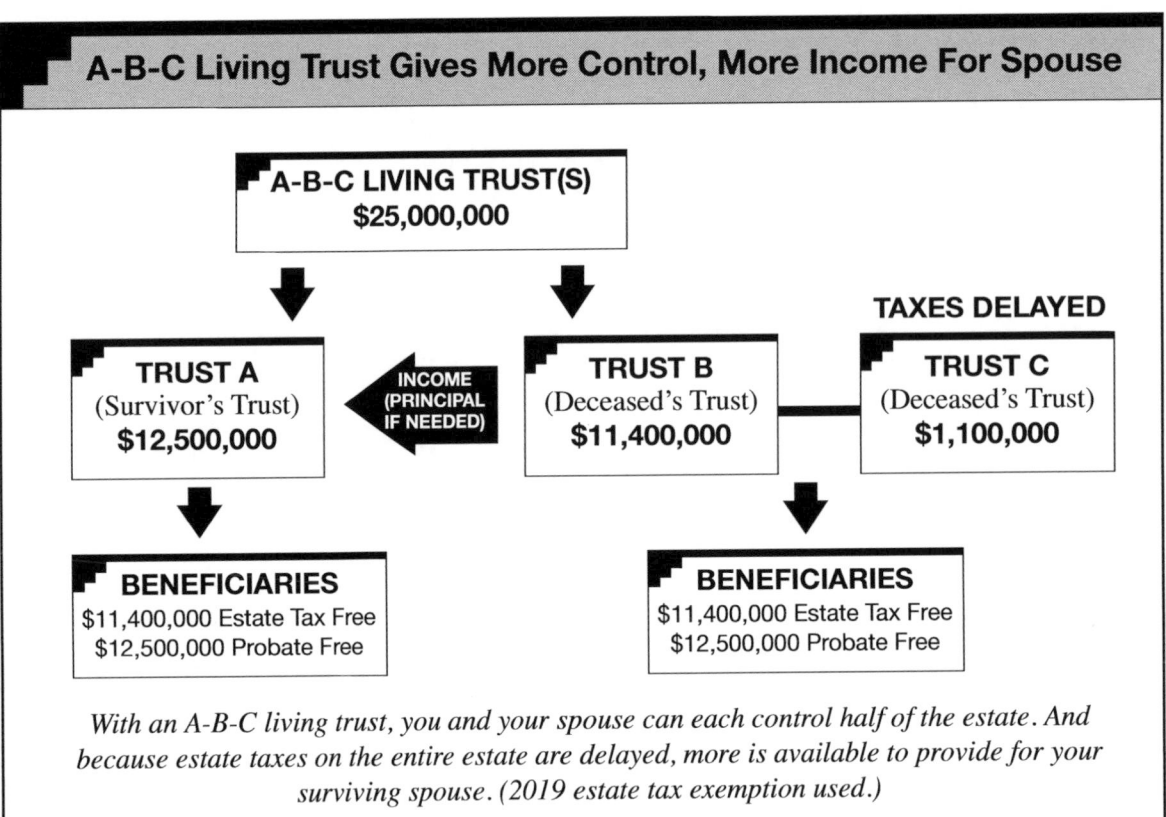

A-B-C Living Trust Gives More Control, More Income For Spouse

A-B-C LIVING TRUST(S)
$25,000,000

TAXES DELAYED

TRUST A
(Survivor's Trust)
$12,500,000

INCOME
(PRINCIPAL
IF NEEDED)

TRUST B
(Deceased's Trust)
$11,400,000

TRUST C
(Deceased's Trust)
$1,100,000

BENEFICIARIES
$11,400,000 Estate Tax Free
$12,500,000 Probate Free

BENEFICIARIES
$11,400,000 Estate Tax Free
$12,500,000 Probate Free

With an A-B-C living trust, you and your spouse can each control half of the estate. And because estate taxes on the entire estate are delayed, more is available to provide for your surviving spouse. (2019 estate tax exemption used.)

Delay Estate Taxes—Provide More For Surviving Spouse

Under current tax law, estate taxes on the assets in Trust C are *delayed* until the second spouse dies. This means *the entire estate* will be available to provide for your surviving spouse.

As explained earlier with the A-B trust (and as the chart above shows), your surviving spouse has complete control over the assets in Trust A, can receive income from Trust B and can also receive principal from Trust B, if needed, for health, education, maintenance and support.

Your spouse will also receive *all* the income from Trust C. Under current law, the spouse *must* receive all the income from Trust C to qualify for this special tax treatment. Your spouse can also receive principal from Trust C, if needed, for health, education, maintenance and support.

Because the estate is not reduced by any estate taxes when you die, a larger amount will be available to invest and provide income to your spouse, and more money will be available in case your spouse needs it. Then, when your spouse dies, the assets in both Trust B and Trust C (50% of the estate at the time of your death) will go to the beneficiaries *you* specify.

Estate taxes on the assets placed in Trust C are not *eliminated*—they are just delayed until the surviving spouse dies. If the assets in Trust A and Trust C *together* are more than the federal estate tax exemption at that time, estate taxes will be due.

Keep in mind that, with the estate tax exemption currently tied to inflation, it is increasing every year (until 2025 under current law). Whether or not estate taxes will be due when the surviving spouse dies will depend on the combined value of the assets in Trust A and Trust C, and the amount of the estate tax exemption at that time.

> **Note:** The "C" trust as explained here is technically called a "Q-TIP" trust, which stands for "qualified terminable interest property." It sounds complicated, but it really isn't. The fact that the surviving spouse *must* receive the income from Trust C and *may* have access to the principal under certain conditions is his/her "qualified interest" in the property. This interest is "terminable" because it ends when the surviving spouse dies.

Dividing Assets Among Trust A, Trust B, And Trust C

Just like the A-B living trust, when one spouse dies, the assets will need to be divided among Trust A, Trust B, and Trust C. As mentioned earlier, it's not so important that the surviving spouse understands exactly *how* to do this because your attorney, CPA, or trust officer will be able to help. However, it *is* important that *both* of you understand what needs to happen and when. If you are thinking about an A-B-C living trust, make sure you and your spouse read Part Seven and discuss it completely with your attorney.

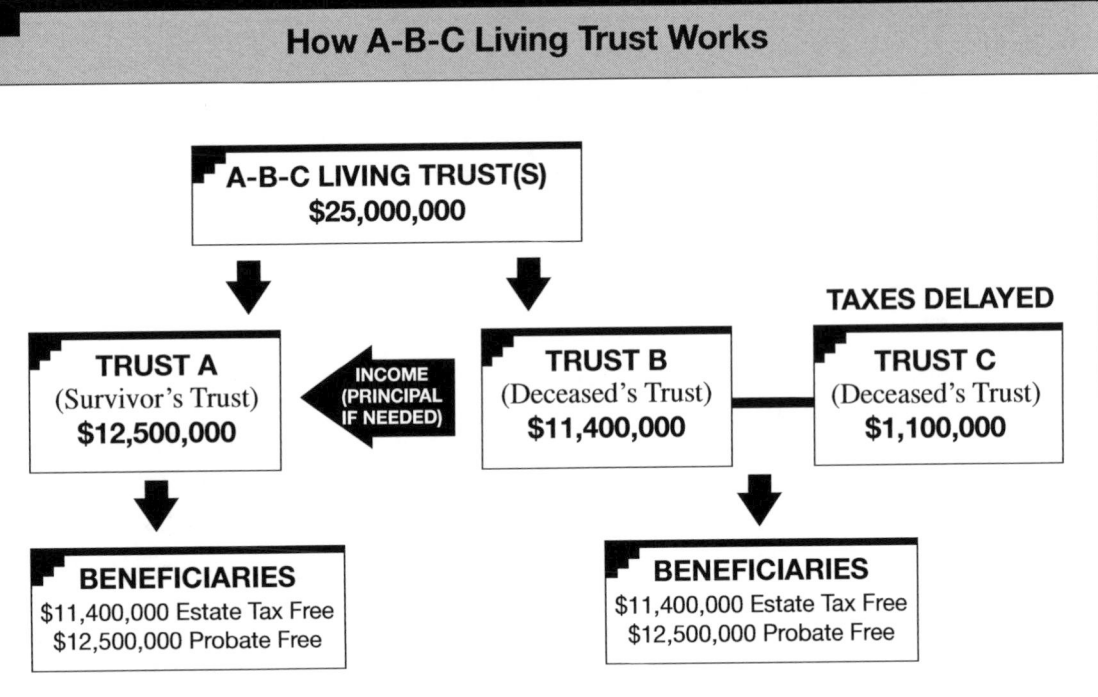

How A-B-C Living Trust Works

A-B-C LIVING TRUST(S)
$25,000,000

TAXES DELAYED

TRUST A
(Survivor's Trust)
$12,500,000

INCOME
(PRINCIPAL IF NEEDED)

TRUST B
(Deceased's Trust)
$11,400,000

TRUST C
(Deceased's Trust)
$1,100,000

BENEFICIARIES
$11,400,000 Estate Tax Free
$12,500,000 Probate Free

BENEFICIARIES
$11,400,000 Estate Tax Free
$12,500,000 Probate Free

How It Works

1. While you are both living, you transfer your assets into one common living trust. Upon the death of one spouse, this trust is divided equally. Half of the estate goes into Trust A for the surviving spouse. The other half (the deceased spouse's share) is divided between Trust B and Trust C. Usually only an amount equal to the federal estate tax exemption is placed in Trust B; the excess is placed into Trust C.

   If you and your spouse start out with separate trusts, the assets will already be divided when one spouse dies. The assets in the deceased spouse's trust are then divided between Trust B and Trust C as explained above.

2. Trust B is taxed when the first spouse dies. Trust A and Trust C are taxed when the surviving spouse dies. In the meantime, the surviving spouse has complete control over Trust A, and can receive income (and principal, if needed, for certain living expenses) from Trust B. In addition, he/she will receive all the income from Trust C, and can receive principal, if needed, for certain living expenses.

(2019 estate tax exemption used.)

How A-B-C Living Trust Works

3. When the surviving spouse dies, the assets in all three trusts are distributed to the beneficiaries.

Benefits

■ **Reduce/Eliminate Estate Taxes**—With an A-B-C living trust, you and your spouse can both use your federal estate tax exemptions. In 2019, this lets you leave your beneficiaries up to $22,800,000 estate tax free, saving up to $4,560,000 in federal estate taxes, plus probate fees.

■ **Provide for Surviving Spouse**—The surviving spouse has complete control over Trust A and receives all income from Trust C. In addition, he/she can receive the income from Trust B and can have access to the principal of Trust B and Trust C, if needed, for certain living expenses.

■ **Control for First to Die**—When the first spouse dies and the common trust is divided among Trusts A, B, and C, no changes can be made to the provisions of Trust B and Trust C—giving the first spouse to die complete control over who will eventually receive the assets in Trust B and Trust C (half of the estate). If you have separate trusts, the spouse who dies first keeps control over the assets in his/her trust, even after they are placed into Trust B and Trust C.

■ **Estate Tax-Free Appreciation of Trust B**—The assets in Trust B are valued and taxed only when the first spouse dies. There will be no re-valuation or estate taxes paid on any appreciation when the surviving spouse dies and the assets in Trust B are distributed.

■ **Estate Taxes Delayed on Trust C**—The assets placed in Trust C are taxed only when the surviving spouse dies. This leaves the estate intact until then, so a larger amount is available to provide income (and principal, if needed) to the surviving spouse during his/her lifetime.

SUMMARY

The ways in which we have explained the A-B and A-B-C provisions here are ways in which they have traditionally been used, and now you have some understanding of how they work. However, depending on your situation, your attorney may recommend some variations that may better meet your needs and objectives.

You may still need additional planning beyond an A-B or A-B-C living trust. If so, your attorney may recommend some of the strategies explained in Part Nine. These would not *replace* your living trust; they would be *in addition to* it. Your living trust is the foundation of your entire estate plan.

With the federal estate tax exemption as high as it is (and, under current law, increasing each year until 2025), and with all of the other planning strategies available to estate planning professionals, there is really no reason for *anyone* to have to pay estate taxes. The key is to plan now, while strategies are still available, and to have enough time to fully implement them.

Part Four—

PLANNING FOR YOUR LIVING TRUST

Now that you have a good understanding of what a living trust is, how it works, and the benefits of having one, let's start thinking about yours.

As you've seen, your living trust can be designed to include just about anything you want. But that also means you will need to make some important decisions.

In this section, we will prompt you to think about what you want to happen to you, your family, and your assets when something happens to you. We will give you information and examples so you can make sound, informed decisions about who will be your trustee, successor trustee(s) and beneficiaries, and when you want your beneficiaries to receive their inheritances.

As you read this section, think about your situation and see which suggestions might be right for you and your family. Feel free to mark up the book and make notes in the margins as you read things you like, have questions about, or just want to think about more.

Later, in Part Ten, we'll help you organize your thoughts and decisions with our Personal and Financial Organizer.

Now, let's start planning for your living trust.

YOU MUST MAKE SOME DECISIONS

What *do* you want to happen to you and your assets if you become incapacitated and when you die? Here are some specific issues you will need to think about and decide.

- If you become incapacitated, whom do you want to take care of you? Whom do you want to manage your financial affairs for you?
- Do you have specific requests about your medical care? Do you wish to receive care in a certain facility? Is there one you wish to avoid?
- Whom do you want to receive your assets when you die? Are there any special gifts of sentimental value you want certain people to have?
- Do you want to leave something to your place of worship, university, or favorite charity?
- If you have minor children, whom do you want to raise them if you (and your spouse) can't? Whom do you want to manage their inheritance?
- When do you want your beneficiaries to receive their inheritances?
- Do you have a child, spouse, or other loved one who depends on you and will need special care?
- If there are stepchildren in your family, how do you want them to inherit from you (if at all)?
- Are there any persons you wish to disinherit?
- If your entire family dies before you, whom would you want to have your assets?
- If you have a business, what do you want to happen to it?
- If you have pets, whom do you want to care for them?

By the time you finish reading this section, you'll probably have the answers to a lot of these questions, and these may prompt you to think of others. Make some notes as things come to mind. Then, in Part Ten, we'll help you get everything organized.

Now, let's start finding some answers.

WHO WILL BE YOUR TRUSTEE?

What Does A Trustee Do?

A trustee basically does what you do right now with your financial affairs—collects income, pays bills and taxes, saves and invests your money for the future, buys and sells assets, provides for your loved ones, keeps accurate records, and generally keeps things organized and in good order.

Who Can Be Your Trustee?

As explained earlier, you can be your own trustee, which is what most people—especially those with smaller estates—choose to do. If you name yourself as trustee, nothing changes after you set up your living trust. You continue to manage your assets and financial affairs just as you always have for as long as you are able.

If you are married, you and your spouse can be co-trustees. This way, if something happens to one of you, the other can continue to handle your financial affairs without interruption. Most married couples who own their assets together—especially those who have been married for some time—are usually co-trustees.

However, you don't have to be your own trustee. You can name anyone you want as your trustee or to be co-trustee with you. Some people choose an adult son or daughter, trusted friend or other relative. Some people like having the experience and investment management skills of a corporate trustee (a bank trust department or a trust company—more about them in a few pages).

Remember, naming someone else as your trustee or co-trustee doesn't mean you lose control. The trustee you name must follow the instructions in your trust and report to you. Plus, you can always change your mind (and your trustee) later.

One big advantage to having a co-trustee is that someone else would already be involved and familiar with your trust if something happens to you. This would eliminate the time a successor would have to spend to become knowledgeable about your trust, your assets, your beneficiaries, and the personalities involved.

You can be your own trustee or name someone else

If you do decide to name someone as your co-trustee (even your spouse), it might be a good idea to have your trust require both signatures to buy or sell assets as long as both of you are alive and able (just like some bank accounts require both signatures). But if you are concerned that you can't trust this person, then he or she probably shouldn't be involved with your trust.

Compensating A Trustee

All trustees are entitled to receive reasonable compensation for their services. However, if you are your own trustee, you probably won't pay yourself. And family members often don't think they should accept a fee. If you name a friend or family member as a trustee or successor trustee, you may want to consider paying them anyway for their time and responsibilities.

Consider specifying the amount of compensation in your trust document. This could go a long way toward preventing hurt feelings and future disagreements over how much your successor trustee will receive.

Who will be your successor trustee(s)?

What Does A Successor Trustee Do?

Successor trustees have a lot of responsibility and should be chosen carefully. Remember, if you (and your co-trustee) become incapacitated, your successor trustee will step in and take full control for you—paying bills, making financial decisions, even selling or refinancing assets. Your successor will be able to do anything you could with your trust assets, as long as it does not conflict with the instructions in your trust document.

When you die, your successor acts just like an executor would—takes an inventory of your assets, pays your final bills, sells assets if necessary, has your final tax returns prepared, and distributes your assets according to the instructions in your trust.

Remember that your successor trustee will be acting without court supervision, which is why your affairs can be handled more efficiently. But this also means it will be up to your successor to get things started and keep them moving along. If needed, your attorney, trust officer, and/or CPA can help guide your successor, so it isn't necessary for this person to know exactly what to do and when. You just need to make sure you name someone who is responsible and conscientious.

Who Can Be Successor Trustees?

Successor trustees can be your adult children, other relatives, a trusted friend, and/or a corporate trustee. If you choose an individual, you should name more than one in case your first choice is unable to act. They should be people you know and trust, whose judgment you respect, and who will also respect your wishes. They do not have to live in the same state you do, although it would be more convenient if they live near you.

When choosing your successors, keep in mind the type and amount of assets in your trust, and the complexity of the provisions in your trust document. For example, if you plan to keep assets in your trust after you die for your beneficiaries (if they are minors, have special needs, or will receive their inheritances in installments), your successor would have more responsibilities for a longer period of time than if your assets will be distributed all at once.

Also keep in mind the qualifications of your candidates. Consider personalities, financial/business experience, and time available due to their own family/career demands. Taking over as trustee for someone can take a substantial amount of time and requires a certain amount of business sense.

■ When Considering Your Children

Many people name one or more of their adult children as successor trustee(s). Just be prepared for possible hurt feelings if you exclude any. (Children can be sensitive about these things.)

As one solution, some people name all of their adult children to act together as *co*-successor trustees. Depending on the number of children you have, where they live, and their personalities, this may or may not be a good idea.

If you have only two or three children who live in the same area as you (and they get along), then it could work out fine. But you don't want your affairs being run by a cumbersome committee that can't agree on anything. Also, keep in mind that all their signatures will be required for any transactions. If they're spread out across the country, that could slow things down.

Choose your successor trustee(s) carefully

An alternative is to name all of your adult children as successors, but instead of having them work together as co-trustees, list them *in order of who you think will do the best job*. That may not necessarily be oldest to youngest. (Being older doesn't always make one wiser.) Only your first choice, then, would become your successor, unless he/she is unable or unwilling to serve at that time, in which case the second would step in, and so on down your list.

If you decide to name an even number of your children (two or four) to act together, you could select just one of them to make decisions. Or you may want to add a corporate trustee as an impartial odd number to prevent any deadlocks in the event your children disagree. (Of course, if your children agree, they could not be overruled by the corporate trustee.)

■ Qualify Your Candidates

Make sure you ask the people you are considering if they want this responsibility. Don't put them on the spot and just assume they want to do this. It would probably be helpful for them (and you) to read Part Seven to see what needs to be done when someone becomes incapacitated and/or dies. You may also want to give each of them a copy of this book so they can become familiar with how a living trust works and understand the duties and responsibilities of a trustee.

If you have any doubts about one of your candidates' abilities or desire to fulfill this responsibility—if you're not sure about his/her business sense or that he/she may not have the time and/or ability, or if you think this person may act emotionally rather than logically and rationally—you should probably name someone else or a corporate trustee as your successor.

One final comment. As much as you love your children and would like to think they will be caring and unselfish once you're gone, *this* is the time to be realistic. If they really don't get along, or if there could be jealousies involved, you and your family will probably be much better off if you select a corporate trustee as your successor trustee. The fee a corporate trustee charges is a small price to pay if it keeps peace in your family.

SHOULD YOU CONSIDER A CORPORATE TRUSTEE?

What Is A Corporate Trustee And What Do They Do?

A corporate trustee is a bank trust department or a trust company that specializes in managing trusts. They can manage your trust for you now and/ or after you die according to your instructions. They can buy and sell assets, handle required paperwork, maintain accurate records, and distribute income and assets as your trust directs.

Why Would You Use A Corporate Trustee?

Family and friends are not always a good choice to be involved with your trust. Even if they do get along, they may be too busy with their own affairs, reside in a distant area, or simply not be responsible or experienced enough to manage the trust assets. You may also want professional help investing and managing your assets.

Do You Lose Control?

No. Even if you name a corporate trustee as your trustee or co-trustee, *you still keep control*. Until you become incapacitated or die, you can always change your trustee if, for any reason, you become unhappy with your choice. And—this is very important—even after you become incapacitated or die, they *must* follow the instructions in your trust. If they don't, they can be held legally liable.

When Would You Use A Corporate Trustee?
■ There's No One You Can Trust

You may have no one you can trust to take care of your financial affairs for you. You may be elderly, widowed, and/or in declining health, and have no children or other trusted relatives living nearby.

A corporate trustee can give you peace of mind, knowing a qualified professional you have personally selected will manage your financial affairs for you now and when you are no longer able to do so yourself. You won't have to worry about becoming a victim of an investment scam or a long-lost relative showing up to take control of your money.

■ You Want Help Managing Your Investments

You may not have the time, desire, or experience to manage your investments by yourself. You may want to travel extensively, don't want to worry about

Corporate trustees are in the business of managing trusts

your investments any longer, or simply feel that a professional could do a better job than you. Maybe you have (or expect to) come into some money from selling a business or other assets, or from an inheritance.

Good investment management is more important now than ever before. With people living longer and health care costs continuing to rise, our savings have to grow larger and last longer. Traditional investments like certificates of deposit used to work well; they were safe and their returns stayed ahead of inflation. But now we have to look at additional investment options to help our savings grow to the point where they can pay for our longer retirement years. And with so many options to choose from, this can be *very* confusing.

A corporate trustee has the experience, time, and resources to manage your trust and help you meet your investment goals. Many also have their own investment funds. You can evaluate them and compare their performance with other investments, including your own results.

You can still be as involved as you wish. You can have them make investment recommendations and present them to you for your decisions. Or you can authorize them to go ahead and make investment decisions *for* you based upon an already determined investment strategy, while you simply monitor their results through regular statements.

■ You Plan to Keep Assets in Trust for Your Beneficiaries

A corporate trustee can also be a good choice if you plan to keep assets in trust for your beneficiaries. These may include minors; those who will receive their inheritances in installments; a child, spouse, or other loved one with special needs; or one who may need help managing finances when something happens to you. Many parents and grandparents choose to keep assets in a trust to protect them from a beneficiary's irresponsible spending, creditors, divorce, bankruptcy, and predators (even spouses) who may have undue influence.

A corporate trustee will follow your trust's instructions objectively and make sure your beneficiaries' needs are taken care of for as long as your trust specifies—even for life. You won't have to worry about a corporate trustee dying before a beneficiary does.

■ **Family May Need Help After You Die (Settling Your Estate)**
The death of a loved one is a difficult time for a family. An innocent error by
a well-meaning but inexperienced relative or friend could negate your careful
planning and cost your beneficiaries thousands of dollars.

Many corporate trustees have experience with settling estates (preparing an
inventory of assets, having appraisals done, preparing tax returns, making
distributions, etc.) and can provide assistance and guidance to your surviving
spouse and/or other family members when you die. Many are also familiar
with various tax saving and estate planning strategies.

Benefits of a Corporate Trustee

■ **Experience**—Managing trusts is their business. They are familiar
with all kinds of trusts, tax and estate planning strategies, and the legal
responsibilities of a trustee.

■ **Professional Asset Management**—Generally, a professional who
has more time, resources, and experience can achieve better results than
an individual.

■ **Regulation**—They are regulated by both state and federal agencies.
Also, most courts consider them to be experts and expect a higher degree of performance from them than from an individual.

■ **Reliability**—They won't become ill or die, go on vacation, move
away, or be distracted by personal concerns or emotions as an individual might.

■ **Objectivity**—They will follow your trust instructions objectively and
unemotionally. A family member may find this difficult to do, especially if he/she is also a beneficiary of your trust.

When Does A Corporate Trustee Start Managing Your Trust?

That's up to you. A corporate trustee can be your trustee now (either acting alone or as a co-trustee with you) or a successor trustee.

Having a corporate trustee involved with your trust now would let them become familiar with you, your trust document, your assets, and your beneficiaries' needs and personalities while you are still around to answer questions and provide direction. At the same time, you can see how the corporate trustee will perform in your absence, evaluate their investment performance and services, and see how comfortable you feel overall. Think of it as a kind of "trustee test drive."

How Safe Are Trust Assets?

Trust assets are not insured by the FDIC. However, by law, trust assets must be kept separate from all other assets. For example, they cannot be loaned out or mixed with the corporate trustee's own assets. And they cannot be used to satisfy the corporate trustee's creditors. So even if a bank or trust company fails, trust assets are safe.

You are also protected against fraud, theft (for example, if an employee takes trust assets and disappears), or if they make an error administering your trust. And, in the unlikely event a corporate trustee did *not* follow your instructions or perform other duties as required by law, your beneficiaries would have a much better chance of being compensated for any loss from a corporate trustee than they would from an individual.

Of course, there is no insurance or bond to protect you if your assets simply lose value due to a decline in market values.

How Much Does A Corporate Trustee Charge?

Their fees are usually based on the value and type of trust assets they are managing and the services you want. Services and fees will vary. Some charge one fee that includes all of their services. Others have add-on fees for certain services. Make sure you ask about them and compare.

Corporate trustees begin charging a fee *only* when they start to act as trustee. So if you name a corporate trustee as your successor trustee, they won't charge you anything until they step in as trustee at your incapacity or death.

Are There Any Disadvantages Of A Corporate Trustee?

Because corporate trustees must objectively follow the instructions for the trusts they manage, some beneficiaries—especially those who want their money now instead of when the trust states—have found them to be inflexible and a bit distant. Of course, in many cases, the reason the trust was established and the corporate trustee chosen was to keep the beneficiary from getting the money until Mom and Dad (or whoever set up the trust) says it's okay.

If, however, you are concerned about a corporate trustee being too impersonal, you can always name a family member or close friend to act with them.

Also, with ongoing mergers and acquisitions, the corporate trustee you select now could become very different in the future. Trust officers also move from institution to institution. You may want to let your beneficiaries be able to change to another corporate trustee if they *all* become dissatisfied. Or you could add a trust protector to your trust, as explained later in this section.

How To Evaluate A Corporate Trustee

Corporate trustees are not all the same. They have different personalities, fees, investment performances, and services. For example, some do not manage real estate or settle estates. Most have minimum requirements on the amount of trust assets they will accept, although at some it is as low as $50,000-$100,000, and you may have that much in life insurance alone.

If you are considering a corporate trustee, talk to some. Visit them if you can. Ask how long their trust department has been in business. Compare their investment performances, fees, and services. Ask to see samples of statements or reports you would receive.

Facts and numbers are important, but so are the people. Do they seem to genuinely care about you and your family? Do they *listen* to you? Do they understand your concerns? Overall, how comfortable do you feel that they will be there for you and your family when you need them?

Should Everyone Use A Corporate Trustee?

No, of course not. If you have a modest estate and your trust is fairly simple, you will probably be just fine being your own trustee and having a capable

Corporate trustees only charge a fee when they begin to act for you

family member step in for you when you are no longer able to manage your trust yourself.

But if your estate is larger, has a variety of assets, if your trust includes tax planning, if assets will remain in your trust for your beneficiaries, or if you don't know whom to name as your successor trustee, a corporate trustee can be a wise choice.

ADDING A TRUST PROTECTOR

Trust protectors have long been used with offshore asset protection trusts to oversee the foreign trustee and make sure the grantor's intent was fulfilled. Attorneys here are increasingly beginning to use trust protectors with both irrevocable and revocable living trusts.

A trust protector is someone you name in the trust document to oversee your trustee and make sure your trust carries on the way you intended. (Alternatively, you can name "an appointer" to appoint the trust protector as needed.) With an irrevocable trust, the trust protector can begin to act right away. With a living trust, his/her active role would start at your incapacity or death.

The trust protector should be someone who knows and understands your motives, family values, and desires when your trust is created. It cannot be you, a parent, sibling, child, or your employee. (Legally, the trust protector must be "independent" of you and your beneficiaries.) It can be a trusted friend or advisor, but if your trust will last a long time, an institution (corporate trustee, bank, etc.) or professional fiduciary should be named.

This will be someone who can speak for you if there is uncertainty in interpreting your trust's instructions and can be the mediator if disputes arise between co-trustees, between the trustee and a beneficiary, or among beneficiaries. He/she can also provide guidance for the trustee and hold it accountable, and protect your beneficiaries from a trustee that is not meeting its responsibilities, is overreaching, or is not being responsive.

How much power you give your trust protector is completely up to you. You can give your trust protector authority to remove and replace the trustee for specific bad behavior (like being unresponsive to the beneficiaries, not providing acceptable record keeping, charging too much, etc.) or even for no reason at all (without cause). If no named successor trustee is available to serve, the trust protector can select a new trustee. If it does become necessary to remove a trustee, it would be easier and less expensive for the trust protector to do this (having already been given the authority in your trust document) than for the beneficiaries to reach an agreement and ask the court for removal.

You could allow the trust protector to change the situs (the location in which the trust is regulated) to a state that has more favorable asset protection or income tax laws. You could even give him/her the ability to amend or revoke the trust agreement, in its entirety or in part, and replace it with another trust (if allowed in your state). This could be extremely valuable in the trust's ability to follow your intentions as tax laws change and to protect the assets from potential predators and creditors.

As a check, an unrelated party could have the power to remove and replace the trust protector.

You keep control over who receives your assets and when they receive them

How to Provide for Your Beneficiaries

Remember, your beneficiaries are the people and/or organizations who will receive your assets when you die. Although most people name family members as their beneficiaries, you can leave your assets to any person(s) or organization(s) that you wish.

And as mentioned earlier, one of the most powerful benefits of a living trust is that *you* keep control over who receives your assets and when they will receive them. Basically, you can do whatever you want.

In the next few pages, we'll give you some things to keep in mind as you decide how to provide for minor children, adult children, and other beneficiaries, including those who may have special needs.

As you read this, think about your situation. But don't worry about all the little details. You just need to have a general idea of what you want. Remember, in Part Ten, we'll help you organize your thoughts and write them down.

Let's start first with special gifts you may want to make.

Special Gifts

You probably own some items of real or sentimental value—jewelry, antiques, or a collection (like coins, stamps, dolls, books)—that you want a certain child, grandchild, other special relative, friend, or organization to have when you die. These are called special gifts or special bequests. (Please note that all guns, even collectibles, require special planning. See Part Six.)

In most states, making these gifts with a living trust is easy. All you have to do is make a list, on a separate sheet of paper, of your special gifts and whom you want to have them. Then, date the list, have it notarized, and keep it with your living trust.

If you change your mind, just make a new list and have it notarized. You don't have to go back to your attorney and change your trust document; you can change your special gifts list at home. Your new notarized list is a legally recognized amendment to your living trust. So you can make changes as often as you like.

If your estate is sizeable, or if a gift is of substantial value, you will want to have your attorney review your list to avoid possible tax problems.

If your list starts getting long, you may want to break it down into smaller, separate lists, one for each person. This way, you won't have to re-do the entire list each time you make a change. Just make sure you date each list and always have new ones notarized.

To prevent possible family disagreements after you die, make your lists as specific as you can. It's much easier for you to do this now than to expect your children and other relatives to reach an agreement after you die that satisfies everyone.

Consider asking your children and other loved ones if there is something of yours they would like to have. There may be an item that has a special meaning to one of your children or grandchildren that you weren't even aware of. Not only would it be nice to know that now, but you may want to personally make some of these gifts now so you can have the joy of seeing the results.

Now, let's look at how to provide for your beneficiaries with other assets.

If You Have Minor Children

Remember, if you have minor children, your living trust should contain a children's trust to prevent the court from controlling the inheritance.

■ Naming a Guardian

You will need to name a guardian for your minor children. This is a *very* important decision. The person you choose will be responsible for raising your children if both parents have died or are incapacitated. As difficult as this decision may be, just remember that if you do not name a guardian and something happens to both parents, a judge will have to select one without knowing your preference.

Guardians must be adults, and you will want to choose someone who respects your values and standards (moral and religious) and will raise your children the way you would want. If you are considering older candidates, such as your parents, be realistic about their abilities to keep up with active toddlers or independent teenagers. If you want a couple to raise your children, it's a good idea to name one of them as your first choice and the other as your second choice, in case they were to divorce in the future.

As mentioned earlier in Part Two, the court must still officially approve your selection. In most cases, the court will go along with your choice. However, remember that if the other natural parent is still alive, he/she will usually be the court's preferred choice.

If you are a single parent with custody and really don't want your ex to be guardian, go ahead and name your preference anyway. Your choice will, at the very least, receive careful consideration by the court. It's also possible that your ex may not be able to take the responsibility (or won't want it). Or the court could agree with you that he/she is not a suitable option and would want to know your choice as an alternative.

■ Naming a Trustee

Remember, the guardian is only responsible for *raising* your children and does not control the inheritance. You also need to name a trustee for your children's trust. The trustee will be responsible for the safekeeping of the inheritance and will provide the money for normal living expenses, education, medical care, and other needs from the assets in the children's trust.

You will need to name a guardian and trustee for your minor children

113

The trustee can be one or more individuals and/or a corporate trustee. (Depending on the size of the inheritance and type of assets, you may want the benefits of having a corporate trustee's experience along with the personal insight of a friend or relative.)

You can name the same person as trustee and guardian and, at first thought, it may seem more convenient to have just one person involved. But keep in mind that the person you want to raise your children may not be your best choice to handle the money — and vice versa.

■ One Common Trust vs. Separate Trusts

Like most parents, you will probably want the trust assets to last long enough to provide for each of your children until they reach a certain age — for example, when the last one completes college.

Usually the best way to do this is to establish *one* children's trust and let the trustee use his/her discretion to provide for each child's individual needs as they arise, just as you would. Any remaining assets could be divided after your children are grown.

Of course, you could have separate trusts for each child with the inheritance split equally among the trusts, but this is less flexible. And although this would, on the surface, appear to treat each child equally, it could result in *unequal* treatment.

First of all, your children are different ages and their needs will last for different lengths of time. The youngest will need to be provided for several years longer than the oldest. With separate trusts, his/her funds could be depleted even before reaching college age, while the oldest one may be able to finish college and have money left over.

Also consider if one child became ill or injured and needed special medical treatment. If you were alive, you wouldn't stop providing for this child's care after you had spent a certain amount of money. You and your other children would probably sacrifice to make sure this child received the treatment he/she needed. But if you create separate trusts for each child, your trustee won't have that option.

■ Give Your Children's Trustee Flexibility

You may want to give your trustee some flexibility in how to use the trust assets. For example, the guardian may need some extra assistance in providing for your children. Put yourself in the shoes of your children's guardian for a moment. Suddenly you have additional children to raise. Is there enough room for everyone in your home, or do you need to add a bedroom? Can you handle the extra work load yourself or do you need to hire a part-time helper? You might even need a larger car.

Caring for your children should not be a financial burden on the person(s) you have asked to be guardian. That's why it's important to plan and leave enough assets to provide for them adequately. If you trust your trustee to manage the inheritance, he/she should be able to use good judgment to provide for the necessary comfort and well-being of your children.

Note: This is a good time to review your assets and insurance with your insurance agent or financial advisor. Do you realistically have enough assets to provide for your children and/or spouse the way you would want if something happened to you today? And if something happened to your spouse, would you have enough to manage without him or her? If you don't have enough assets to provide for your family as you would like, increasing your life insurance is often a relatively inexpensive solution.

■ Allowing for Loans/Advances for Your Older Children

To ensure the trust assets provide for all of your children, you probably want to keep the trust intact until the youngest has reached an appropriate age.

But, at the same time, you may not want to penalize your older children who may need funds to help purchase a home, pay for a wedding, or start a business while they are waiting for the youngest to grow up.

You might consider allowing for an advance or loan from their inheritance, which would be subtracted later when the trust assets are distributed. Your trustee should, of course, make sure the advance is appropriate and justified both in amount and purpose, so that the amount withdrawn from the trust does not adversely affect the other children. You may want to give your trustee some guidelines, such as specifying a limit on the amount of the advance to be considered.

Treating your children fairly may mean giving more to one than to another

If You Have Minor Grandchildren

Your living trust can also include a children's trust for your grandchildren. You will need to name a trustee (perhaps a parent and/or a corporate trustee) to manage the assets until each child reaches the age(s) at which you want him/her to receive the inheritance.

If your estate is substantial, you could consider transferring some of your assets to a separate trust for your grandchildren *now,* while you are living, to reduce your estate tax liability. Just make sure you don't leave anything *directly* to your minor grandchildren—you don't want to cause a guardian-ship. (Sizeable inheritances left directly to grandchildren may be subject to a generation-skipping transfer tax. See Part Nine.)

If You Have Adult Children

Once your children (and other beneficiaries) are adults, you have many options for giving them their inheritances. You'll first need to decide how much you want each one to receive and then when you want them to receive it. Keep in mind that your beneficiaries and their circumstances are different—and what may be right for one is not necessarily right for another.

■ How Much Do You Want Each to Receive?

As we mentioned earlier, most parents want to treat their children fairly. This may mean giving each an equal share *or* it may mean giving more to one child than to another.

For example, you may want to give more to a son who is a teacher than to a daughter who is a doctor. You may want to compensate a son or daughter who takes care of you during an illness or your last years. Or, instead of leaving a family business to all of your children, you may want to leave it to the one who has taken an active role in the business, then compensate the others with life insurance proceeds and/or other assets.

Some parents worry about leaving their children with too much money. They want their children to have enough that they can do anything they want, but not so much that they will do nothing! If this concerns you, just remember that no one said you have to leave *everything* you own to your children. In fact, you may decide it would be better not to give them anything *at all*—and keep the assets in trust for your grandchildren and future generations, and/or make a generous contribution to a favorite charity.

■ When Do You Want Them to Receive Their Inheritances?

Next, you need to decide *when* you want them to receive their inheritances. Let's look at some commonly used options.

Distribution Option 1: Give Some Now

If you can afford it, you may want to consider giving your beneficiaries some of their inheritance now, while you are living. Of course, you must take care of yourself first. Most people want to make sure they first have enough to last for as long as they live. And if they are married, they want to make sure there is enough to provide for the surviving spouse. As a result, most people typically hold onto *all of* their assets until the second spouse dies.

But with people living longer, this approach doesn't work as well as it used to. It's not unusual for parents to be in their 90s when they die, which means their children may be in their 70s when they inherit. If the surviving spouse is much younger (for example, if this is a second marriage), the kids may *never* see their inheritances.

If you can afford to give your beneficiaries some of their inheritances now, you will experience the joy of seeing the results—of seeing your children buy a home or start a business, or seeing your grandchildren go to college—and knowing it may not have happened without your help.

You may also have a child who wants to do worthwhile, but low-paying (even non-paying) work like teach, be a full-time volunteer, or even be able to stay at home to raise your grandchildren. You could provide them with additional income now so they could afford to do it.

Giving now can also reduce estate taxes. For more information on gifting, see Part Nine. Just remember, *never* give away more than you can afford.

Distribution Option 2: Lump Sum

You could have your trust distribute all of your assets to your beneficiaries in one lump sum as soon as possible after you die. This is a very common method of distribution. If your beneficiaries are responsible adults, this may

Installments give your beneficiaries more than one chance to act wisely

be a good choice, especially if they are older and you are concerned that they may not have many years left to enjoy the inheritance.

However, keep in mind that once a beneficiary has possession of the assets, he/she could lose them. A creditor could seize the assets for payment of debts or settlement of a lawsuit. An ex-spouse could end up with a good portion (or even all) of the inheritance through a divorce settlement. Even a current spouse can have access to assets that are placed in a joint account or if your beneficiary later adds his/her spouse as a co-owner.

If it bothers you that a son- or daughter-in-law could end up with your assets, or that a creditor could seize them, a lump sum distribution may *not* be the right option. If you want to be sure your assets stay in the family, you may want to consider installments or even keeping the assets in your trust.

Distribution Option 3: Installments

Many people prefer to give their beneficiaries more than one opportunity to invest or use their inheritances wisely, which doesn't always happen the first time around. So, instead of giving their beneficiaries their inheritances all at one time, they give it to them in installments.

Using the installment method also provides some protection against creditors, even an ex-spouse. They can only have access to assets that the beneficiary has actually received. So, in most cases, they would *not* be able to access the assets that are still in the trust. (However, if your beneficiary is not paying child support or spousal support as ordered by a court, in some states trust assets can be used to pay these obligations.)

Installments can be done just about any way you wish. Here are some you could consider.

At Certain Intervals

One way is to have your trust distribute portions of the inheritance at certain intervals after you die. For example, one-third when you die; another third, five years later; and the final third, five years after that. (If you are married, you may want distributions to begin after both you and your spouse have died.)

Just make sure you review this part of your trust from time to time to see if it still works for your situation. Depending on how old your children are at any given time, and how long you live, you may not want to make them wait for years after you die before they receive the full inheritance. There's the chance they may not live long enough to receive all of it.

At Certain Ages

As an alternative, installments could be distributed after you die as a beneficiary reaches certain ages—for example, the first installment at age 25, a second at age 30, a third at age 35, etc.

Again, if you choose this option, make sure you review your trust periodically. Otherwise, your beneficiaries could have already passed those ages by the time you die and would receive their inheritances in one lump sum, defeating your intention of distributing it in installments. To prevent this, your trust can specify that if your beneficiaries have passed these ages when you die, the inheritance would then be paid in installments every so many years (as above).

At Certain Occasions

Be careful about linking the distributions to certain milestones like marriage, birth of a child, etc. It could be that your beneficiary doesn't marry or have children. (This could also encourage an insincere marriage, and part of the inheritance could end up outside the family.)

Using graduation from college as a distribution time can also present some potential problems. For example, how would you define "college?" Two-year, four-year, trade school? What if a beneficiary pursues a career (performing arts, a trade, etc.) for which a college degree isn't necessary?

Distribution Option 4: Keep Assets in Trust

You may decide to keep assets in the trust and *provide* for a beneficiary, but not actually give the assets to him or her. Here are some situations with which you may be able to identify.

An Irresponsible Beneficiary

If you feel a beneficiary is too irresponsible to receive outright control of his/her inheritance (or has a problem with drugs, alcohol, gambling, etc.),

You may decide to keep the assets in trust

you can specify that the inheritance remain "in trust" for his/her lifetime or until he/she reaches a more mature age.

The trustee will manage and invest the inheritance, and provide for the beneficiary's basic needs as you instruct. If you don't think your beneficiary is responsible enough to receive a regular income from the trust, the trustee can pay rent and other expenses directly so the beneficiary never actually has the money.

Give some thought to your choice as trustee. A family member acting alone may be too sympathetic and easily swayed—or just the opposite. You may want to have a corporate trustee be a co-trustee to add some objectivity and share the responsibility. You'll also need to specify who will receive any remaining inheritance if the beneficiary dies before receiving the full amount of the inheritance.

You may also want the trust to include a *spendthrift clause* to protect the trust assets from creditors. Generally, this says that the beneficiary cannot voluntarily spend any trust assets or income before they are paid to him/her. So if, for example, your irresponsible son or daughter buys an expensive sports car, the trust cannot be held responsible for payment.

Protection from Creditors/Spouse
As mentioned earlier, if you are concerned that a son- or daughter-in-law or a creditor could have access to the inheritance, you may want to keep the assets in trust and just provide periodic income to your beneficiary.

Incentive to Work
Maybe you want to give a beneficiary a little extra incentive to work and lead a productive life. For example, one father was concerned that his beach-loving son would continue to simply ride the waves while he waited around for Dad to die. The son saw no reason to seek regular employment because he knew he would receive a sizeable inheritance when Dad died. To encourage his son to be more productive, Dad arranged for the inheritance to *stay* in trust. And for every dollar the son earned on his own, the trust would match it.

Note: If you decide to income-match, make sure your trust will provide for your beneficiary if he/she is *unable* to work due to illness or injury.

And don't forget about retirement. Do you want your beneficiary to work *for as long as he/she lives* in order to receive an income from the trust?

Beneficiary Doesn't Need the Money

You may have a child who is already financially secure and doesn't really need the money. Instead of giving the inheritance to this child, you could keep the assets in trust for your grandchildren and future generations. You can still provide periodic income to your child and have the assets available as a safety net should circumstances change (due to illness or injury, divorce, death of a spouse, investment loss, job loss, etc.), and he/she needs some money.

Loved One with Special Needs

You may have a spouse, child, sibling, parent, or other loved one who is disabled or may simply not be able to handle an inheritance by him/herself after you die. This is a perfect time to keep the inheritance in trust and have the trustee provide for this person as you would. (This is another good time to consider a corporate trustee.)

If this person is receiving government benefits, the next two sections will be of particular interest to you. The first one explains how a *special needs trust* lets you provide for a beneficiary without jeopardizing valuable government benefits. The second section explains some recent changes in the law you need to know about if your spouse is currently eligible for or may require Medicaid.

Providing For Dependents With Special Needs

If you have a spouse, child, sibling, parent, or other loved one who is physically, mentally or developmentally disabled—from birth, illness, injury or drug abuse—he/she may be entitled to government benefits (Supplemental Security Income and/or Medicaid) now or in the future. However, most of these benefits are available only to those with very minimal assets.

Like many others, you may find yourself faced with a difficult choice. If you leave a substantial inheritance to this person, he/she will be disqualified from receiving the government benefits which may be crucial for his/her care. On the other hand, you may not want to have to disinherit this person in order to preserve these benefits.

Providing for a loved one with special needs takes special planning

There is a third option. With a *special needs trust* you can provide for a disabled child or other loved one without interfering with his/her benefits.

The special needs trust should be very specific in stating that its purpose is to *supplement* government benefits—that is, to provide only benefits or luxuries *above and beyond* the benefits the beneficiary (the disabled person) receives from any local, state, federal, or private agencies.

It is extremely important that the special needs trust not duplicate any government-provided services and that the beneficiary not have any resemblance of ownership of the trust assets. Otherwise, it is very possible that the government would attempt to seize the trust assets for repayment of services provided or determine that the beneficiary does not qualify for future benefits because he/she has ample assets and income to provide for adequate care.

To make sure the beneficiary does not have any implied ownership in the trust assets, the special needs trust should give the trustee complete control over the distribution of the assets and any income they generate. The beneficiary should not be able to demand any principal or interest from the trust.

You should also instruct the trustee to purchase only goods and services that government benefits do not provide, such as airline tickets to visit relatives, furniture, a stereo, etc. The trustee should make the purchase directly, instead of giving the money to the beneficiary and letting him/her make the purchase. A spendthrift clause (see page 120) is also a good idea for extra protection.

■ Who Should Be Trustee?

Of course, you (and your spouse, if you are married) will continue to provide for this person while you are alive and able. But someone will need to assume this responsibility after your death or incapacity, so you will need to name a trustee.

The most obvious choice is another family member or close personal friend who has a deep concern for this person's welfare. This may be one or more of your healthy adult children. Your attorney or CPA may also be willing to serve as trustee.

As with any trustee, be sure to discuss this with the person(s) you have in mind. Make sure they have the time, ability, and desire to take on this responsibility. Also, be aware of a possible conflict of interest, especially if your other children will inherit the trust assets after your special needs beneficiary has died. They may be more interested in preserving the trust assets than in putting the care of the special needs person first.

A corporate or professional trustee can be a good choice, especially if you do not want to burden other family members with this responsibility or don't want to worry about a possible conflict of interest. And, of course, you don't have to worry about your beneficiary outliving a corporate trustee; they'll be around to provide for your beneficiary for as long as he/she lives.

You may want to consider using both. For example, the corporate or professional trustee can manage the assets and a relative can be responsible for determining and purchasing the goods and services that will make your beneficiary more comfortable. You may also want to consider having a corporate trustee work with you now to take advantage of their investment skills and to have them become familiar with your beneficiary and his/her needs.

■ How Much Should You Put Into the Trust?

There is no way to know for sure how much money will be needed. Among other things, you will want to take into consideration how long you expect this person to live, the kind of care he/she will need, the benefits available (now and projected), how much income the assets can be expected to generate, how much you can afford to put into the trust, and how much you want to give to other beneficiaries. Life insurance on the life of a parent, grandparent, or other relative is often used to fund a special needs trust.

■ Seek Professional Assistance

As you can see, providing for someone with special needs takes more thought and is more complicated than providing for your other beneficiaries. Also, the laws vary from state to state. *Make sure* you use a local attorney who has experience in setting up special needs trusts. Standard beneficiary wording just will not work.

Special Needs Trust For Your Spouse

If your spouse is receiving (or may need to qualify for) Medicaid benefits, you may want to set up a special needs trust to provide your spouse with some extra services and benefits that are not covered by Medicaid. It would work

Disinheriting a child is permanent

like a special needs trust for any other beneficiary. But, because of a recent change in the law, it would have to be set up a little differently.

For now, at least, to preserve Medicaid eligibility, a special needs trust for your spouse must be created *by a will* after you die. To set it up now, your attorney will write a brief will, the only purpose of which is to create this special needs trust when you die. Then you designate which assets you want to go into this trust. (Your other assets stay in your living trust.) The downside is the assets that will go into this special needs trust will probably have to go through probate.

Now, remember, laws can change. In fact, several attorneys have been working to have the wording changed so a special needs trust for your spouse can be set up through your living trust—*without* a special will and probate. An attorney who specializes in Elder Law can help keep you informed. (See Part Two for two excellent sources for Elder Law attorneys.)

Remember, you only need a special needs trust if your spouse is currently eligible for or is likely to require Medicaid—and Medicaid is only available to those who have very limited assets. If you have long term care insurance or you pay for medical expenses yourself, you don't need a special needs trust. In that case, you can provide for your surviving spouse as you wish through your living trust for the rest of his/her life.

Disinheriting

Sometimes a parent chooses to intentionally disinherit one or more of their children. There may be what the parent considers to be legitimate reasons, such as if one child has been more financially successful than the others, or not wanting a special needs child to lose government benefits, or not wanting to leave an inheritance to an irresponsible or drug-dependent child. (In the previous pages we have shown you that there are viable alternatives to disinheriting in these situations.) And sometimes a parent wants to disinherit a child who is estranged from the family, or use disinheriting as a way to get even and have the last word.

Regardless of the reason, disinheriting a child is hurtful, permanent, and will undoubtedly affect that child's relationship with his or her siblings. Courts are full of siblings who sue each other over inheritances but even if they don't sue, it is highly unlikely they will be having holiday dinners together. Finances aside, there is symbolic meaning to receiving something from a parent's estate.

How you choose to include your children in your estate plan says a good deal about your values and your faith. Not disinheriting a child who has caused you grief and heartache can convey a message of love and forgiveness, while disinheriting a child, even for what seems to be good cause, can convey a lack of love, anger, and resentment.

If your decision to disinherit a child is final, it should be included in your trust. It's a good idea to tell your child so it doesn't come as a complete surprise. Explaining your reasons personally (not in your trust) will allow for honest discussion, and may keep the child from blaming siblings or contesting your trust. If you have a change of heart, have your trust changed immediately.

If Your Beneficiaries Die Before Receiving Their Inheritances

As we've said before, most people leave their assets to family members. And if a beneficiary dies before receiving the inheritance, you basically have two choices to determine how this beneficiary's share will be distributed.

The legal phrases in your trust document that specify how this is done are *per capita* and *per stirpes*. This may seem confusing at first, especially if you have trouble following family trees. But it is important for you to understand how these provisions work because they distribute the assets very differently. The flow charts on the following pages should help you understand them.

You should also think about whom you would want to have your assets if *all* of your beneficiaries die before you. Many people specify their place of worship, a favorite charity, or foundation.

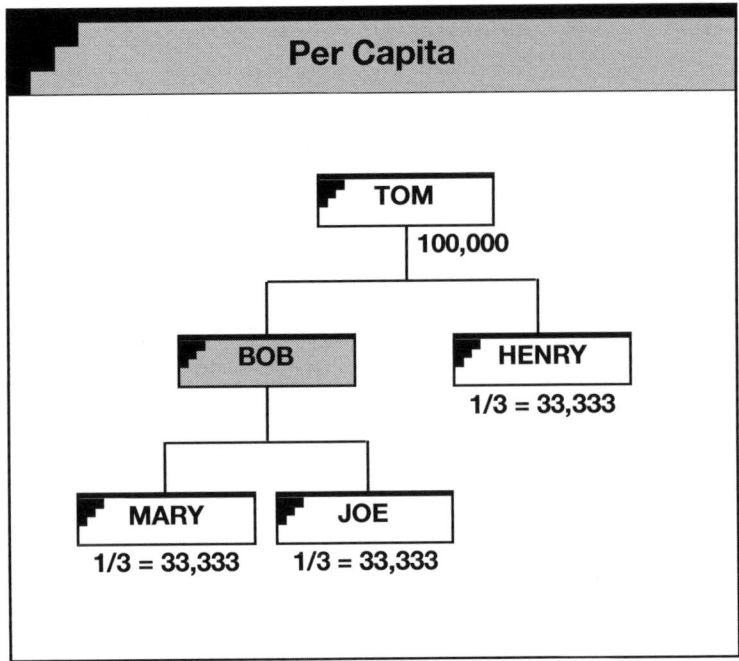

Per Capita

Distribution per capita (or by pro rata or share and share alike) means that the surviving descendents will receive equal shares of the inheritance, regardless of generation. Let's say Tom, a widower, has two grown sons—Bob and Henry. Bob dies before his father Tom. Henry and his brother's two children (Tom's grandchildren—Mary and Joe) will each receive one-third of Tom's estate.

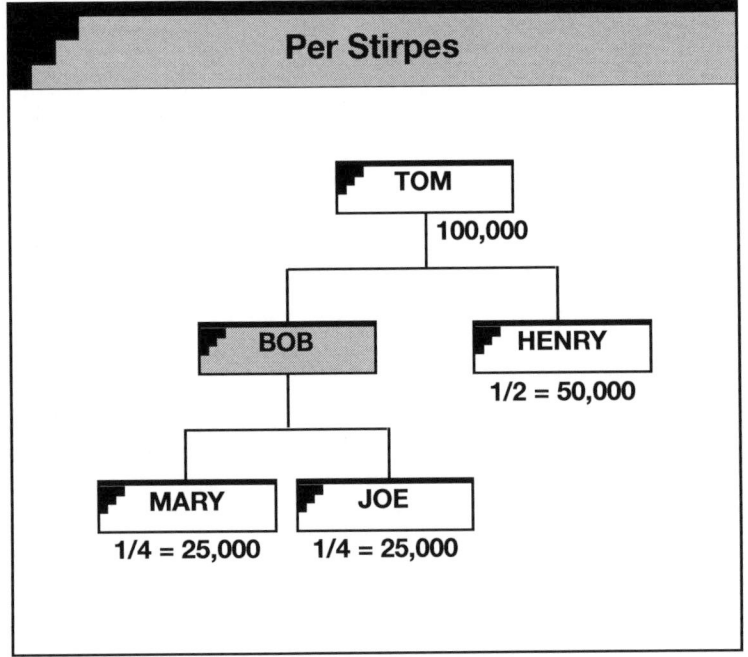

Per Stirpes

Distribution per stirpes (or by representation) means that your surviving descendents will only receive what their immediate ancestor would receive. Using the same example, Henry will receive 50% of his father's estate. Bob's children (Mary and Joe) will each receive 25% of their grandfather's estate, splitting the 50% their father would have received.

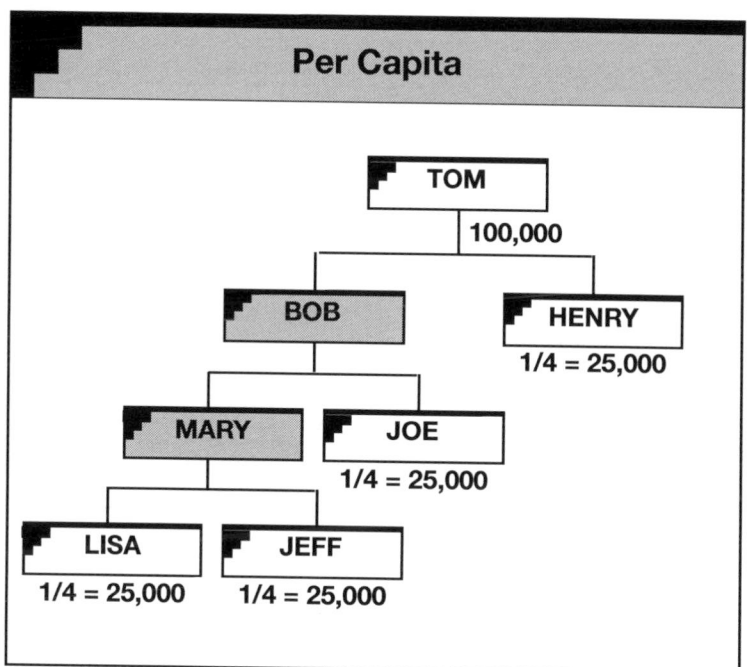

Now let's carry this a generation further. Let's say that Bob's daughter Mary, who had two children (Lisa and Jeff), also dies before her grandfather. When Tom dies, under the *per capita* instructions his four beneficiaries—son Henry, grandson Joe and great-grandchildren Lisa and Jeff—will each receive one-fourth of his estate.

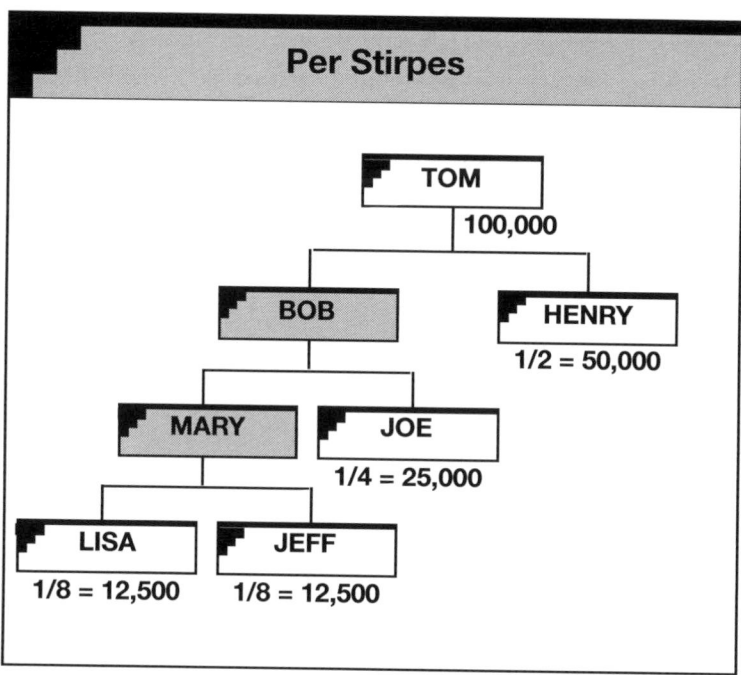

However, under *per stirpes* instructions, Mary's children would split the inheritance their mother would have received. Henry receives 50%, Mary's brother Joe receives 25% and Mary's two children will each receive 12.5% (splitting Mary's share).

If You Have Pets

For most pet owners, their pets are part of the family. In fact, some people are closer to their pets than to their own children! Many pet owners want to provide for the continuing care of their pets after their own deaths. You may have read that Lauren Bacall left $10,000 for the care of her dog, Sophie.

As you think about your desires, the pet's needs, and how best to accomplish them, here are some things to consider:

- Identify your pet to prevent a different animal from benefiting, especially if the pet is valuable or a large sum of money is involved. This can be accomplished with photos, veterinary records, a microchip, even DNA testing. You may have heard about the couple who, in exchange for taking care of a deceased lady's beloved cat, were allowed to live in her home rent-free for as long as the cat lived. Well, over the course of several years (longer than the cat's expected lifetime), they were caught replacing the original cat with a series of similar looking, younger cats!

- You can name the same person to serve as trustee and be the caretaker, but you may want to name two different people so they will be accountable to each other. You may want to require the caretaker to sign an agreement to provide proper care and relinquish care to a successor if the promised care is not provided. Name successors in case your initial choices become unable or unwilling to act, and include a sanctuary, pet adoption service, or shelter of last resort if none of your chosen caretakers survives the pet or is able to serve. Be sure to ask the people you wish to name if they are willing to serve.

- Define what proper care is. Expenses may include food, housing, veterinary and dental care, toys, exercise routines, grooming, compensation for the caretaker, and burial/cremation fees. Farm animals, race horses, and other large or valuable animals could require a full time caretaker.

- You may want to purchase liability insurance to cover any potential damage caused by the pet to people and/or property.

- Think about how much money will be needed to provide for this care. Will it end when the pet dies, or will it continue for the pet's descendants?

A life insurance policy on your life can provide the needed funds. Then what should happen to any remaining funds? Do you want them to go to family members or to a charity?

Charities, Religious Organizations, And Other NonProfits

As you think about who will be your beneficiaries, consider including a favorite charity or foundation. Take a few minutes to think about organizations or causes that are special to you—some national, perhaps international, and some local. There are many excellent ones, and they are all in need of funding to continue their work. There is sure to be one or more that you would like to help. In addition to the tax benefits of charitable donations, you have the power to do something good, to express yourself, and to give something of value back into the world.

For example, you may have been very active in your church, synagogue, or other religious, fraternal or charitable organization. Perhaps it provided support to you at a critical time in your life and you would like to return the support. Maybe someone very close to you died from cancer, Alzheimer's or another disease, and you would like to help fund research to find a cure. Many people give in the memory of a loved one. You may feel very strongly about helping our veterans, education, child abuse, the hungry and homeless, protecting the environment, world peace, animal rights, the arts, organ donation—the list of worthwhile causes is endless.

Your gift can be as specific or as general, as large or as small, as you want to make it. For example, you could set up a scholarship program for underprivileged children. You could buy new chairs or religious textbooks, or help fund a building project, for your place of worship. The charity or foundation of your choice will be glad to make suggestions and help you set up your gift program. (Some may even be able to recommend an attorney who can prepare your trust.)

Including a charity as a beneficiary of your living trust lets the charity receive the maximum benefit of your gift. It will not be reduced or delayed by the probate process as would happen if you made the gift through a will. Also, because a) a living trust is more private, b) distributions can usually be made more quickly, and c) the process to contest is more difficult, there is less chance your gift will be contested than if it were made via a will.

With a living trust, the charity receives the maximum benefit of your gift

Plan for successors in all areas of your life

Some people have told us that they take some or all of the money they will save by not going through probate and give it to a charity.

> **Note:** Make sure you specify the legal name and the location (including address) of the organization you want to receive the gift. For example, if you want the local office of a national organization to have it, make sure you clearly state so. Otherwise, the local office and the national office could end up fighting each other in court to see who will receive the gift.

Also, if you are unsure whether or not the organization will be around to receive the gift, list an alternate charitable beneficiary. This will prevent a court from having to decide who will ultimately receive your gift.

In Part Nine, we explain ways you can give to a charity or foundation so you (or your estate) will receive special tax advantages.

ESTATE PLANNING IS SUCCESSION PLANNING

Estate planning is about making sure your assets and belongings will go to the people and organizations you want to have them after you die, with as little delay and costs as possible. It is about planning for the possibility of incapacity before you die. But, as you are starting to see, it is also about planning for successors in all areas of your life when you are no longer here and able to perform your responsibilities.

Think of all the areas in your life where someone would need to step in and take your place in your absence. Whom do you take care of? Whom do you provide for? Whom do you guide or mentor? Consider, for example:

Your Business

If you own a business, it provides for your family, your employees, and your clients. Business succession planning is critical for the business to continue in your absence. You may want the business to be run by one of your children, a business partner, or a key employee. You may want your employees to own the business through an Employee Stock Ownership Plan (ESOP).

But without a written plan, the funding to make it happen, and careful grooming of the right successor, the business you spent most of your life building and running will likely disintegrate without you. A 2001 study by *Small Business Review* found that only 30% of all family-owned businesses survive to the next generation; only 12% make it to the third generation; and a meager 3% are functioning into the 4th generation and beyond. The overwhelming reason is that most owners do not plan for their exit. And you *will* eventually exit your business due to retirement, incapacity, or death.

Your Family

You already know that you need to name a successor for those who depend upon you: minor children, an aging parent, your spouse or a child with special needs and, yes, your pets. Life insurance or your assets may provide the needed funds, but someone will need to manage the money and make financial decisions. You also need a plan for their care if they outlive you. The more you can plan and put into place now, the smoother the transition will be in your absence.

Your Legacy

Consider your role as patriarch or matriarch for your family. Who will succeed you as the one others come to for advice, wisdom, and counseling? Have you been teaching your children and grandchildren the values and lessons you want to pass down to future generations as part of your legacy? Are you grooming anyone as your family successor?

Consider also your business and charitable endeavors. You have probably gained valuable experience in your chosen field of work or life passion. Are you mentoring someone younger than you who can continue your work?

Planning for successors in all areas of our lives provides an excellent example to others and shows how much we care.

IF YOU NEED MORE HELP MAKING DECISIONS

By now, you probably have a pretty good idea of whom you want to be your trustee, successor trustee(s) and beneficiaries, and how and when you want your beneficiaries to receive their inheritances.

But if you are still unsure about anything, here are some things you can do:

- Re-read the appropriate section(s) a couple of times. Make notes in the margins of things you don't understand, want to know more about, or want to think about some more. Then…

- Discuss it with your spouse, close friends, or professional advisors. Talk to as many people as you feel comfortable discussing these matters. Ask what they have done or what they might do if they were in your place. Sometimes just talking out loud with someone helps you make a decision or makes you feel better about one you've already made.

- On a sheet of paper, write down your options and list the advantages and disadvantages of each one.

- Write down your questions and concerns, and ask your attorney about possible solutions. Attorneys are called "counselors at law" for a reason. Most have counseled many families and have seen the results of proper and improper planning. An experienced attorney will be able to guide you through difficult decisions and help you reach the right ones for your unique situation.

If you're having trouble with a decision, try not to worry about it too much. Sometimes you just have to clear your head and come back to it later. You'll eventually make a decision that is right for you.

Now, let's look at how you can find the right attorney and the steps you will need to take to have your living trust prepared.

Part Five—

HAVING YOUR DOCUMENTS PREPARED

Now that you have a general idea of whom you want to be your trustee, successor trustee(s), and beneficiaries (and how you want them to inherit), let's go through the process—step-by-step—of setting up your living trust.

In this section, we'll help you find the right attorney to prepare your trust document. We'll even give you specific questions to ask as you interview attorneys. Then we'll explain the information your attorney will need and what to expect when you meet with your attorney. Finally, we will explain other documents your attorney should prepare that will give you extra protection.

DO YOU NEED AN ATTORNEY?

Since the first edition of this book was written, there has been an explosion of do-it-yourself (DIY) websites, kits, books, and forms, many of which were created with assistance from attorneys. You may think your needs are so simple you don't need an attorney's help. Or maybe you just want to save money.

The truth is you *can* do your own estate planning. But *should* you? It may seem easy and straightforward while you are completing the forms, but simple mistakes or omissions can have far-reaching complications that will only come to light after you are gone. With you not here to explain your intentions or correct mistakes, your loved ones could end up paying much more in legal fees than you might save by not using an attorney now.

If you are contemplating DIY estate planning, consider the following:

Benefits Of Using An Experienced Attorney

■ **Legal Expertise**: Experienced estate planning attorneys have the technical expertise to draft documents correctly. Yes, they may use computerized forms to work from, but they know what to change and how to change it to make your plan work the way you want. They also understand the technical terms and legal requirements in your state. Laws vary greatly from state to state, and a DIY program or kit may not tell you everything you need to know to prevent your plan from being thrown out by the court.

■ **Counseling**: Attorneys are called "counselors at law" for a reason. Most estate planning attorneys have counseled many families, and they have seen the results of proper and improper planning. An experienced attorney can guide you with delicate decisions, including who should be the guardian of your minor children; how to provide for a special needs child or parent without jeopardizing government benefits; how to provide for your children fairly; how to protect an inheritance from creditors and irresponsible spending; and how to provide for a significant other if you are not married.

■ **Assistance with Transferring Assets**: Remember, you must transfer your assets (change titles) to your living trust for it to work properly. As explained in Part Six, many attorneys will transfer your home to your trust at no additional cost, and they usually have legal assistants who can transfer other assets for a small fee. If you want to save some money and transfer some assets yourself, the attorney will provide written instructions; legal assistants are usually available to answer questions and/or provide assistance.

■ **Explanation of Intentions**: If there is any confusion as to what your intentions were after you are gone, the attorney who counseled you will be able to explain them. This unbiased interpretation from someone who does not stand to benefit from your plan can help avoid costly litigation by your beneficiaries and even maintain the validity of your documents.

■ **Coordination of Assets**: You probably own your assets in a variety of ways. Some may be titled in your name. Others (real estate, IRAs, retirement benefits, life insurance, annuities) may be controlled by a contract, joint ownership and/or beneficiary designations. An experienced attorney will know how to coordinate these so that your assets are distributed the way you want.

■ **Tax Planning**: With the federal estate tax exemption so high, most people do not need federal estate tax planning. But some states have their own death or inheritance tax, often with much lower exemptions than the federal tax, and other taxes (income, capital gains, Medicare surtax, gift, and generation-skipping) are still on the table. Careful professional tax planning is a must if you have tax-deferred accounts and long-term capital gains.

Start with referrals from people you know and trust

Again, most people think their estate planning will be simple. But the reality is that most of us do need some personalized planning, and you may not realize that without the guidance and counseling of an experienced attorney.

How to Find the Right Attorney

You have to be careful and maybe even a bit skeptical as you search for the attorney who will prepare your living trust for you. You'll want an attorney is experienced *specifically* with living trusts. Just having "a lot of experience in estate planning" may not be enough. That could mean wills and probate.

Your attorney should also be someone with whom you feel comfortable sharing your personal and financial situation, and who will charge you a fair price. In the next few pages, we'll help you find such an attorney.

Before you start your search, it would be a good idea to complete the Organizer in the back of this book. This will encourage you to actually *write down* your decisions and thoughts about your trust, questions you want to ask your attorney, information about your assets, and the size of your net estate.

You don't need to make *all* of the decisions yet; you will want to have some counsel from your attorney. But having your information and questions organized will make it easier to evaluate attorneys and select one who is right for you. You'll feel more confident as you interview them, you'll save time, and you may even save some money.

Finding Referrals
■ People You Know
The first step in locating your attorney is to ask for referrals from people you know and trust. Ask your friends and associates if they have living trusts

and, if so, who prepared them. Are they satisfied? Are they aware of other attorneys you should consider?

You can also ask other professionals who work with estate planning attorneys. Your banker, trust officer, CPA, life insurance agent, and financial planner are usually good sources. Your investment broker, family or business attorney, place of worship, or a charity may also be able to provide recommendations.

Here's a question to ask professionals: "If your mother needed a living trust, whom would you recommend for her?"

■ Certified Estate Planning Attorneys

The bar associations in some states have certification programs for attorneys who specialize in estate planning. Requirements vary, but usually the attorney must devote a certain amount of his/her practice to estate planning, complete a certain number of hours of continuing education courses each year, and may have to pass periodic exams.

You can call your local bar association to find out if your state has a similar program, what the requirements are, and to see if they will give you a list of attorneys in your area who meet them. (You can find the phone number online or you can call directory assistance.) At the least, the information will help you better qualify the attorneys you interview. However, as explained on the next page, be cautious about attorney referrals from your local bar.

■ Seminars

Some attorneys still present free seminars on living trusts in their offices, at hotels, in retirement centers, and at libraries. This is an excellent way to observe and evaluate an attorney without making a commitment. It's also a good opportunity to ask questions and hear other people's questions.

Does the attorney speak in plain English that you can understand? Is the presentation organized and well done? How well does the attorney answer questions? Does the attorney give you something to take home and read?

Usually, attorneys will stay for a few minutes afterwards to meet the attendees, answer individual questions, and schedule appointments. Some will offer a free consultation. Some even give attendees a discount. This can be good for both of you: the attorney saves time by explaining the basics to several people at one time and you save money on your trust.

If you are interested in attending one of these seminars, check your local newspaper for advertisements or listen to a local talk radio station. If you do attend one, remember that the quality of the seminar is only part of it. In the end, what counts is the quality of the documents the attorney prepares for you. You will still want to interview and evaluate the attorney.

■ **Prepaid Legal Services Plans**

Some employers, associations, and unions offer prepaid legal services plans to employees and members. Several are also being offered directly to the public through credit card companies. Under these plans, some legal services, such as review of legal documents and consultations, are free. Other services are offered at discounts, and the attorney's normal hourly rate may be reduced. Most of these plans use local attorneys to provide the services.

If you belong to or qualify for membership in one of these plans, this may be a way to have your trust done at a lower cost. However, a referral from the plan does not guarantee an attorney has experience in living trusts. You will still need to personally interview the plan's attorneys. Just remember, a lower cost is no bargain if your document is not properly prepared.

■ **Local Bar Association**

Your local bar association can also give you names of some estate planning attorneys. But that's about all they can do; they cannot recommend one attorney over another. Attorneys often pay a fee to be on the referral list, and the bar just goes down the list, usually with no knowledge of the attorney's experience or qualifications. Some bars charge to give you referrals. In that case, you might as well use the yellow pages or internet—at least they're free.

■ **Avoid Scams and Rip Offs**

Watch out for all kinds of scams and rip offs. They are definitely out there. It was probably inevitable that some unethical people would find ways to make some quick money by capitalizing on the growing popularity of living trusts and taking advantage of other people.

The most publicized scams, of course, are non-attorneys, using high pressure tactics, selling cookie cutter living trusts in seminars and door-to-door. But

Become an informed consumer and use common sense

you could also be taken advantage of by an attorney. Some routinely draft living trusts and don't fund them. Others write testamentary trusts in wills when their clients really wanted revocable living trusts.

How can you make sure you find the right attorney and not become a victim of one of these scams or rip offs? Your best protection is to become an informed and educated consumer—which you are doing now—and use common sense. The next section on how to evaluate an attorney will be especially helpful.

How To Evaluate An Attorney

Once you have several attorneys to consider, you will need to start narrowing your list. First, look to see if any attorneys have been recommended to you by more than one source—and see who recommended them. If you keep hearing some of the same names from people you respect and trust, that's a pretty good sign you are on the right track.

Next, find out where the attorney is located. You might as well start with those who are near you. But, while convenience is a consideration, the right attorney may be worth a little *in*convenience.

Keep in mind that you are looking for an attorney who has experience, has the right personality for you, and whose fees, services, and qualifications match your needs.

■ Telephone Interview—An Eleven-Point Checklist

The next step is to call the attorneys on your list. You don't need to have a lengthy conversation at this point. Try to keep it to about five minutes. That's plenty of time to find out whether or not this attorney may be right for you. If the attorney can't speak with you when you call, leave a message with your name and who referred you. Then see how long it takes before the attorney calls you back. Keep in mind that *you are the customer.* Don't be intimidated or afraid to ask questions. Here are some to consider.

1. Tell the attorney you want a living trust document that will avoid probate when you die and a conservatorship (guardianship) if you become incapacitated. Then ask the attorney if he/she does revocable living trusts. If the attorney tries to talk you out of a living trust, suggests a will or joint ownership, or tries to convince you that a living trust is complicated and expensive, or that most people don't own enough to need one (implying

they're only for the wealthy), ask him or her to explain why. If you are not satisfied with the explanation, find another attorney.

2. Ask the attorney how many years he/she has been doing living trusts and about how many he/she has done. Ask what percentage of his/her practice is devoted to living trusts.

    If the attorney has done hundreds of living trusts but only started doing them a year ago, that tells you the attorney has done a lot of them but it may not tell you the quality of the documents. On the other hand, if the attorney has been doing living trusts for ten years but has only done 12, that may not be enough experience. Ideally, you will find someone who specializes in living trusts and has done a lot of them over a long period of time. This is not a *guarantee* that the attorney knows what he/she is doing, but it's a good indicator.

    Here's the point. If you needed a triple bypass operation, would you choose a doctor who has only done a few or would you choose the specialist who devotes most of his/her time to this very operation? It's essentially the same thing; with the doctor, we're talking about your health, and with the attorney, we're talking about your wealth.

    Now, this is not to say that a less experienced attorney couldn't do a great job, especially for a smaller estate. It's not uncommon for less experienced attorneys to work with more seasoned mentors. Find out whom the newer attorney goes to for advice and who reviews his/her work. Common sense will take you a long way here.

3. If your estate is more than the federal estate tax exemption, ask how many living trusts with estate tax planning the attorney has done and over how many years. (After you complete the Organizer, you'll know how much your estate is worth and if you need these provisions.) Again, the more of these the attorney has done and the longer he/she has been doing them, the better off you will probably be.

4. Ask who will actually write your trust document. In larger firms, it would not be unusual for the attorney you meet with to collect your information, instruct an associate to draft the document, then review it to make sure it is accurate. This is perfectly acceptable and will be less

Remember, you are the customer

costly than if a senior attorney did the actual writing. What you want to avoid is an attorney who knows little about living trusts, who just collects your information and then sends it to an attorney in another state who prepares a cookie cutter trust document.

5. Ask how many living trusts the attorney has administered (or settled) when clients became incapacitated or died. Some attorneys have written a lot of living trusts, but have little or no experience administering them. An attorney who has hands-on experience administering living trusts at incapacity and death, and has seen how well his/her trust documents have worked, could be very helpful to your family later if they have questions or need assistance with your trust.

6. Ask how much the attorney charges for a living trust. Some charge a flat fee if you are single and your estate does not need estate tax planning, and a slightly higher flat fee if you are married and need no estate tax planning. (See Part Three for a discussion of the federal estate tax exemption.) Be sure to ask if there are any charges that are in addition to this fee, such as for transferring assets into your trust.

If the attorney charges by the hour, it will be harder to get an estimate over the phone. Tell the attorney how much your estate is worth, and ask if he/she can give you a ballpark estimate or what the cost has been for estates that are similar in size to yours. Be cautious if the attorney is reluctant to talk about pricing at all. If you are concerned about price, tell the attorney and ask if you can pay in installments or by credit card.

7. Ask how long it will take and decide if that is acceptable to you. Because you will be prepared and organized, the attorney may be able to provide you with a first draft of the documents within a couple of weeks. It may take another couple of weeks for you to review them and have any corrections made. However, if you or the person who needs the trust (for example, a parent) is ill, that may be too long. If you need the documents prepared more quickly for a valid reason, ask if the attorney will accommodate you. Remember, *you're* the customer.

8. Ask the attorney for a biography. Most will be happy to provide one or will refer you to the firm's website. Look to see where the attorney

went to school. Does he/she have any advanced degrees or professional designations? Does the attorney take continuing education courses? Does he/she teach or write on topics for other attorneys?

9. Ask how much malpractice insurance the attorney has. If your assets are worth $10 million, would you want to go to an attorney who only has $1 million of malpractice insurance?

10. Ask if you can you come in for a free consultation. Many attorneys are willing to spend 15-20 minutes with you at no charge for a meet and greet, and will answer some general questions. But if the attorney charges a reasonable fee for this meeting, it still may be worth it depending on the size of your estate, the qualifications of the attorney, and the strength of the referral.

11. Evaluate the conversation. What do you think? Were you comfortable with the attorney? Did the attorney seem willing to answer your questions, or did you feel you were only taking up his/her time? Could you understand him/her? Did the price estimate seem reasonable? (Remember, you're comparing the cost of a living trust to the potential costs and inconveniences of probate *and* a possible conservatorship.) Don't be afraid or embarrassed to shop around and to compare prices. But, at the same time, be careful not to sacrifice quality for price. You want the best *value*, not the cheapest price.

You want the best value— not the cheapest price

■ Personal Interview—A Nine-Point Checklist

The next step is to schedule a personal meeting with the attorneys who are at the top of your list. Be considerate and keep your time limit in mind. If your meeting is for 20 minutes, take no more than 20 minutes. Again, remember that *you* are the customer. *You* are interviewing the attorney. Most attorneys will want your business—and *you* will decide who gets it. Here are some points to consider.

1. Is the attorney prompt? Is the staff courteous? Is the attorney's office neat and clean? Does the attorney appear to be well-organized?

2. Show this book and your completed Organizer to the attorney. If the attorney tries to downplay the information and discourage you from wanting to avoid probate, keep looking. The attorney you want to deal with should endorse any information that correctly explains living trusts.

3. Confirm the price estimate. The attorney should be able to look quickly at your completed Organizer and give you a pretty good estimate.

4. What documents are included in this cost? Most attorneys will prepare the following documents *in addition to* your living trust document for the same fee. (These are explained at the end of this section.)

- Pour over will;
- Durable power of attorney for property management;
- Living will, durable power of attorney for health care and HIPAA Release Authorizations.

5. How much assistance does the attorney provide with changing titles and beneficiary designations? Does the attorney do any for you? Is there an additional charge? If you have a problem, will the attorney call on your behalf? Is there an additional charge for this? Or does the attorney just do the documents and leave this part of the process up to you? Most attorneys include pre-written letters you can send to your bank, savings and loan, etc. with instructions for changing titles. (These are very helpful.) How much assistance the attorney gives you is usually another good indication of the quality of work he/she does.

6. Ask if the attorney will notify you of any changes in the law that might affect your trust. The more conscientious attorneys think of you as a lifelong client and want to make sure your trust does not go out of date.

7. Ask if there are any clients you can call for a referral. (If clients have given their permission, this is perfectly okay.)

8. Ask to see a sample of the documents you will receive. (If there is not enough time during your meeting, you can look at these in the reception area or another office afterwards.) Look for the living trust document, then the additional documents mentioned above in Question #4. The documents should be well organized and easy to follow. Some attorneys put them in a binder with a table of contents, divided sections, and a summary of each document in simple English. However, while the way the documents are organized can be a good reflection of the type of work the attorney does, a pretty package does not necessarily mean that the documents are well written. (If you are acting on a referral from another respected estate planning professional or trust officer, the attorney probably does good work.)

9. Evaluate the meeting. How do you feel now that you have met the attorney? Do you feel confident in his/her abilities? Does he/she speak in plain English that you can understand? Did the attorney seem to be genuinely interested in you and your family's welfare? Did the attorney seem willing to answer your questions and encourage you to voice your concerns, or did you feel you were only taking up his/her time?

A pretty package doesn't mean the documents are well written

Trust your instincts. If you feel good about the meeting, this may be the right attorney for you. But if something doesn't feel right, then it probably isn't—and you'll want to keep looking.

Meeting With Your Attorney

Once you've selected the attorney to prepare your living trust, here's generally how the process should go.

1. Call the attorney's office to schedule an appointment to have your living trust prepared. Ask what information you should bring with you. Many attorneys will send you a list of the documents they will need. Here are some your attorney may want to see:

   - Copies of deeds;
   - Existing wills or trusts;
   - Pre-marital and/or divorce agreements;
   - Most recent statements from accounts (checking, saving, brokerage, money market, etc.);
   - Copies of stock certificates/bonds you have in your possession;
   - Insurance policies;
   - Plan documents for company retirement/saving plans;
   - Certificates of ownership for vehicles (especially if valuable);
   - If you are owner of a sole proprietorship: balance sheet, list of assets, Schedule C of latest income tax return, fictitious business name statement, list of licenses or permits;
   - If you are owner of a closely-held corporation: articles of incorporation, bylaws, minutes, most recent corporate income tax returns, annual statement, balance sheet, buy-sell agreements, voting trust agreement, stock certificate;
   - If you are a partner in a partnership: the partnership agreement, buy-sell agreement, amendments, most recent partnership income tax returns, balance sheet, annual statement.

Your attorney isn't asking to see all this just because he/she is nosey. The reason is that *your attorney can only help you create a plan that is as good as the information you provide*. For example, if you underestimate the value of your assets, the attorney won't be able to help you plan properly and you could end up paying too much in taxes.

The information you share with your attorney is confidential. (You've probably heard of the term attorney/client privilege.) By law, your attorney cannot reveal any of this information. You should feel comfortable enough with your attorney that you can be completely honest. If not, maybe you should look for another attorney.

2. Send a copy of your completed Organizer to your attorney in advance, so he/she will have time to review it *before* your meeting.

3. At your first meeting, the attorney should review your information, ask you some questions, answer your questions, and will probably make some suggestions for you to consider. Just like a doctor, your attorney needs to "examine" you (your information and needs) before administering the treatment (preparing your documents). If your attorney charges by the hour, you should be able to get a more definite cost now that he/she has seen all of your information and knows what you want and need.

4. Your attorney will then prepare a draft of the documents for you to review and approve. As mentioned earlier, in most cases, this will only take two or three weeks, but if your plan is complicated it may take a little longer. (It could also happen more quickly, depending on your needs.)

5. When you receive the drafts, make sure you read them carefully. Be sure you understand everything. Don't be afraid to ask questions.

6. After you have approved the drafts, the final documents will be prepared. You (and your spouse) will sign them, and usually they will be notarized. There often are two original documents, so that if you misplace one, you will have another original.

7. Some attorneys will prepare a schedule of assets and attach it to the trust document. This is a list of all the assets that will be transferred to the

trust. Often, there are three schedules—one for each spouse's separate assets, and one for jointly owned assets.

Listing assets on a schedule does not mean they are in your trust. You still have to change titles and beneficiary designations to do that. The main purpose of this is for convenience. It will give you a checklist of assets that are to be transferred, and it will be helpful for your successor trustee as a guide as to what the trust assets are.

8. Titles and appropriate beneficiary designations will then need to be changed; otherwise, you've just wasted your time and money. *Remember, your living trust can only protect the assets you transfer into it.* This "funding" process is explained thoroughly in Part Six.

Your attorney can only create a plan that is as good as the information you provide

OTHER DOCUMENTS YOUR ATTORNEY SHOULD PREPARE

As mentioned earlier, there are some other documents your attorney should prepare in addition to your living trust to give you extra protection, convenience, and control.

Some will act as a safety net for assets inadvertently left out of your trust. For example, something may happen to prevent you from changing all of the titles and beneficiary designations, or you could receive an inheritance or win the lottery and not have time to put the assets in your trust. Or you could just forget an asset.

Other documents will give you control over decisions that may need to be made about your medical care when you are not able to make them. Let's look at what these documents are and what they can do for you.

For Control Over Assets Left Out Of Your Living Trust
■ **Pour Over Will**

A pour over will is a very short will that acts as a safety net. It states that if an asset is discovered after you die that was inadvertently left *out* of your living trust, the asset is to go *into* your trust. The forgotten asset will probably have to go through probate, but at least your pour over will catches the asset and sends it back (pours it over) into your living trust so it can be distributed as part of your overall living trust plan.

There is another reason you may need a pour over will. In some states, the guardian for minor children must be named in a will. So if you have a children's trust in your living trust, your attorney will also name the guardian in your pour over will to satisfy this requirement. This keeps your living trust private, because only the pour over will would have to be admitted to court when the guardian is appointed. Even in states that do not require this, many attorneys will name the guardian in the pour over will anyway, so your living trust would not have to be admitted to the court and made public.

For example, we know that Michael Jackson named his mother as guardian for his children because his will, which named her, was admitted to the court when she was legally appointed as their guardian. But that's about all we know about his estate planning because he had a trust.

■ Durable Power of Attorney for Asset Management

Your living trust document can only give your successor trustee (or co-trustee) the authority to manage the assets you put in your trust. A durable power of attorney for asset management gives your successor limited authority to manage assets that are *not* in your trust.

For example, if you are incapacitated and your successor trustee finds that you forgot to put an asset into your trust—or you receive an inheritance or win the lottery in your personal name—this document, when properly written, can give your successor the authority to change the title and put the asset into your trust for you. Your successor will also be able to do this for you if you are well and simply out of the country or otherwise unavailable.

Another benefit of this document is convenience. Although your living trust gives authority to your successor trustee (or to your co-trustee) to act for you, some people and institutions (like hospitals and nursing homes) still may not be that familiar with living trust documents. Instead of trying to educate them in an emergency, your successor can show them the durable power of attorney document which is readily recognized by just about everyone. (Again, you will probably consider your living trust plan to be private, and you may not want it shown to strangers.)

A durable power of attorney can also give your successor trustee the power to sign your tax returns, which cannot be done in a living trust.

It is important that these powers are given only to the same people you name as your successor trustees (and co-trustee, if you have one) and in the same order as you have listed them. In other words, the powers are given to the trustee who steps in for you; they go to the trustee position, rather than to a specific individual. So, if your first choice for successor trustee is unable to act, your second choice (or third, if necessary) will have this authority.

■ These Are Only Extra Precautions
These extra safety nets should never take the place of changing titles and beneficiary designations to your trust while you are alive and able. Don't put off completing your trust thinking that these provisions will do it for you.

Certificate Of Trust—For Convenience
As you begin to change titles, some institutions may insist upon having a copy of or reviewing your trust. For example, your bank will probably want to see your trust before changing your accounts, safe deposit box, etc. You shouldn't think of this request as a nuisance or invasion of your privacy because it's for their protection—*and yours*.

Before they change the titles on your accounts, they need to see the name of your trust, who is authorized to be trustee and successor trustee, if the trustee has the necessary powers to transact business for the trust, that you have signed your trust, and that it is notarized. The reason is they do not want the liability of giving control of your assets to someone *unless they are sure* you want this person to have control—and you wouldn't want that, either.

However, they do not need to see a listing of your trust assets, who the beneficiaries of your trust are, and how you will provide for them. So that you do not have to show them your entire trust document, your attorney can prepare a *certificate of trust* or a *certified copy of your trust*. This is a shortened version of your trust that will usually satisfy these requests. It verifies the existence of your trust, explains the powers given to the trustee, identifies the successor trustees, etc., but it does not reveal any of your confidential information (your assets, your beneficiaries, their inheritances). Your attorney may call this document by another name, but he/she will know what needs to be prepared.

> *A pour over will sends a forgotten asset back into your trust*

For Control Over Decisions About Your Medical Care

Throughout this book, we have been discussing how to keep control of your assets if you become incapacitated and when you die, so you already know how the court can take control of your assets at incapacity. The court can also get involved when a person is severely ill or injured and there is disagreement between family members and/or the medical community as to what actions the person might have wanted in such a situation.

Two cases have stood out in the fairly recent past: Terri Schiavo's is documented at www.terrisfight.org; Karen Ann Quinlan's at www.karenannquinlanhospice.org. (It is worth taking the time to read about these two young women's plights and share them with your family.) Recently, Casey Kasem was in the news when his wife and children went to court over his care in his last days.

When your attorney prepares your living trust document, he/she will also prepare the following documents to give you control over medical decisions that may need to be made when you are not able to make them yourself. This can be very important for you and for those who will care for you.

■ Living Will

Many people think a living trust and a living will do the same things because the names are so similar. But they do very *different* things.

A living trust, as you have learned in this book, is for your *financial* affairs. It lets you keep control over your assets if you become incapacitated and after you die. A living will is for *medical* affairs. It is a simple document that lets your physician know the kind of life support treatment you would want in case of terminal illness or injury. The wording for a living will is short and standard. You can get a copy of one from your attorney, doctor, hospital, or nursing/medical association.

Living wills became popular after Karen Ann Quinlan fell into an irreversible coma in the 1970s. You may recall that, because she was legally an adult and had left no written instructions regarding what she would have wanted in this situation, her family was forced to wage a lengthy court battle to gain control of her care and have her removed from life support.

Limitations of Living Wills

You should be aware that a living will may or may not do what you expect it to do. In some states, for example, a living will is binding. If a doctor or hospital refuses to honor it, they must withdraw from the case. But in other states, it is not legally binding on anyone. It is simply a "directive" to your physician. Many doctors and hospitals are reluctant to discontinue any life sustaining treatment, primarily because they have been trained to *save* lives. And if a family member objects to your wishes as expressed in your living will, it's almost certain the doctor and hospital will not follow through as you have requested; they do not want to be held liable.

Also, a living will addresses the use of life support only in very specific *terminal* situations where death is imminent. It would not be of any use to someone who may exist for years in a coma or a vegetative state. In many states, a living will does not allow for nutrition (food and water) to be discontinued. Also, because a living will is a *statutory* document, the wording cannot be altered or personalized.

■ Durable Power of Attorney for Health Care

This document, sometimes called a health care proxy or medical power of attorney, gives you more control than a living will. It lets you give legal authority to another person (called your agent or surrogate) to make *any* health care decisions for you if you are unable to make these decisions for yourself. And, unlike a living will, a durable power of attorney for health care *is* legally binding and enforceable.

Your agent would be able to make decisions regarding the use of life support not only if your condition is terminal, but also if you are in a coma or vegetative state. In many cases, your agent would also be able to order nutrition (food and water) stopped.

A living will lets you make known your wishes for treatment at the end of your life; a durable power of attorney gives your agent the legal authority to make them happen. A durable power of attorney for health care can also be useful if you need surgery or medical treatment of *any* kind and there is a chance you will not be able to make medical decisions for even a short time.

Living wills and living trusts do different things

■ HIPAA Release Authorizations

The Health Insurance Portability and Accountability Act (HIPAA) of 1996 was created by Congress to protect the privacy of your health information. Unfortunately, it may also limit your privacy in ways you do not want.

Unless you have provided a signed HIPAA release form, medical professionals are not allowed to discuss any aspect of your health information or care with others, even family members. If they do so without your permission, they could be subject to substantial fines.

Think about whom you would want to be able to receive updates on your situation and care. Certain family members, an unmarried partner, close friends, clergy, even your attorney may come to mind. Also, your trustee, co-trustee and/or successor trustees would need to be able to know your condition and prognosis in case they need to step in for you. Your attorney will be able to help you make these decision.

SUMMARY

It would be a good idea to share your thoughts and desires about end of life issues with your family and other loved ones. You should also talk with your doctor. Find out how he/she feels about a durable power of attorney for health care and living wills, explain your opinions, and confirm that your doctor will honor your wishes. (If your doctor is not supportive of your position, you may want to find one who is.)

If you live part of each year in two states, consider having documents prepared in both states. Then you won't have to worry about whether or not your doctors will accept documents that don't look like the ones they are used to seeing.

Finally, every adult member of your family (that's age 18 and older) should have these basic estate planning documents. Otherwise, you could end up battling the courts and medical providers, adding unnecessary stress and financial strain to an already emotional situation.

Now that you have found the right attorney and had your documents prepared, let's look at what's involved in transferring assets to your living trust.

Part Six—

FUNDING YOUR LIVING TRUST

After you have signed your living trust document, the next step is to change titles and beneficiary designations to your trust. This is called "funding" your living trust.

This is probably the most important part of getting a living trust. If you have signed your living trust document but haven't changed titles and beneficiary designations, you've simply wasted your money. You may have a great trust, but until you fund it, it doesn't control anything—because your living trust can only control the assets you put into it.

Remember, when you put assets in your living trust, you do not lose control of them. You can continue to buy and sell assets just as you did before. And anything you put into your living trust can always be taken out later.

In this section, we'll discuss who is responsible for funding your trust and how difficult this process is. Then we'll explain the general procedures for changing titles and beneficiary designations for the most common types of assets people own. We suggest that you look for the ones you own and skip over the others. If you own something that is not included here, your attorney can tell you how to put it into your trust.

WHO WILL FUND YOUR TRUST?

You should know, before your trust is set up, how much of the funding process the attorney will do. The most conscientious attorneys we know will do *all* of the funding. They want their clients' trusts to be as effective

*Your living
trust can only
control the
assets you
put into it*

as possible so they personally make sure everything is put into the trust properly.

Usually, however, it is a combination of the attorney doing some and you doing some. Ideally, your attorney should review each asset with you, explain the procedure to you, and together you should decide who will be responsible for each asset. Many attorneys will put your home in your trust for you at no additional cost. Some also have legal assistants who can put other assets in your trust for you at a lower hourly rate than if the attorney does it.

Depending on how much the attorney charges, how comfortable you are with the process, how much time you have, and how interested you are in keeping your costs down, you may want to do many of them yourself.

Most attorneys have pre-written letters you can send to your bank, investment broker, insurance company, etc. that tell them how your assets should now be titled. At the least, your attorney should give you very specific instructions and the exact wording to use for titles and beneficiary designations. The wording will include the name(s) of the trustee(s), the name of your trust, and the date you sign the trust document. So it will be something like this: " John Doe and Mary Doe, Trustees of the Doe Family Trust, dated month/day/year."

How DIFFICULT IS THE FUNDING PROCESS?

As you will see in the next few pages, most titles and beneficiary designations are not difficult to change. Some are changed by an assignment. This is a short (usually one-page) document your attorney will prepare that identifies the asset and states that you are transferring its ownership to your living trust.

Others will require written instructions from you, giving the institutions the exact wording to use on the titles and beneficiary designations. Usually the pre-written letters from your attorney will be all you need, but some institutions have their own forms you will need to complete. For example, life insurance companies have standard forms to change the beneficiary on policies.

Most changes can be handled through the mail, by telephone, or by fax. Some will require your signature to be notarized or guaranteed. (See "Stocks/Bonds/ Mutual Funds" later in this section.)

Even though the process itself is not really difficult, it will take some time. How *much* time will depend on how many titles and beneficiary designations you have to change and how quickly the institutions respond. Most will be cooperative. However, you *may* encounter a few people who are still unfamiliar with living trusts. (As living trusts have become more widely used, this doesn't happen as often as it used to.) If you do have any difficulties, usually a quick call from your attorney will clear things up.

If you decide to do most of the funding yourself, we suggest that you make it a priority and keep going until you're finished. Start with your assets that have the largest values, then work down to the smaller ones. Remind yourself *why* you are doing this—and look forward to the peace of mind you'll have when your living trust is complete.

Now let's look at how titles and beneficiary designations are changed.

How TO CHANGE TITLES AND BENEFICIARY DESIGNATIONS

If You Live In a Community Property State
If you live in one of the ten states that allow community property ownership, your attorney may suggest that jointly-owned assets—especially real estate—be retitled as community property *before* they are put in your trust.

As explained in Part One, when one spouse dies, community property assets receive a *full* step-up in basis. This reduces the capital gains tax that would be due when the assets are eventually sold. With joint ownership, *only the deceased's share* would receive a step-up in basis—so you would have a bigger gain (profit) when the assets are sold, and would pay more in capital gains tax.

Community property status can be retained when the assets are put in your living trust. So, by retitling jointly owned assets as community property *first*, you will get the full step-up in basis when one spouse dies.

If You Live in a Noncommunity Property State

If you live in a noncommunity property state and have owned an asset jointly with your spouse since before 1976, the asset may be entitled to a full step-up in basis when one spouse dies. If you change the title on it now (even to your living trust), you could lose the full step-up; the deceased spouse's share would still get a step-up, but the surviving spouse's share would not. This could cause your surviving spouse to pay more in capital gains tax if he/she decides to sell the asset after you die.

If the asset is your personal residence, losing the full step-up will not be a problem unless the gain is more than $500,000. (If you are married, up to $500,000 of the gain on the sale of your personal residence is exempt from capital gains tax. See "Exemption From Capital Gains Tax When Residence Sold" later in this section.) But it could be a problem for other assets like farmland, commercial real estate, or stocks.

If this sounds like it could apply to your situation, check with your attorney or tax advisor *before* you change the title. (For more information, see *Gallenstein v. United States*, a 1992 Sixth Circuit Court of Appeals case. Other circuit courts have followed this ruling in similar cases.)

Your Home, Real Estate, Land, Condominium, Etc.

Depending on the state in which the property is located, a correction deed, grant deed, warranty deed, assignment, or quitclaim deed will be used to change the titles of real estate to your living trust.

The new deed will include how the property is titled now (before you put it into the trust), what the new title should be (to put it into your trust), and the legal description. The deed for each property will be signed by you, witnessed, notarized, and recorded in the county where the property is located.

Again, your attorney will probably put your home in your living trust for you at no extra cost. This is usually a good idea since the home is the most valuable asset most people own, and the legal description and titles must be exact.

■ Out of State Property

If you own property in another state, you will want to transfer it to your living trust to prevent a conservatorship and/or probate there. Your attorney can contact a title company or attorney in that state to handle the transfer for you.

You may also be able to do part or all of it yourself. First, find out what is involved. Check with an attorney or escrow office in that state to find out the proper form to use, to verify the process, and to get the name and address of the recording office. In some states, your trust may have to be recorded. If so, a certificate of trust should be all that is needed. However, it may be more convenient (and wise) to have the local attorney or escrow office handle the transfer for you.

■ Current Mortgage

Putting real estate—especially your home—into your living trust should not disturb your current mortgage in any way. Even if the mortgage contains a "due on sale or transfer" clause, retitling your home in the name of your living trust should not activate the clause. Even so, it would still be a good idea to contact the lender *before* you transfer the property so you don't inadvertently activate the clause, especially if you own rental property or commercial real estate. (The lender may charge a small fee to approve the transfer.)

In the past, some people who wanted to put their homes into their living trusts were met with resistance. Many banks, savings and loans, and mortgage companies who write home mortgages (called primary lenders) simply did not understand living trusts. Many were also afraid the *secondary* lenders—institutions who buy home mortgages from these primary lenders, providing them with more money to loan out—would not buy mortgages if the borrower was a living trust instead of an individual.

But things have changed. Fannie Mae, Freddie Mac, and Ginnie Mae (which buys FHA home mortgages)—the major secondary lenders—all now consider a revocable living trust to be an "eligible borrower" as long as normal guidelines are met. For example, the property must be owner-occupied, they want to make sure the trustee is authorized to borrow against the property, and they usually want the owner to be a trustee, which most people are anyway.

These published guidelines will make it much easier to transfer your home into your living trust, to refinance your home after it is in your living trust (without having to temporarily remove it from the trust), and even to purchase new real estate in the name of your living trust.

If you do run into resistance, it will probably be from a lender who has not informed its loan officers or simply doesn't want to change the way it does

Putting your home into your living trust should not disturb your mortgage

business. If this happens to you, you can always take out the mortgage in your personal name and then transfer the property to your living trust after the closing—or you could look for another lender.

■ Homeowner's, Liability, and Title Insurance

Your homeowner's and liability insurance should be changed to reflect your living trust on the title and the trustees as additional insureds. (If you are your own trustee, it will show you as trustee instead of you as an individual.) Your agent will be able to make this change for you, probably at no charge. Usually all the insurance company will need is a letter of instruction from you and a copy of the new deed.

Title insurance should also be changed. Check to make sure your title insurance company will still insure title when your living trust is the owner of the property. Most will. In fact, one of the largest title insurance companies routinely issues title insurance when the property is in a living trust, and they do not require a separate title search.

■ Property Taxes

Most owners of real estate pay a property tax every year based on the appraised value of the property. Transferring real estate to a living trust should not cause your property to be reappraised because the underlying ownership is the same (remember, it's *your* trust) and because the trust is revocable (remember, you can take the property *out* of your trust and put it back into your individual name at any time).

Even so, you may need to notify the tax assessor's office. In California, for example, a "Preliminary Change of Ownership Report" must be filed. This is a simple form (with check boxes) that the attorney usually completes at the same time the new deed is prepared.

■ Transfer Tax

Generally, a transfer tax is charged whenever property is sold. Putting real estate into a living trust does not constitute a sale, because you can take the property out of the trust at any time. So, in most states, there will be *no* transfer tax when you transfer property to your living trust.

However, a few states and counties are looking for creative ways to raise revenue and they may charge a transfer tax anyway. For example, Pennsylvania *used* to charge a transfer tax when real estate was transferred into a living trust and *any* beneficiary was someone other than a spouse, grandparent, parent, child, grandchild (and spouse) or sibling (and spouse). So if you named a friend or a charity as a beneficiary of your living trust (even as an alternate beneficiary), you had to pay a transfer tax on real estate you put into your living trust. This tax was repealed, specifically for living trusts.

■ Exemption From Capital Gains Tax When Residence Sold

Previously, if you were over age 55, you were allowed a one-time $125,000 exemption of the gain (profit) on the sale of your home. Also, if you sold your home and bought a new one for at least the same price within two years, the profit from the sale of your previous residence was exempt from capital gains tax, providing you had owned and made this house your principal residence for at least three of the previous five years. Putting your home in a living trust had no effect on either of these exemptions.

The Taxpayer Relief Act of 1997 included a "new" exemption that replaced these two previous ones. Currently, if you are single and sell your home, up to $250,000 of your gain (profit) will be exempt from capital gains tax, providing you have owned and made the house your principal residence for at least two of the past five years. (If you are married, up to $500,000 will be exempt.) You can use this exemption only once every two years. Having your home in a living trust will have no effect on your being able to use this capital gains tax exemption.

■ Homestead Exemption From Creditors

As we explained in Part Two, part or all of the value of your home may be protected from creditors' claims under your state's homestead laws. Putting your home in a living trust should not cause you to lose this protection.

■ Rental Real Estate

Under current tax law, the expenses you have from rental real estate (including mortgage interest, property taxes, insurance, repairs, depreciation, and other operating expenses) can usually be deducted *only* from rental income.

If you don't have enough rental income (passive income) to offset your expenses (passive losses) in the year they are incurred, you can carry the excess losses (net losses) forward and deduct them from rental income in subsequent tax years. If you have not been able to deduct all of your losses by the time you sell the property, you can write them off then.

Putting your home in your living trust has no effect on your capital gains exemption

As usual, there are exceptions:

1. If you earn your living mainly in the real estate business (for example, you are a contractor, builder or broker), you may not be affected by these passive loss rules.

2. If your adjusted gross income (AGI), as defined on IRS Form 1040, is less than $150,000 and you actively participate in the management of the property (approve repairs and new tenants, write checks, make management decisions, etc.), you can deduct up to $25,000 ($12,500 if married filing separately) of net losses each year from your *ordinary* income (wages, tips, etc. as defined by the IRS on Form 1040). If your AGI is more than $100,000, the $25,000 is gradually phased out so that, by the time the AGI is $150,000, the amount of passive net losses that can be deducted from ordinary income is reduced to "0."

Transferring rental real estate to your living trust does *not* affect the way you handle these losses while you are living. However, if you are currently allowed to deduct up to $25,000 in net losses from your ordinary income, these losses may be handled differently *after* you (and your spouse) die. For a full explanation, see Part Eight.

■ If You Suspect the Property is Contaminated

You can still put contaminated property in your living trust, but the trustee can personally be responsible for any clean up. As explained in Part Two, if you are your own trustee, this won't affect you because you are *already* responsible. But, remember, if the clean up is not complete by the time your successor trustee steps in, he/she (and, ultimately, your beneficiaries) can also be liable. If you suspect that property you own may be contaminated, be sure to read the discussion of this in Part Two. And make sure you tell your attorney *before* you transfer the property to your trust.

Credit Cards, Notes You Owe

Setting up a living trust should not affect any credit cards, loans, or notes you owe. These are not assets, so you don't need to do anything with them. You just continue making your required payments as usual.

Mortgages, Loans, And Notes Owed To You

If you have owner-financed any assets (for example, you "took back" a note on a house you sold), loaned someone money, or have any other notes payable to you, you will need to *assign* these mortgages/loans to your living trust. This is done by an assignment which is signed by you only (not the other party), notarized, and attached to the original document. If the original mortgage was recorded, some attorneys will also record the assignment.

If you have loaned someone money without documenting the loan, this would be a good time to put it in writing to prevent disputes over the terms and nature of the loan. Write up the terms of the loan and have it signed by the other party. An assignment can then be prepared to transfer the loan to the trust.

Checking, Saving, And Pay-on-Death Accounts

You will need to change the ownership of your checking and saving accounts to your living trust. New signature cards will then need to be signed by the trustee(s). If you are your own trustee, you can sign the signature cards with just your usual signature.

You may need to sign new account agreements. Some institutions will require a new account, with a new account number, and new checks. If you are your own trustee, the information on your checks does not need to change. They can still be printed with just your name, address, and telephone number (if desired). You continue to sign checks the same way you always have.

If you have named beneficiaries on any accounts, you'll want to change them to your living trust. For example, you may have established an account and named your spouse, child, or grandchild as the beneficiary. These are called Totten Trusts. The account title probably includes the words "in trust for" (ITF), "as trustee for" (ATF), "payable-on-death" (POD), or "transfer on death" (TOD).

Remember, by changing the beneficiary on these to your living trust, you prevent the possibility of the court taking control of the funds if your beneficiary is a minor or incapacitated when you die, or dies before or at the same time as you. The institution will probably have its own form to change the beneficiary.

Change beneficiary of pay-on-death accounts to your living trust

To change the ownership or beneficiary of an account, the institution will probably ask to see a copy of your trust document. Remember, this is for your protection and, as explained in Part Five, a certificate of trust should satisfy their requirements.

Certificates Of Deposit

These should be retitled in the name of your trust. Some let you name a beneficiary. If yours does, the beneficiary should also be your trust. You do not need to cash these in to do this.

Some institutions will retitle the certificates immediately with no penalties. If yours requires you to wait until the certificate matures, you can go ahead and change the beneficiary and use an assignment to transfer your ownership interest to your trust. Then, when the certificate matures, you can change the title to your trust before you renew it.

Note: This process does not apply to IRAs that are invested in CDs. IRAs are discussed later in this section.

What About FDIC Insurance?

The Federal Deposit Insurance Corporation (FDIC) insures deposits at banks and savings associations that are FDIC members. Since its creation in 1933, depositors at every FDIC-insured bank that has failed have been fully reimbursed for the insured amount on their accounts. In 2008, FDIC insurance was temporarily increased from $100,000 to $250,000. In 2010, the increase was made permanent, providing up to $250,000 of coverage per owner per account category per institution. The coverage is free and automatic.

FDIC categories include single accounts, joint accounts, qualifying retirement accounts, revocable and irrevocable trusts, and government accounts. "Deposits" include checking and saving accounts, retirement accounts (including IRAs and Keoghs), NOW accounts, and CDs. Securities, mutual funds, other such investments, and contents of safety deposit boxes are not considered deposits and therefore are not covered by the FDIC. (To read more about the categories, and what is and is not insured, visit www.fdic.gov.)

When you retitle FDIC-insured accounts in the name of your living trust, the insurance coverage may change. In fact, your living trust accounts may qualify for *much more* FDIC insurance. That's because the amount of coverage is determined by the number of owners (grantors) and the number of named beneficiaries.

For example, if you and your spouse are co-grantors of your trust and you have named your three children as beneficiaries, the trust account will be insured for up to $1.5 million. (Three beneficiaries times $250,000 times two grantors = $1.5 million.)

By contrast, if you and your spouse had a joint account instead of a trust account, it would only be insured for up to $500,000. With a joint account, there are no beneficiaries and each owner's share is insured for up to $250,000.

With a trust account, deposit insurance is provided to the owner (grantor), but the amount of coverage is based on the number of beneficiaries named in the trust. If the trust account has more than one owner—for example, if you and your spouse are co-grantors—each owner's coverage is calculated separately (three beneficiaries times two grantors, as in the example above).

Trust beneficiaries can be an individual, regardless of the relationship to you, or a charity or nonprofit organization as defined by the IRS. (Previously, a qualifying beneficiary could only be a spouse, child, or grandchild of the grantor; a parent, sibling, niece, nephew or non-relative did not qualify.)

There are some limitations and complications in the calculations. For example, if you have named more than six beneficiaries and they will not receive equal shares, a different formula applies. Also, revocable trust coverage is based on *all* revocable trust deposits held by the same owner at the same bank, so any pay on death (POD) accounts would be added to your living trust account, and then coverage would be determined.

The FDIC has a calculator on its website that will help you determine how much insurance coverage you have on your accounts (www.fdic.gov/edie). You can also call the FDIC at 877-275-3342 and speak to someone who can help you understand your coverage.

Credit Union Accounts

Most credit union accounts can easily be transferred to your living trust. To do this, you will need to set up a new account titled in your trust's name and transfer your existing account(s) to it.

Accounts titled in the name of your living trust may qualify for more FDIC insurance

Of course, to have an account at a credit union, you must be a member. And in order for your trust to qualify, all "parties" of your living trust—the grantor(s), trustees, *and* beneficiaries—must be eligible for membership. This is not usually a problem for most people because their living trusts include only family members, who are usually eligible to join anyway.

If you have named a corporate trustee as a successor trustee, this may still be okay because, when it steps in, the corporate trustee will usually close the credit union account and transfer it to an account it manages.

If your living trust does not qualify as a member, there are still some things you can do. You can name your living trust as the "pay on death" beneficiary on the account or add your living trust as a "joint owner with right of survivorship" (joint owners do *not* have to be members). Then, when you die, your credit union accounts will automatically be owned by your trust.

No special membership card or agreement is usually required when you open the new account for your living trust. The credit union will probably ask to see your trust document to make sure it qualifies for membership, what the trustee's powers are, who the successor trustees are, and when they are authorized to step in. (Although they may need to see who your beneficiaries are, they do not need to know how you will provide for them.)

Your trust, just like any other member, will be entitled to vote at annual meetings. However, since the trust is not a person, someone (usually the trustee) will need to be given the authority to vote for the trust.

These rules apply to federal credit unions (more than half of the 14,000 credit unions are federally regulated), but even those that are state regulated will often follow these guidelines.

> **Note:** If you think you may want to take out a loan at some point, you should probably keep an individual account with the minimum required balance. That's because your trust would only be allowed to borrow an amount equal to its own value.

Safe Deposit Box

You will need to change the box authorization card to your trust and the trustee(s) will need to sign the card. This will allow your successor trustee to have ready access at your death or incapacity. Your banker or savings and loan officer can help you do this.

Stocks/Bonds/Mutual Funds

■ Street Accounts

If you maintain an account in the name of your bank or brokerage company (called a "street account") or invest in a mutual fund, they will need written instructions from you to change the name on your account to your trust.

Call them first to see if you should send a letter of instruction (remember, your attorney will probably include sample letters with your trust) or if they have their own form they can send you—or if they have their own procedures you will need to follow.

They may request that your signature be guaranteed. Your local banker or broker can probably do this for you. (Just call ahead and make sure.) You will sign the form or your letter in your banker's or broker's presence, and he/she will affix a stamp that "guarantees" your signature.

They may also ask to see a copy of your trust document. Again, the certificate of trust should be all they need.

■ If You Possess Certificates

If you have possession of actual stock and securities certificates, you can set up an account at a brokerage house or other financial institution. They will transfer the titles to the name of your trust for you and keep the certificates for you. This way you do not have to worry about misplacing them, losing them in a fire, or making frequent trips to your safe deposit box.

If you are more comfortable keeping the actual certificates yourself, you will need to have new certificates issued in the name of your trust. (Never write or mark on an original stock or bond certificate.) Your broker or banker can have them reissued for you; they may charge a small fee for this service.

You can also do this yourself. Your attorney can prepare a "stock power," a short document that assigns the securities to the trust, identifies what is being transferred (for example, 50 shares of General Electric stock), the certificate numbers, and the name(s) of the trustees. You'll sign the stock power and have your signature guaranteed (as above).

You'll then need to locate the stock transfer agent. This is the organization that is authorized to transfer title on stocks and bonds. For bonds, the transfer agent is usually the institution from which you receive payments on the bond. If you have stock certificates, don't rely on the name of the transfer agent on the certificate; it may be outdated. Call a brokerage house and ask someone there. Your attorney may also be able to find out the transfer agent for you.

Send the transfer agent a letter by certified mail instructing them to issue new certificates in the name of your trust; a certificate of trust; and the certificates. Send the stock power separately, also by certified mail. (Do not send the stock power and the certificates together in the same envelope; if someone intercepts them, they would be able to negotiate them.) Make sure you keep copies. And check the new certificates as soon as you receive them.

If you have lost a certificate, contact the transfer agent and request an "Affidavit of Lost Certificate and Indemnity Agreement." Complete and sign the affidavit, and follow the instructions to furnish bond.

Savings Bonds

Savings bonds can be transferred to your living trust with no adverse tax consequences. To have savings bonds re-issued in the name of your living trust, you'll need to complete Form PD F 1851. If you have named a beneficiary on a savings bond, you can change it to your trust using form PD F 4000.

These downloadable forms are available on the website www.treasurydirect. gov. Select the Forms menu tab, then select the Savings Bonds section. You can complete the forms online before you print them, or print them and then complete them. You will need to sign them in the presence of a bank officer so your signature can be verified. (Instructions are included with the forms.)

You can call the Federal Reserve Bank to order forms or if you have questions. Their customer service number is 800-245-2804. The representative with whom we spoke was friendly, knowledgeable, and helpful, and said they frequently receive calls from people who want to re-issue their savings bonds in the names of their living trusts.

Automobiles/Boats/Other Vehicles

Most states will permit a vehicle title to be re-issued in the name of your trust. Also, some states now allow you to name a beneficiary for your vehicle. If yours does, your trust should be the beneficiary. In some states, however, this will require the payment of an excise (transfer) tax, just as if the trust had purchased the vehicle.

Take Florida, for example. Currently, Florida has a $225 initial registration fee (in addition to other registration fees). This fee does not apply if you trade in your existing car for a new one. But it does apply if you buy an additional car or if you have never owned a car before. So, because your trust has not owned a car before, you will have to pay this fee when you transfer it into your trust. But you will only have to pay it once; you won't have to pay it again if you replace that car with another one.

However, a car is considered "exempt" property in Florida. So, if you plan to leave your car to your spouse or an heir, you don't need to transfer it to your trust and spend the $225. Your spouse or heir can transfer the car title after you die for less than $100. But if you plan to leave your car to someone else, then it may be worth putting it into the trust and paying the $225 fee. (Don't you just love finding out what's going on in Florida?!)

You may want to call your state's license bureau to find out the process where you live. Depending on the costs involved and the value of the vehicle, you may want to wait until you purchase your next one and title it in the name of your trust.

Your attorney may advise you to leave your car and/or other vehicles out of your trust, especially if the value is within the amount your state allows to transfer without probate. Also, if you are using a corporate trustee, they may not want to manage your car, unless it is of considerable value.

Asset protection is another reason to keep vehicles out of your trust. For example, if you are at fault in an auto accident and the injured party sees that your car is owned by a trust, he or she may think you have "deep pockets" and be more inclined to sue you.

Some states let you name a beneficiary for your car

Your living trust can be owner and beneficiary of your life insurance policies

If you do title a vehicle in the name of your trust, notify your insurance company. They may want to change your policy to reflect the change of ownership and list the trustee as an additional insured. If you are your own trustee, it will show you as trustee instead of you as an individual. The insurance company may request a copy of the new registration and a letter of instruction from you. They will probably make the change for you at no charge.

Personal Untitled Property

Your attorney will probably prepare an assignment to transfer your personal property (furniture, artwork, clothing, jewelry, cameras, sporting equipment, books, etc.) to your trust. If these articles are of substantial value, you would want them in your trust.

However, if the value of these articles is low enough that a probate would not be required in your state (as explained previously), your attorney may recommend leaving them out of your trust. They could also be intentionally left out if there was a desire to cut off creditor's claims in probate (as explained in Part Two).

Life Insurance

In many cases, you will want your living trust to be both the beneficiary and the owner of your insurance policies.

Naming your trust as the beneficiary gives you maximum control over the proceeds. It keeps the courts from getting involved if your loved ones are incapacitated, die before you (or at the same time as you), or are minor children. You can keep the proceeds in trust until you want your loved ones to receive the money. You can be sure the money is used to pay your final expenses. And by naming your trust instead of your spouse as the beneficiary, you can even keep control of the funds if your spouse should remarry.

> **Note:** If you live in a community property state and the insurance was purchased with community property funds, your spouse is entitled to half of the proceeds—and may need to sign a consent form if you want to name your living trust as beneficiary.

Naming your trust as the owner of your policies gives you more flexibility and maximum control over the policies. For example, if you name your spouse or someone else as the owner, you might worry that they will cancel the policy or change the beneficiary.

If you have a policy that has a cash value and you name your trust as the owner, your successor trustee would be able to borrow on the policy at your incapacity to help pay for your care. If your illness becomes terminal, your successor could apply for a "living benefit" currently offered by many insurance companies. Under this program, the death benefit is paid to you *before* you die—instead of to your beneficiary *after* you die—so the cash is available to help meet expenses during your illness.

If your estate is large enough that it would have to pay estate taxes, you should probably consider having an irrevocable life insurance trust. Estate taxes are explained in Part Three and life insurance trusts in Part Nine.

Employer-Provided Insurance

These would include life insurance (including split dollar insurance), accidental death insurance, and disability income insurance your employer provides for you. Your living trust should be the beneficiary when you have the option. Your employee benefits or personnel department will have the appropriate forms and can help you complete them.

Sole Proprietorship

Business licenses and DBAs (doing business as) should be changed to show your living trust as the owner. An assignment is used to transfer business property to your trust.

Closely-Held Corporation

First check to make sure that transferring your interests to a living trust will not trigger an event covered by a buy-sell agreement. (If it does, you can request that the document be changed.) The appropriate corporate records will then need to be prepared to transfer title. Share certificates will also need to be re-registered in the name of your trust. To do this, a stock power (prepared by your attorney) and the certificates will need to be sent to the attorney or officer who handles the transfers.

Subchapter S Corporation

With a subchapter S corporation, both the earnings and any losses of the corporation are passed through to the owners personally. Earnings are taxed only once at the personal level and any losses can be deducted from ordinary income. (With a "C" corporation, earnings are taxed twice—once at the cor-

Business interests can be transferred to your living trust

porate level, and again at the personal level when the earnings are distributed. Until the corporation is sold or liquidated, losses can only be deducted from corporate earnings.)

Transferring subchapter S corporation stock to your living trust does not cause any change or any problem while you are living. After you die, however, the stock can only stay in your living trust for up to two years; after that, it would lose its "S" status and become a "C" corporation.

But this rarely happens because two years is usually plenty of time to distribute the stock to the beneficiaries so the "S" status can be retained. If you don't want your beneficiaries to receive the stock outright, the IRS also allows it to be transferred to other trusts that meet its qualifications to retain the "S" status. The IRS creatively calls these "qualified subchapter S trusts" (QSST).

Your attorney should plan for the distribution of subchapter S stock when he/she prepares your living trust document.

Limited Partnerships/Corporations/Limited Liability Companies

If you are involved in any real estate (or other) partnerships, corporations, or limited liability companies, your interest should be assigned to your trust. This probably will not disturb the existing agreement or affect your partners in any way, but you should check the agreement or corporate bylaws just to be sure.

The general partner may already have a form to assign your interest to your trust. If not, your attorney can prepare one. The assignment should identify your interest that is being transferred, how the interest should be titled, and that the trustee accepts any liabilities as well as benefits.

Send the assignment to the general partner with a letter instructing him/her to make the transfer. Because other documents may need to be prepared to complete the transfer, you may want to give the general partner a limited power of attorney to sign the other documents for you. (The general partner may charge a fee to do this.)

General Partnership Interests

This transfer is handled in the same way as a limited partnership. However, your signature will probably need to be notarized, and the assignment should include a provision for the other partners to consent to it. The partnership agreement may also require you to send the assignment to the other partners or general partner to sign—as verification of their acceptance—and return the assignment to you.

If you are using a corporate trustee with your trust, they may not be able to serve as a general partner. A special trustee may have to be appointed instead.

Copyrights, Patents, And Royalties

Intellectual properties such as these can usually be transferred to your living trust with an assignment drafted by your attorney. (Make sure your attorney is familiar with these.)

Oil And Gas Interests

Transferring proven oil and gas interests—mineral leases, overriding royalty interests, production payments, and working and operating interests—can all be transferred to your living trust without losing the percentage cost depletion deduction (similar to depreciation). Your trust and/or beneficiaries can continue to claim the deduction after you die.

The process to put these interests into your trust will vary, depending on the state in which the property is located. You may want to have your attorney do the transfers for you. They can be tedious—legal descriptions and depletion allowances must be exact—and you want to be sure they are done properly.

Club Memberships

As long as the membership agreement does not prohibit it, a club membership can be assigned to your trust. Some membership agreements allow you to name a beneficiary. If yours does, it should be your living trust.

Foreign Assets

Foreign assets can be transferred to a living trust if revocable living trusts are recognized in that country. You or your attorney will need to contact an attorney in the country where the assets are located to find out if there are any specific advantages—or disadvantages—to putting these assets in your trust and the process that should be followed.

ASSETS REQUIRING SPECIAL CONSIDERATION

While you should start with the general premise that *all* titles and beneficiary designations should be changed to your living trust, there are a few assets that you may not want in, or cannot be placed into, your living trust. Here are some you may own.

Guns

A large number of Americans own guns for hunting, target shooting, and self-defense. Many families also have heirloom guns that they would like to keep in the family and pass down from generation to generation.

Unlike other assets, firearms possession and transfer is regulated pretty heavily, which presents unique estate planning challenges. Federal, state, and local firearms laws strictly regulate possession and transfer of a firearm between persons.

The four critical words are "possession," "transfer," "firearm," and "person." These four words are not defined consistently under federal law and/or in state law and care must be taken to avoid criminal liability. This has been called the "accidental felony"—wrongful possession or transfer by well-meaning, generally law abiding persons who are simply unaware of how gun law works.

"Prohibited persons" are not allowed to possess or transfer firearms. These include, but are not limited to, convicted felons; persons with a history of mental illness; persons convicted of misdemeanor domestic violence offenses; users of illegal drugs; dishonorably discharged veterans; and persons who have renounced U.S. citizenship. Prohibitions exist in both federal and state law, and they may differ. For example, a number of states regulate possession of firearms by age and/or by use.

A responsible gun owner usually understands and follows gun law. But after the gun owner becomes disabled or has died, successor trustees or family who step in may not be familiar with guns or gun law—and they can innocently and unintentionally violate gun laws.

For example, transferring a firearm to a beneficiary could subject both the trustee/executor and the recipient to criminal penalties. The beneficiary could be a prohibited person, the firearm might require federal approval prior to transfer, or the transfer might require a Federal Firearms Licensee (FFL) to handle the transfer and conduct a background check. Interstate transfers are permitted but must be done in accordance with both federal and state law, and depend in part on the particular firearm involved. Any firearm left to an out-of-state beneficiary creates issues that must be understood before a transfer occurs.

Guns require special planning

Using A Gun Trust

A gun trust or firearm trust is a revocable living trust designed specifically for the possession, transfer, and lawful enjoyment of firearms between persons. It can help a gun owner or successor trustee to comply with complex gun laws by providing written guidance and documentation. Possession and transfer guidelines are very helpful to have, whether a person is the grantor, a trustee, or a beneficiary. Written guidelines help to protect them from potential criminal liability.

Generally, the trust becomes the owner of the firearms in a manner recognized by state and/or federal law. There are some complexities involved because a trust is not a "person" under Title I, so it cannot actually purchase a handgun, rifle, or shotgun in its own name. Also, the National Instant Criminal Background Check System (NICS) does not recognize a person in their capacity as a trustee but only as an individual. However, depending on state law, a firearm can generally be assigned to a trust just like any other tangible personal property such as a table or chair could be.

For Title II or National Firearms Act (NFA) firearms, a trust *is* a person, so it can purchase and take possession in its name via a trustee. Because the two Titles are inconsistent in the definition of "person," the ATF requires a Federal Firearms Licensee (FFL) to have the trustee picking up to have a background check (NICS) and to sign a letter (which the FFL retains) stating that he/she is acting as trustee.

Use of trust property must be compliant with state law, and a trust cannot violate public policy if it is to be valid, so this is not a way to "beat the system." It exists within the system as a useful estate planning tool.

A trust can have one or more trustees, including the gun owner. A trustee is entitled to possess and administer trust property. A trust must have at least one beneficiary other than the gun owner/grantor to be valid, although the second one could become a beneficiary only after the death of the grantor.

Any non-prohibited person could be a gun trust beneficiary entitled to enjoy trust property now or later. But possession by a trustee is critical, even if not required for a particular firearm, due to liability concerns. With firearms, it is simply a best practice to have a trustee in actual or constructive possession at all times, as federal and state laws are complex and not consistent. A person named as both a trustee and beneficiary could conceivably possess and enjoy trust firearms without the trust grantor being present, but state law might dictate otherwise.

For example, Washington State passed a law about transfers that makes this unclear for a trust or any other entity. Some other states have similar laws or are considering them. Generally, a trustee of a trust may lawfully possess the trust property without triggering a "transfer," although state law must be carefully considered. A beneficiary of a gun trust may enjoy trust property, but should generally do so in the presence of a trustee when a firearm is involved, and absolutely when an NFA firearm is involved. A trustee must also consider a beneficiary's capacity to safely use the firearm, as civil liability may also be a concern to the trust, and possibly for a trustee, depending on state law.

Most National Firearms Act (NFA) firearms require prior approval from the Bureau of Alcohol, Tobacco, Firearms, and Explosives (BATFE) before being removed from the state where registered, even temporarily. Transportation of firearms must comply with federal and state law. Certain firearms may be legal to possess in one state but not in another, and the gun trust does not change this fact.

A gun trust can continue beyond your lifetime for your beneficiaries over multiple generations, can accomplish charitable planning, and could even direct that a collection be sold to another gun enthusiast upon your death. Depending on firearms possessed, some might require BATFE approval prior to transfer to a beneficiary (for example, Title II or NFA firearms such as silencers, machine guns, short barrel rifles or short barrel shotguns, destructive devices, and the category known as "any other weapon" or AOWs). If there is a state registry of handguns or firearms, compliance would also be required. In any event, a gun trust can and should avoid probate, keeping the gun collection private and unexposed to potential thieves.

The trust document must be carefully written to account for the different types of firearms held and to comply with both federal and state law. While any valid trust could technically be used to possess firearms, a conventional living trust, no matter how well written, will simply not contain meaningful guidance on lawful administration of a firearms collection. A gun trust should be prepared by an attorney who fully understands the nuances of gun laws, both federal and in your state or states of residence. For more information, visit www.gunlawcommunity.com.

IRA, 401(k), 403(b), Pension, Profit Sharing, Keogh, And Other Tax-Deferred Plans

These are plans that were created to encourage you to save for your retirement. They are called *tax-deferred* plans because you did not pay income taxes on this money when the contributions were made. The income taxes are *deferred* until you withdraw the money at a later time—ideally, at your retirement when your income (and tax bracket) are lower.

You cannot leave your money in these accounts forever. At a certain point (your *required beginning date*), Uncle Sam says you must start taking money out. Generally, this is April 1 following the year in which you become age 70 1/2. However, if you have money in an employer plan (pension, profit sharing, etc.), you continue working beyond age 70 1/2 *and* you own less than 5% of the company, you can delay your required beginning date on those accounts until your actual retirement date. (This exception does not apply to IRAs.)

Determining the amount you are required to take out each year (your *required minimum distribution)* is much easier now than it used to be. Each year you divide the year-end value of your account by a life expectancy divisor found on The Uniform Lifetime Table as provided by the IRS (shown on the following page). The result is your required minimum distribution for that year.

For example, the divisor for age 72 is 25.6. If your year-end account balance is $100,000, you divide $100,000 by 25.6. The amount you are required to withdraw for that year, then, is $3,906.25.

You can withdraw *more* than the required minimum distribution amount at any time. But if you don't need all of your money, or if you die before you use it all, you'd probably like to let it continue to grow tax-deferred for as long as you can, with as much as possible going to your spouse and/or children, and as little as possible going to taxes.

The Uniform Lifetime Table

Age of Account Owner	Divisor	Age of Account Owner	Divisor	Age of Account Owner	Divisor	Age of Account Owner	Divisor
70	27.4	81	17.9	92	10.2	103	5.2
71	26.5	82	17.1	93	9.6	104	4.9
72	25.6	83	16.3	94	9.1	105	4.5
73	24.7	84	15.5	95	8.6	106	4.2
74	23.8	85	14.8	96	8.1	107	3.9
75	22.9	86	14.1	97	7.6	108	3.7
76	22.0	87	13.4	98	7.1	109	3.4
77	21.2	88	12.7	99	6.7	110	3.1
78	20.3	89	12.0	100	6.3	111	2.9
79	19.5	90	11.4	101	5.9	112	2.6
80	18.7	91	10.8	102	5.5	113	2.4
						114	2.1
						115 and older	1.9

To determine the amount you are required to withdraw each year from your tax-deferred account, divide the year-end balance by the life expectancy divisor next to your current age.

For years, this was difficult to do because the rules governing these distributions were complicated and confusing. But in 2001 and 2002, the IRS changed many of the rules, finalized the regulations (which had been temporary for several years) and actually made it *easier* to get the results you want.

You cannot change the ownership of your tax-deferred plans to your living trust. You *can,* however, name your living trust as the beneficiary. But before you do, be sure to consider all of your options. As you will see in the next few pages, whom you name as beneficiary will have a significant impact on how long the tax-deferred growth can continue, and how much of your tax-deferred savings will go to Uncle Sam in income and, possibly, estate taxes.

While not every possibility is covered in this section, the following information will help you begin to understand the basics of this planning. We cannot emphasize enough that you need to seek guidance from an attorney who is experienced in planning for these assets, especially if your estate is significant and/or you have significant amounts in tax-deferred plans.

■ Who Should Be Your Beneficiary—If You Are Married
Option 1: Spouse as Beneficiary
Most married people, especially those who have been married for some time, name their spouse as beneficiary. In many cases, this will be your best option.

The two main reasons are 1) the money will be available to provide for your surviving spouse, and 2) it gives you the spousal rollover option.

Also, if your spouse is more than ten years younger than you are, you can use a different life expectancy chart that will make your required distributions less. (This lets the tax-deferred growth continue longer on more money.)

Here's how the spousal rollover option works. If you die first, your surviving spouse can "roll over" your tax-deferred account into his/her own IRA, further delaying income taxes until your spouse must start taking required minimum distributions at his/her required beginning date. When your spouse does the rollover, he/she names a new beneficiary(ies)—preferably much younger ones, as your children and grandchildren would be.

After your spouse dies, the beneficiary's *actual life expectancy* will be used for the remaining required minimum distributions. Depending on the beneficiary's age at that time, that could mean decades of tax-deferred growth.

For example, let's say your grandson is 20 when he inherits a $100,000 IRA from your spouse. Assuming a 7% annual return, and that he takes out only the required minimum distribution each year, over the next 63 years (the life expectancy of a 20-year-old), this $100,000 IRA will provide your grandson with over $1.7 million in income!

What if you name your spouse as beneficiary and your spouse dies before you? Under the old rules, this was often a problem. Unless you remarried, you lost the spousal rollover option. You could name a new beneficiary, but the distributions after your death were still based on your and your deceased spouse's life expectancies. But now, if your spouse dies first, you can name a new beneficiary—and after *you* die, the distributions will be based on *the new beneficiary's* life expectancy.

Possible Disadvantages

There are some possible disadvantages of naming your spouse as beneficiary that you need to consider. Keep in mind that, after you die, your spouse will have full control of this money, which may not be what you want. You may have children from a previous marriage or feel that your spouse may be too easily influenced by others after you're gone.

Choose the beneficiary(ies) for your tax-deferred plans carefully

Supreme Court: Inherited IRA is available to a beneficiary's creditors in bankruptcy

Your spouse doesn't *have* to do a rollover; a lump-sum distribution could be very tempting, even though all of the income taxes would have to be paid at once. If your spouse becomes incapacitated, the court could take control of this money. The money could also be lost to your spouse's creditors.

Naming your spouse as beneficiary could also cause you to pay too much in estate taxes. Remember, in Part Three, we explained how you can waste your estate tax exemption if you leave everything to your spouse. If your estate is large enough to pay estate taxes and most of your estate is made up of your tax-deferred savings, naming your spouse as the beneficiary could cause you to waste some or all of your exemption. (If you have other assets that can be applied to your exemption this might not be a problem.)

Option 2: Children, Other Individuals as Beneficiary

If your spouse will have plenty of assets—or if you have reason to believe your spouse will die before you—you could name your children, grandchildren or other individuals as beneficiary(ies).

The tax benefits can be great. Because you are not leaving this money to your spouse, your estate tax exemption can be applied to it, which could save estate taxes. And if your beneficiary is much younger than you (as your children and grandchildren would be), you can "stretch out" the tax-deferred growth over their life expectancies.

Possible Disadvantages

As we explained in Part Two, any time you name an individual as a beneficiary, you lose control. After you die, your beneficiary can do whatever he/she wants with this money, including cashing out the entire account and destroying your carefully made plans for long-term, tax-deferred growth. There is the risk of court interference if your beneficiary is a minor or becomes incapacitated.

And then there are a beneficiary's creditors. Money that has been withdrawn has always been considered to be available to a beneficiary's creditors, spouse, and ex-spouse(s). But in 2014, the Supreme Court ruled that the entire inherited IRA is available to a beneficiary's creditors in bankruptcy court.

The justices reasoned that because the beneficiary cannot make additional contributions or delay distributions until retirement, an inherited IRA is not a retirement account of the beneficiary. There is, in fact, nothing to prevent the beneficiary from withdrawing funds, or even clearing out the account, at any time. Therefore, these funds must also be available to satisfy the beneficiary's creditors during bankruptcy. Following the same logic, an inherited IRA is also subject to divorce proceedings.

One more note of caution: If you leave a substantial amount to a grandchild, it could be subject to the generation-skipping transfer tax, which is equal to the highest estate tax rate in effect at that time *and is in addition to* estate and income taxes. (See Part Nine for a full explanation.)

Option 3: Trust as Beneficiary

Naming a trust as beneficiary will give you maximum control over your tax-deferred money after you die. That's because the distributions will be paid not to an individual, but into a trust that contains your written instructions stating who will receive this money and when. Using a trust as beneficiary will allow the tax-deferred growth to continue over a beneficiary's life expectancy *and* protect your hard-earned savings from the beneficiary's creditors and/or irresponsible spending.

For example, your trust could provide income to your surviving spouse for as long as he or she lives. Then, after your spouse dies, the income could go to your children or grandchildren.

While you are living, the required minimum distributions will be paid to you over your life expectancy. After you die, the distributions can be paid to the trust over the life expectancy of the oldest beneficiary of the trust. Just as you can do now, the trustee of your trust will be able to withdraw more money from the tax-deferred account(s) if needed to follow your instructions, but the rest can stay in the account(s) where it is protected and growing tax-deferred.

Possible Disadvantages

You will not be able to provide for your spouse *and* stretch out the tax-deferred growth beyond your spouse's actual life expectancy. That's because you must use the life expectancy of the oldest beneficiary of the trust which, in this case, would probably be your spouse.

Also, many trusts pay income taxes at a higher rate than most individuals, but this only applies to income that *stays* in the trust. (With a revocable living trust, this would apply only *after* you die.) Distributions from your tax-

Naming a trust as beneficiary will let you keep maximum control

deferred account that are paid to the trust are subject to income tax, and if they were to stay in the trust, the higher tax rates would apply. But usually this is not a problem because the trustee has authority to distribute the income to the beneficiaries of the trust, who then pay the income tax at their own (usually lower) rates. (See Part Eight for more on trusts and income taxes.)

Finally, in order for a trust to qualify as beneficiary of a tax-deferred account, it must meet certain IRS requirements:

- It must be valid under state law.
- It must be irrevocable or become irrevocable at your death.
- The beneficiaries must be individuals (no charities or other non-persons) and they must be identifiable from the trust document.
- A copy of the trust document and any subsequent revisions must be provided to the Plan Administrator or IRA trustee, custodian or issuer.

Revocable Living Trust or Stand Alone Retirement Trust?

A revocable living trust becomes irrevocable at your death, so it would meet the requirements above. But because the trust's oldest beneficiary's life expectancy must be used to determine the distributions, many attorneys now recommend a separate share, or even a separate trust, for each beneficiary. These are called "stand alone retirement trusts" because they are created solely for retirement plan and IRA assets. (A revocable living trust would still be used for your general estate planning purposes.)

Here are some terms you should know:

- A *conduit trust* requires that all distributions from the IRA or retirement plan must be distributed to the trust's beneficiary(ies). The trust simply acts as a "conduit" from the plan to the beneficiary. These distributions are not protected from a beneficiary's creditors and provide no asset protection.
- An *accumulation trust* allows the distributions to be kept within the trust instead of being distributed to the beneficiary. Assets that remain in the trust are protected from the beneficiary's creditors, but any undistributed income kept in the trust will be subject to the higher income tax rates. (An accumulation trust is usually used to provide for a special needs beneficiary so that government benefits are not jeopardized.)
- A *trust protector* can be given the power to change from a conduit to an accumulation trust. This can be valuable if there is a change in the benefi-

ciary's circumstances (due to disability, divorce, dependency issues, etc.) that would make it desirable to keep the distributions in the trust. (See Part Four for more about trust protectors.)

Option 4: Charity/Foundation as Beneficiary

If you are planning to leave an asset to charity after you die, a tax-deferred account can be an excellent asset to use. That's because when you name a charity as the beneficiary, there will be *no income or estate taxes* on this money after you die.

If you name a charitable remainder trust as beneficiary, your spouse, children, or others can receive an income for a set number of years or for as long as they live—and you can still save income and estate taxes. You can also set up your own charitable foundation and have the foundation pay your kids a salary to run it. (See Part Nine for more information about these.)

The only downside of naming a charity as beneficiary is that it has no life expectancy. Under the old rules, if you named a charity as beneficiary, you had to use just your life expectancy when determining distributions during your lifetime. This made the distributions larger than they would have been with another beneficiary. But now, even with a charity as your beneficiary, you still use the Uniform Lifetime Table to determine your required minimum distributions, so this is not the problem it used to be. However, you still need to be aware of a charity's "zero" life expectancy, as you will see next.

Option 5: Some or All of the Above as Beneficiary

You don't have to choose just *one* of these options. You can split a large IRA into several smaller ones and name a different beneficiary for each one. If your money is in an employer plan, you can roll it into an IRA and then split it.

You could name several beneficiaries for one IRA, but then you must use the life expectancy of the oldest beneficiary for the entire IRA, just as when you use a trust as beneficiary. This is especially important if a charity is involved. Remember, it has a life expectancy of zero, so the IRS would consider it the oldest beneficiary. Depending on when you die, this could cause the entire IRA to be paid out in just five years.

With separate IRAs—one for each beneficiary—you can use *each one's* life expectancy. This will give you the maximum stretch out over *all* their ages.

You can divide a large IRA into smaller ones

It will also be more fair to your beneficiaries, especially if there is a wide difference in their ages, or if you want to include a charity. (A stand alone retirement trust for each beneficiary is still advantageous.)

When should you divide a larger IRA? That will depend on your planning decisions. Doing it now, while you are living, is the cleanest approach. If you die first, your surviving spouse can also split your IRA when he/she does a rollover and names new beneficiaries. And now, under the new rules and under certain circumstances, your IRA can be divided into separate accounts in the year *after* you die.

Setting up separate IRAs now will make it a little more complicated for you when calculating your required minimum distributions each year, because one will have to be calculated for each IRA. But you can take the total of your distributions from any IRA you wish. If your estate is substantial, dividing a large IRA can also help you use your estate tax exemption more effectively.

> **Note:** Any time you name someone other than your spouse as the beneficiary, you need expert advice. You'll need to find an attorney who is experienced in this area, especially if you have large amounts in these plans. Also, your spouse may need to sign a consent form. Even in non-community property states, spouses now have rights to retirement plan and other benefits.

■ Who Should Be Your Beneficiary—If You Are Not Married

If you are not married, your decision will be less complicated. You can name any individual, a trust, or a charity as the beneficiary. If you want an individual to receive this money after you die, consider using a trust to keep more control. And make sure the individual is aware of the rules for an inherited IRA.

Before you make a decision, consider all of your options carefully. Make sure your attorney has experience in this area, especially if you have a sizeable amount in your tax-deferred plans.

■ If You Die Without a Beneficiary

What happens if you die without a valid beneficiary? That depends upon when you die. If you die *before* your required beginning date, your account must be paid out within five years. If you die *after* your required beginning date, distributions will be paid over the remaining years of your "fixed life expectancy," determined from an IRS table based on your age in the year you die. In either case, the proceeds would have to go through probate to determine who is entitled to receive these benefits, as explained in Part One.

■ How to Change the Beneficiary Designation for Your Tax-Deferred Plans

With the new rules, you can change your beneficiary at any time while you are living and the distributions after you die will be paid over that beneficiary's life expectancy.

In fact, your final beneficiaries do not have to be determined until September 30 of the year *after* you die, which allows for some neat clean-up planning to be done after you're gone. For example, your spouse could disclaim (refuse) some benefits so a grandchild could inherit. No new beneficiaries can be added after you die, however, so you must be sure to name all appropriate beneficiaries while you are living.

To change the beneficiary of employer-sponsored plans (such as a 401(k), pension, or profit sharing plan), contact your employee benefits or personnel department for the proper form. To change the beneficiary of your IRA or Keogh, you will need to contact the institution where your account is located.

Some plans have restrictions on what you can do on the beneficiary designations. Be sure to read the document carefully. If the plan will not let you do what you want to do, consider rolling your money into an IRA as soon as you can. (However, some states' laws provide less protection for IRAs than for other types of tax-qualified plans, so be sure to check first.) If your money is already in an IRA and the institution will not agree to what you want, consider moving your IRA to another institution.

■ Roth IRA

If you qualify, you may want to consider converting some or all of your tax-deferred money to a Roth IRA. You can only convert from a traditional IRA, so if your money is in a different tax-deferred plan, like a pension or profit sharing plan, you must first roll your money into a traditional IRA and then convert it to a Roth IRA. You will have to pay ordinary income taxes on the amount when you convert. Why go to all this trouble? Because it can be worth it. Here's why:

- Unlike a traditional IRA that requires you to start taking your money out at age 70 1/2, with a Roth IRA there are *no* required minimum distributions during your lifetime. So you can leave your money there *for as long as you wish*.
- Unlike a traditional IRA, you can continue to make contributions to a Roth IRA after you have reached age 70 1/2.
- As a general rule, after five years or age 59 1/2 (whichever is later), *all distributions to you and your beneficiaries will be tax-free*.
- You can stretch out a Roth IRA just like a traditional IRA. After you die, distributions can be paid over the actual life expectancy of your beneficiary. Your spouse can even do a spousal rollover and name a new beneficiary.

Your tax advisor can help you determine if converting to a Roth IRA would be a good move for you.

Tax-Deferred Annuities

Tax-deferred annuities sold by insurance companies are not IRAs or qualified plans. As a result, they are not governed by the same IRS rules as the plans listed above and the preceding discussion does not apply to them.

Before you name a beneficiary, read your contract carefully. There may be some restrictions or income tax issues you need to be aware of when making this decision.

For example, if you are married, naming your spouse as beneficiary may allow the tax-deferred payments to continue over your spouse's lifetime after you die, while naming someone other than your spouse (like your living trust) could cause the balance to be paid out all at once after you die. (One solution may be to name your spouse as first beneficiary and your living trust as second beneficiary.)

Incentive Stock Options

Stock options are often used as a form of compensation for valued employees, who are given the right to buy company stock at some point in the future at a predetermined, and usually very favorable, price.

Usually, you have to wait until a certain amount of time has passed before you can exercise the option (buy the stock). You do not pay income taxes until the stock is later disposed of which, according to the IRS, is a "sale, exchange, gift, or transfer of legal title."

The laws are not clear about whether putting stock options into your living trust would cause you to violate the waiting time or if this would be considered a transfer of legal title, which would cause you to pay income taxes at that time.

However, we are aware of at least one company that has written to the IRS, asking for an opinion on whether transferring incentive stock options to a revocable living trust would be considered a disposition. The response from the IRS states that it would not be.

You or your attorney will probably want to read the plan document to see if there are any restrictions on transferring these options to your living trust. You may also want to write the plan administrator for approval. Depending on how long you have before an option expires, you may decide to wait until *after* you exercise the option and then transfer the stock to your living trust.

Section 1244 Stock

Business owners know that many new businesses fail, so they often incorporate under Section 1244 of the Internal Revenue Code. If the business is later sold or liquidated at a loss, this allows the stockholders (the owners) to take the loss on the stock as an *ordinary* loss instead of a *capital* loss.

Normally, when you sell stock (and other investments) and have a loss, it is considered a *capital loss* and can only be used to offset *capital gains* (your profits when investments are sold). If your capital losses exceed your capital gains for that year, under current tax law you are only allowed to deduct $3,000 ($1,500 if married filing separately) of the excess loss per year from your ordinary income (wages, tips, etc. as defined by the IRS on Form 1040).

But with 1244 stock, the stockholders can deduct the loss from *ordinary* income instead of from just capital gains. Individuals can currently deduct up to $50,000 in these losses per year; married couples filing jointly can deduct up to $100,000 in losses per year. Any excess loss can be rolled forward to subsequent tax years.

Under current tax law, transferring Section 1244 stock to a living trust would cause you to lose this tax benefit. Whether or not you will want to put this stock in your living trust will probably depend on how long you have been in business and how profitable the business is.

If you think the business may have to be sold or liquidated at a loss, you probably do not want to put Section 1244 stock in your living trust. However, if the corporation is successful and there is little chance of a loss, you may want to go ahead and do so. We suggest you discuss this with your attorney and accountant before you decide.

Professional Corporations

State laws require shareholders of professional corporations (like doctors and dentists) to be licensed members of their professions. Because a living trust is revocable and you keep control of the assets you put in it, some attorneys reason that transferring a professional corporation to a living trust would not be a problem. But because the laws do not specifically mention living trusts, many attorneys suggest that you leave these out of your trust for now—at least until the laws are changed to include living trusts.

Part Seven—

THE FINAL STEPS TO YOUR PEACE OF MIND

Now that you have your living trust prepared and you have funded it with your assets, you may be wondering what you need to do next. Actually, you don't *have* to do anything else for your trust to work—except, of course, to remember that any assets you acquire from now on need to be titled in the name of your trust.

However, there are some things you can do now that will make things much easier for your family when something happens to you. For example, when you funded your trust, you had to locate title documents and find out exactly what assets you own. Instead of just dumping all that information back into a drawer (or several drawers), we'll show you how to organize this information so it will actually *mean* something to your spouse, children, and/or successor trustee when it is needed.

Also, as your personal, family, and financial situations change, you may need to change your trust. In this section, we'll give you some examples of changes in your life that may affect your trust, and we'll explain what you need to do to change it.

And, finally, we'll explain step-by-step what your surviving spouse or successor trustee needs to do if you become incapacitated and when you die.

Once you understand what will need to happen and the information your family will need, you'll be able to organize things and prepare them. Then you'll know you've done *the best you can do* for your family—and that will give *you* great peace of mind.

Organize Information for Your Family

Think for a few moments about what would happen if you became incapacitated or died today. Would your spouse, family, and/or successor trustee know what to do?

Would they know where to find your trust document and the health care documents you signed? Do they know who should be notified? Do they know about the insurance you have and benefits they can apply for? Do they know about assets you own and where they are located? Do they know who your attorney and accountant are? If you own a business, do they know what to do to keep it operating or how to arrange for its sale? Do they know whom to call if they need help?

Maybe you don't want anyone to know everything about your assets right now. That's okay; you don't have to tell them details. But, as you will see as you read this section, it's very important that they know where to find this information *when they need it*.

Here is a checklist of things you can do now that will make things much easier for your family later.

■ Read the Rest of This Section Carefully.
When you understand what your spouse, family, and/or successor trustee will need to do when something happens to you, you'll want to make things as easy for them as possible—and you'll be motivated to organize things for them.

■ Inform Others.
Give copies of your health care documents (durable power of attorney, health care proxy, living will) to your physician and designated agent. You may want to purchase additional copies of this book for your successor trustee(s) and beneficiaries so they will understand what a living trust does, why you have chosen to have one, and what they may need to do.

■ Store Original Documents in Safe Place.
Keep originals of your documents (titles, living trust and health care documents) in one safe place like a fire-proof safe or a safe deposit box. Make copies for the notebook or files described next.

■ **Create a Notebook or Files of Financial and Personal Information.**
We suggest that you buy one or two three-ring binders to hold this information. Alternatively, you could organize it in a file drawer and/or on your computer. (If you organize the information on your computer, you'll still need a paper system for some of the documents so print hard copies and add them to the paper files.) The main thing is to *do* this and then keep it current.

Speaking of your computer, be sure to back up your files and store the back-ups in a safe place in case your computer is lost or stolen. If a password is required, include it in your notebook or files. Clean up your desktop and label any relevant files clearly so they will be easy for someone to find.

The following list of items to include will help you put together the information that will be needed.

- A copy of this book.

- A copy of your living trust and ancillary documents (financial power of attorney, pour over will, etc.)

- A copy of your health care documents.

- Your special gifts lists. (See Part Four.)

- A listing of your assets, where they are located, current values, account numbers, date of purchase, purchase price, date transferred to your trust, and name of contact person. (The Organizer in the back of this book will be helpful.)

- A copy of year-end bank and investment account statements. If you bank online, include websites, passwords, and login information.

- Safe deposit box location, list of contents, and location of the key. Also, any post office boxes, locations, and combinations.

- A listing of your creditors (people to whom *you owe* money, including mortgages, credit cards, etc.). Include names, addresses, phone numbers, amount owed, and any documentation. If you pay any of these online, include websites, passwords, and login information.

Does your family know where to find the information they will need?

Review your trust and other information annually

■ A listing of people who *owe you* money. Include names, addresses, phone numbers, amount owed, and any documentation.

■ A listing of insurance policies (health, long-term care, disability income, life) and other benefits to which you or your family may be entitled if you become incapacitated and when you die. Include policy numbers, company, location, amount of benefit, phone numbers, and contact person. Place the actual policies in the notebook/files.

■ Birth and marriage certificates, divorce papers, adoption papers, citizenship/naturalization papers, diplomas, and death certificate if one spouse is deceased. If you or your spouse is a veteran (or was, if deceased), include discharge papers and records of VA benefits received.

■ Names, addresses, and telephone numbers of your personal advisors including attorney, banker and/or trust officer, insurance agent, accountant or CPA, financial advisor/broker, physicians, etc.

■ A calendar or timeline of important financial dates. Include monthly, quarterly, and annual bills (utilities, insurance, property taxes, etc.), when to meet with the accountant to prepare income taxes, etc. If you receive bills online or have bills set up on autopay from your bank account or credit card, document this so someone else will know.

■ Access to your email, social media (FaceBook, LinkedIn, Twitter, Instagram, etc.) and any online photo and document storage accounts.

■ A list of medications you take, dosages, and when you take them.

■ At least two letters of instruction, one to be opened if you become incapacitated and the other when you die. (You could also make an audio or video recording.)

At incapacity: Include any special instructions or wishes regarding your care, the care of others who depend on you (minors, parents, pets, etc.), people to notify (include address/phone), and continuation or sale of a business.

At your death: Include people to notify (and their addresses/phone numbers), instructions for funeral/burial/cremation (and organ donation), the care of others who depend on you (minors, parents, pets, etc.), and continuation or sale of a business. Some people like to preplan their memorial service, even to the point of selecting photos and narrating a slide show of the highlights of their lives. You may also want to outline your obituary, as family members may not be aware of details of your life story that you would want known.

- If you have minor children or other dependents who rely on you, you may want to do separate instructions (letter, video or audio) to the person who will care for them. You may want to include particular likes, dislikes, places to go, foods to eat, friends, etc. This can give you peace of mind, knowing that you will be able to pass this information on if something should happen to you unexpectedly.

- You may also want to write letters (or make an audio or video recording) to your spouse, children, grandchildren, and other loved ones. You may want to share wisdom you have gained, express your faith and values, and/or tell them of special memories you have and how much they mean to you. Perhaps you want to make amends. You may also want to tell your family why you are taking the time now to put everything in order for them—and encourage them to do the same for their families. These letters can give you tremendous peace of mind and be a source of great comfort to your loved ones for years to come.

■ Show Your Spouse, Family Member, and/or Successor Trustee Where This Information is Located.

Remember, you don't have to show them all the details yet if you don't want to. But you should at least let one or two people know that you have organized this information and where they can find it when it is needed.

■ Review This Information Annually.

Once a year, pull out your notebooks or files, read through them (and this section of the book), and see if anything needs to be updated. Just like an annual physical, think of this as your annual *trust* checkup. Link this review to an annual occasion—a holiday, your birthday, beginning of the year, after tax time—so it becomes something you do every year.

Have you bought or sold any assets? Did you remember to title the new ones in the name of your trust? Have you changed any passwords? Do your instruction letters still say what you want them to say? Do you need to make any changes to your trust document? (See below for situations that could create a need to change your trust document and how to change it.)

■ **Have a Trial Run.**

Tell your spouse and/or successor trustee to pretend that you have just become incapacitated. Have them go through the checklists on the following pages and see if they can find the information they will need. Then, have them repeat the process as if you have just died.

Will this take some time? Yes. But it's a very *unselfish* use of your time. Remember, you don't have to do all this. After you set up your trust and transfer your assets to it, the trust will work.

So, what do *you* get out of this? The satisfaction of knowing you have done everything you can to make things easier on your family. You do it out of love—it's your final gift to them. You are also setting an example for your family, and perhaps they'll do the same for theirs.

CHANGING YOUR LIVING TRUST

Your living trust is a snapshot of you, your family, and your assets right now, at this point in time. But people and situations change, and your trust may need to change, too.

Basically, you should change your trust any time it no longer does what you want. If you review your trust every year as we suggest, you will become very familiar with it and you will be able to keep it current with your life.

Here's a checklist of events that could prompt a change in your trust. We suggest that you review this list each year when you review your trust.

Changes in Your Family Situation
You and Your Spouse
■ You marry, divorce or separate;
■ Your health (or your spouse's health) declines, or your spouse dies.

Your Children, Grandchildren, Parents, and Other Beneficiaries
■ Birth or adoption;
■ Marriage, divorce, or separation;
■ Finances change (good or bad);
■ Parent or other relative becomes dependent on you;

- Minor becomes an adult;
- Attitude toward you changes;
- Health declines;
- A child, grandchild, or other beneficiary dies.

Changes in Your Economic Situation

- Value of assets changes dramatically (up or down);
- Change in business interests (new partnership or corporation, you plan to sell a business, etc.);
- You buy real estate in another state;
- You are planning to retire and/or need to designate a final beneficiary for tax-deferred plans before distributions begin.

Outside Changes

- Changes in the laws, state or federal. Find out if your attorney will keep you informed when changes occur that would affect your trust.

Note: Here is an excellent example. If your A-B living trust was prepared prior to 2012, it may state that when the first spouse dies, an amount equal to the federal estate tax exemption is to be placed in Trust B and any excess in Trust A. This language was commonly used to maximize the federal estate tax exemption of the first spouse to die. But with the exemption at $11.2 million, this wording could cause all of the assets to be placed in Trust B with nothing left for the surviving spouse's Trust A.

- You plan to move to a different state;
- Successor trustee (or guardian for minor children) moves away, becomes ill, dies, or changes his/her mind about accepting the responsibility.
- You change your mind about a successor trustee or guardian for your minor children.

Remember, you do *not* need to change your trust when you buy and sell assets. But you *do* need to title newly acquired assets in the name of your trust.

How to Change Your Trust

If you decide you want to make a change, don't write on your trust document. Once you have signed the trust document, it must not be altered. If you want to change something that is in the trust document itself, your attorney will prepare an amendment to your trust which you will sign, and it will probably be notarized, just like your trust document. Amendments are usually pretty

Your living trust can and should change with you

simple. It should not take your attorney very long to prepare one, nor should it cost you very much. You do not need to do anything to your assets—they are already in your trust. Your attorney will just change the trust document that *controls* your assets.

Remember, in most states, if you keep a separate list of your special gifts (specific items that you want to go to certain people or organizations), you do not need to make any changes to your trust. You just need to update the list and have it notarized.

On the following pages, you will find checklists for your surviving spouse and for your successor trustee so they will know what needs to be done when something happens to you. As you will see, some of the steps are the same. But we felt that having separate checklists would make it easier for them.

My SPOUSE IS INCAPACITATED. WHAT DO I NEED TO DO?

If you and your spouse have transferred your assets to your living trust, you will be able to continue to manage your financial affairs without court interference. Even if the incapacity is not expected to be lengthy (for example, if your spouse has had a stroke or heart attack and is expected to recover), not having to deal with the courts will be a great relief.

Here's a checklist that will help you get started when you may not know where to begin. Because many married couples have one living trust together—they are co-grantors and co-trustees—that is how this checklist is written.

If you and your spouse have separate trusts and you are successor trustee of your spouse's trust, this list will still be helpful. But you should also read the checklist for the successor trustee which follows.

■ Take Care of Your Spouse First.
Make sure your spouse is receiving quality care in a supportive environment—and that you are comfortable with the hospital or nursing home, doctors, and staff.

■ Notify Insurance Company, Spouse's Employer, and Others.

Be sure your insurance company has been notified, and that the physician has a copy of the health care documents (durable power of attorney for health care, health care proxy, living will) you and your spouse signed when your trust was prepared.

Notify your spouse's employer, friends, and relatives. (You may want to have a family member or friend help you with this.) If your spouse wrote you a letter (as explained earlier in this section) explaining what you should do at his/her incapacity, it may be very helpful.

■ Find the Trust Document.

Hopefully, you already know where it is. See if you are able to write checks and sell assets with just your signature. Many trust documents are written so that one spouse can act alone after the other becomes incapacitated. However, some documents name a co-trustee (like a son or daughter, or a corporate trustee) to act with the well spouse. If a co-trustee is required, notify him/her as soon as possible.

■ Notify Your Attorney.

Notify the attorney who prepared the trust document. He/she should be aware of the incapacity in case you have questions. Remember, you've never done this before, and it may be comforting for you to know there is someone you can call.

■ Find Out What Your Insurance Covers.

If you don't already know what your insurance covers, you will need to find out now. Assuming your insurance will cover a certain procedure or facility could be a very costly mistake. Find out your alternatives *before* making a major decision. If you need help understanding your coverage, your insurance agent or your spouse's personnel/benefits department may be able to help you. Most insurance companies also have a toll free telephone number you can call 24 hours a day if you have questions. If you have long term care insurance, make sure you are familiar with the coverage if it turns out the incapacity will be lengthy.

■ Have Doctor(s) Document Spouse's Condition.

It may be necessary to have the appropriate physician write a letter documenting your spouse's condition. Some trust documents will only require a letter from an M.D., some from one or two specialists, others require none.

You will probably need to show this letter to the bank and others so you can sign checks and sell assets, if that becomes necessary.

■ Apply for Benefits.

Apply for any disability benefits to which your spouse may be entitled, including your spouse's employer, private insurance, Veteran's benefits, and Social Security.

■ Become Familiar with Your Finances.

You need to know what assets you have, where they are located, and what your income sources are. You may need to put together a budget. Familiarize yourself with any business dealings your spouse was involved with. If you own real estate, make sure you have keys, take care of any utilities, etc. If your spouse has a business, you will probably need to make arrangements for its continuation.

Hopefully, you and your spouse organized this information as we suggested. (You can see now how much easier things will be if you did.)

If you find any assets that were left out of the trust, use the durable power of attorney to transfer them into the trust as soon as possible so they will not have to go through probate when your spouse dies. However, it's possible that an asset was *intentionally* left out of the trust for creditor protection (see Part Two). You may want to check with your attorney *first*.

■ Put Together Team of Advisors.

Depending on the value of your assets, and the expected length and severity of your spouse's incapacity, you may want to put together a team of professional advisors to help you. These will probably include your attorney, accountant, banker and/or trust officer, financial advisor, and insurance advisor. You may also want to include an adult child or a close friend.

Be sure to consult your advisors *before* you sell *any* assets, especially stocks, real estate or a business. There could be serious tax consequences, and they may be able to suggest some better alternatives. If your spouse owns a business, your advisors can help with decisions about its continuation.

My Spouse Is Incapacitated. What Do I Need To Do?

☐ **Take Care of Your Spouse First.**

☐ **Notify Insurance Company, Spouse's Employer, and Others.**

☐ **Find the Trust Document.**

☐ **Notify Your Attorney.**

☐ **Find Out What Your Insurance Covers.**

☐ **Have Doctor(s) Document Spouse's Condition.**

☐ **Apply for Benefits.**

☐ **Become Familiar with Your Finances.**

☐ **Put Together Team of Advisors.**

☐ **Keep Records, Take Care of Taxes and Accountings.**

☐ **Keep Successor Trustee(s) Informed.**

■ **Keep Records, Take Care of Taxes and Accountings.**
Keep careful record of medical expenses and file claims promptly. Keep records of the bills you have paid and any income received. And don't forget that income tax returns must be filed by April 15 each year. Contact your accountant early to find out what information he/she will need so you will have plenty of time to locate statements, etc.

■ **Keep Successor Trustee(s) Informed.**
It may be appropriate, depending on the trust document, to keep your successor trustee(s) informed in case something happens to you.

Above all, try to keep a balanced perspective. Nothing should be more important right now than spending time with your spouse. If you find that managing your financial affairs and caring for your spouse is becoming too much for you to handle, consider having someone you trust help you with the finances—like an accountant, capable son or daughter, or even a corporate trustee (they can manage your investments *and* do the bookkeeping for you). You can always resume more of the responsibilities later.

MY SPOUSE HAS DIED. WHAT DO I NEED TO DO?

When your spouse dies, there are some things you must do to settle your spouse's estate and plan for your future. This will be especially important if your trust has A-B or A-B-C provisions (explained in Part Three), or other tax/additional planning.

If you and your spouse changed titles and beneficiary designations to your living trust, this will be much easier for you. Because there will be no probate, you will be able to do things privately and on your own schedule, instead of the court's.

You may be able to handle much of this yourself. But it would be wise to seek guidance from your professional advisors (attorney, bank/trust officer, accountant, financial advisor, etc.). You may also want to ask some family members to help you.

Here's a checklist to help you get started. Because many married couples have one living trust together (they are co-grantors and co-trustees), that is how this checklist is written.

If you and your spouse have separate trusts and you are successor trustee of your spouse's trust, this list will still be helpful. But you should also read the checklist for the successor trustee which follows.

■ Take Care of the Funeral.
Enlist a family member to help with funeral arrangements, flowers, cemetery marker, announcement in paper, special wishes for service, notifying friends, relatives, employer, etc. If your spouse left you some written instructions regarding the service, burial, people to notify, etc. (as we suggested earlier), this will be much easier on everyone involved.

■ Find the Trust Document.

Hopefully, you already know where the trust document is. See if you will be able to act alone or if a co-trustee has been named to act with you. If a co-trustee is required, notify him/her as soon as possible.

■ Contact Attorney to Review Trust Document/Process.

It would be wise to schedule an appointment with an attorney (or a corporate trustee, especially if named as co-trustee) as soon as possible to review your trust document, your assets, and your responsibilities, and to develop a schedule. You may want to have a family member or friend go with you.

Even if you have a modest estate, an hour or so with an attorney can be worth the time and expense to confirm what you need to do. It's also comforting to know there is someone you can call if you have a question.

If your estate is larger, if there are assets of sizeable value, if there is an IRA or retirement plan account, if your trust has tax planning or complicated provisions, or if you're just not sure about what needs to be done, this meeting will more than pay for itself.

You don't have to go back to the attorney who prepared your trust, although he/she would certainly be more familiar with the document. You can go to another attorney (see Part Five if you need to find one). A corporate trustee experienced with trust administration can also help you.

■ Order Death Certificates.

Order at least 12 certified death certificates (you can usually get these from the funeral home). You will need these to collect benefits and conduct other business. Multiple copies will help speed things up, as you won't have to wait to get copies back before you can give one to someone else.

■ Take Care of Ongoing Bills, Final Expenses.

You can continue to pay your regular bills (utilities, telephone, etc.). However, depending on the size of your estate and the provisions in the trust document, there *may* be some tax reasons why you should not pay the mortgage on your home and other real estate. Notify the lender of your spouse's death and that the next mortgage payment may be delayed a few days—just until you are able to meet with your attorney to start settling the estate.

Understanding Living Trusts®

Keep careful records of final medical bills and funeral expenses as they may be deductible. Submit medical claims promptly.

■ Put Together a Team of Advisors.

It's very important for you to realize that you are not alone in this and that no one expects you to be able to do everything all by yourself. Nor should you even try. This is a very emotional time, and even routine tasks may seem overwhelming. An innocent error could turn out to be a very expensive mistake.

You will probably want to put together a team of professionals to advise and/or help you. These will likely include your attorney, accountant, banker and/or trust officer, financial advisor, and/or insurance advisor. You may also want to include an adult child or a close friend as a sounding board.

Before you sell any assets, apply for any benefits (especially your spouse's IRA and other retirement plans), or change any investments, talk to your professional advisors about your options. They will be able to recommend choices that will provide you with maximum income and save substantial amounts in taxes. *Don't rush these decisions*; they usually do not have to be made right away.

Also, if your spouse owned a business, your advisors will be able to help you make arrangements for its continuation or sale.

■ Inventory Assets/Determine Current Values.

Before you meet with your attorney, it would be a good idea to put together a preliminary list of all of the assets and their estimated values. Later on, the exact values will need to be determined for accounting and tax purposes.

This information is very important for several reasons:

1. You need to know exactly what assets you have and what your income sources are. You and your advisors will need to plan for your future.

2. Your attorney, accountant, and/or trust officer need to know this information so they can suggest ways to save taxes, help you settle the estate, file tax returns, and advise you. (Remember, a federal and/or state estate tax return is required if the value of the estate is more than the exemption at that time.)

3.   Documenting the value of assets when your spouse dies can save a considerable amount in capital gains tax when they are eventually sold.

Remember, when an asset is sold, capital gains tax will be due on the gain (profit). This is the difference between what you paid for the asset (your cost *basis)* and the selling price. The death of a spouse changes the basis of your assets.

If you live in a non-community property state, only your deceased spouse's interest in the assets in your common trust will receive a new basis equal to the value as of his/her death. If your spouse owned an asset separately (either in a separate trust or identified as separate property in your common trust), the entire asset will receive a new basis equal to its value. (Also, as discussed in Part Six, if you and your spouse jointly owned an asset since before 1976, *both* interests may get a new basis.)

If you live in a community property state, both your spouse's interest and your interest in each community asset will receive a new basis.

If the assets have appreciated *over* their cost, the new basis will be a *stepped-up* basis. (See Part One for an explanation of stepped-up basis.) If the value of the assets is *below* their cost, the new basis will be a *stepped-down* basis.

4.   If your trust has A-B or A-B-C provisions or other tax/additional planning, your attorney, accountant or trust officer will need this information to help you decide which assets should go into each trust to maximize the objectives of this planning.

If you find that an asset is still in your spouse's name and was not transferred to your living trust, it may have to be probated. Depending on the value and type of asset, you may be able to do this yourself, or your attorney can help you. However, it's possible that an asset was *intentionally* left out of the trust for creditor protection or another valid reason (see Part Two). It's best to check with the attorney first.

How to Determine Values

It is important that current values are appropriately determined; otherwise, the IRS will not accept them. The IRS has specific rules that must be followed in establishing "fair market value" when an estate tax return is required or when calculating basis for income tax purposes. In other words, a ballpark estimate by a neighbor who happens to be a real estate agent—or your own best guess—usually will not do.

Your banker or investment advisor can provide you with the values of accounts on the day your spouse died. *The Wall Street Journal* for that day can also be a good source for values of stocks and mutual funds. Some items (especially real estate and collectibles) will need to be appraised, and this should be done as soon as possible. Your attorney or trust officer can recommend a reputable appraiser. There are also companies that do estate valuations; your attorney or trust officer will know about those, too.

■ Do Tax Planning.

You will need to consider the income tax consequences before you apply for benefits or sell any assets. For example, you may have several choices for how your spouse's IRA and other retirement benefits can be paid to you (including rolling over the proceeds into your IRA, a lump sum, payments over your lifetime and, perhaps, over someone else's lifetime). You should know the tax implications of each *before* selecting one. Your advisors will be able to help you and determine a payout option that is best for your situation.

Also, don't forget that income tax returns must be filed by April 15 each year. Contact your accountant early to find out what information he/she will need so you will have plenty of time to locate statements, etc. A state inheritance tax return may also need to be filed.

> **Note:** If the value of the estate is more than the federal estate tax exemption, or if there is an A-B or A-B-C provision in your trust, there are other steps that need to be taken, as explained beginning on the next page.

■ Apply for Benefits.

After consulting with your advisors, you will know which payout (distribution) option to choose when applying for benefits from life insurance companies, retirement plans, your spouse's employer, Veteran's benefits, Social Security, associations, and any others that might pay a death benefit.

■ **Pay Bills.**

Verify and pay all bills and taxes. Make a final accounting record of all assets and bills paid, and keep it with your records. (A bookkeeper, accountant or corporate trustee can show you how to do this or do it for you.)

■ **Make Special Gifts.**

If your spouse had a list of items he/she wanted certain people or organizations to have, you can go ahead and make them.

■ **Keep Things Organized for Your Successor Trustee(s).**

Keeping good records from now on will be very helpful for your successor trustee(s). You may also want to keep your successors informed so they will know what to do if you become incapacitated and when you die.

Tax Planning if the Estate is More Than the Federal Estate Tax Exemption (or the Trust Contains A-B or A-B-C Provisions)

In addition to a final income tax return, if the gross value of the estate is more than the estate tax exemption in effect at that time, a federal estate tax return will need to be filed within nine months of the death—even if no estate taxes are due. Also, a state return may need to be filed, even if no tax is due.

■ **If The Trust Does Not Have Tax Planning**

If the value of all of the assets is more than the estate tax exemption and your living trust did not include any tax planning provisions, your attorney will probably use the marital deduction to transfer all of the assets to you so no estate taxes will be due now. (But, remember, estate taxes *will* be due when *you* die if your estate is more than the exemption at that time.) Your attorney will probably also file a federal estate tax return to preserve your spouse's federal estate tax exemption under the portability provision. (See Part Three.)

Disclaiming

Your attorney may suggest that you *disclaim* some assets. This is a legal "no thank you." Instead of going to you, these assets would go to the beneficiary(ies) who would receive them if you were not living. This is often done to reduce estate taxes or to continue the tax-deferred growth of a retirement plan or IRA over the life expectancy of a younger beneficiary. This can be a good idea, as long as you don't need some of the assets *and* you are willing to give them up. However, to be able to disclaim an asset, you must not have received any benefit from it. So it would be wise to wait until you meet with your attorney before you sell any assets, change any titles, or apply for any benefits.

■ If Your Trust Has Tax Planning

If you have an A-B or an A-B-C provision (or other tax planning) in your trust document, your attorney will help you put into place the provisions that you and your spouse wanted for additional control and/or to save estate taxes.

This planning process should begin as soon as possible. Because the assets will be divided, it's important not to sell or retitle any assets, or apply for any benefits, until after you meet with your attorney. In preparation for this meeting, it would be a good idea for you to review Part Three (where we explain the A-B and the A-B-C provisions) and the following pages.

Because the surviving spouse is often named as the trustee of Trust B (and Trust C), this section has been written with that in mind.

Assets Will Be Divided

You and your attorney (and trust officer when there is a corporate trustee involved) will decide how to divide the assets between Trust A and Trust B (and Trust C). Sometimes this is done by placing specific assets in each trust, and sometimes by putting a percentage of each asset in each trust.

A listing of the assets that are placed in each trust will be prepared, including their estate tax values and their values at the time the division is made.

Remember, the assets in Trust A are *yours*. You can sell, spend, or invest them however you wish. You can change any provisions in Trust A, including the beneficiaries if you wish. As long as you are a trustee of your trust, you continue to file your regular income tax return using your social security number.

However, the assets in Trust B (and Trust C) are *not* yours. They belong to the beneficiaries your spouse named. The assets will stay in Trust B (and Trust C) so they can be used to help support you for as long as you live. In the meantime, as the trustee, *you are safeguarding* the assets for the beneficiaries. (The information for successor trustees, which follows, will help you understand this responsibility.)

Note: As explained in Part Three, depending on the provisions in the trust document, you may be entitled to receive the income earned by the assets in Trust B (and principal, under certain conditions). The beneficiaries of Trust B may also be allowed to receive some benefits while you are living.

If there is also a Trust C (QTIP), you will receive *all* of the income the assets in Trust C earn. You may also be able to receive principal from Trust C—again, depending on the provisions in the trust. The beneficiaries of Trust C will not receive its assets until after you die.

Investing

You will undoubtedly want to have some professional help investing the assets, especially the assets in Trust B (and Trust C). Because you will probably be receiving all of the income, you will want investments that produce income. At the same time, the beneficiaries would like to see their assets increase in value—or at least not lose value. Your investment advisor or a corporate trustee can help you decide how to invest them and avoid a conflict of interest.

Record keeping

Certain bookkeeping procedures must be followed for Trust B and Trust C. These are not especially difficult, and you may be able to handle them yourself after they are set up and explained to you. (If you don't want to do the accounting, you can have a bookkeeper, accountant, or corporate trustee do it for you.) For example:

You cannot mix your assets in Trust A with any of the assets in Trust B or Trust C, so Trust B and Trust C will have their own separate bank accounts. All income and expenses must be applied to the appropriate trust. For example, if you receive a check for income that was generated by the assets in Trust B, it must be deposited in Trust B's account first, even though you will eventually receive the income. You can then write yourself a check for that amount.

Trust B and Trust C will have their own separate tax identification numbers and separate tax returns will be filed for them each year. (Your accountant can do this—or if you use a corporate trustee, they will do this for you.)

Keeping the assets separate is not really that difficult. You just have to understand that there are now two (or three) trusts and *only one is yours*. The other trust(s) belonged to your spouse, and you are taking care of the assets until you die.

My Spouse Has Died.
What Do I Need To Do?

- ☐ **Take Care of the Funeral.**
- ☐ **Find the Trust Document.**
- ☐ **Contact Attorney to Review Trust Document/Process.**
- ☐ **Order Death Certificates.**
- ☐ **Take Care of Ongoing Bills, Final Expenses.**
- ☐ **Put Together a Team of Advisors.**
- ☐ **Inventory Assets/Determine Current Values.**
- ☐ **Do Tax Planning.**
- ☐ **Apply for Benefits.**
- ☐ **Pay Bills.**
- ☐ **Make Special Gifts.**
- ☐ **Keep Things Organized for Your Successor Trustee(s).**

It may help to remember *why* you are doing this. Usually it's for keeping additional control over the assets and possibly to save taxes. And that's probably worth a little extra time and paperwork.

Keeping the trust assets separate and the bookkeeping up to date will be *tremendously* helpful when your successor trustee(s) steps in if you become incapacitated and when you die. If you don't do this, your successor trustee, your accountant and your attorney might be able to re-create the records—but just think how time consuming and expensive that would be. And if they *can't* recreate the records, all of that hard work could come undone.

By the way, this record keeping is required because of the extra planning—*not* because you have a living trust. If this planning had been done in a will, you would have to do it then, too—*and* you would have had to go through probate.

I'M THE SUCCESSOR TRUSTEE. WHAT ARE MY RESPONSIBILITIES?

If you have been named as successor trustee for someone—perhaps your spouse, parents or a good friend—you don't do *anything* until this person becomes incapacitated or dies. But you may be wondering what you need to do then.

You may not know very much about the trust—why it was set up, what it does, what your responsibilities will be. As a start, we suggest that you read this book to get an overview of the benefits of a living trust and how it works. The checklists which start on the next page will also be helpful.

The most important thing for you to remember as trustee is that *these assets are not yours*. You are safeguarding them for others—for your incapacitated spouse, parent(s) or good friend while they are living and later, until the assets are distributed after this person dies, for the beneficiaries. When you sign your name and conduct business, it will be as the trustee—not as you, personally.

As a trustee, you have certain responsibilities. For example:

- You must follow the instructions in the trust document.
- You cannot mix trust assets with your own. You will need to keep separate checking accounts and investments.
- You cannot use the trust assets for your own benefit.
- You must treat all beneficiaries the same. You cannot favor one over another.
- The trust assets must be invested in a prudent (conservative) manner, in a way that will result in reasonable growth with minimum risk.
- You are responsible for keeping accurate records, filing tax returns, and reporting to the beneficiaries as the trust requires.

As you can see, these responsibilities are based on common sense, especially when you keep in mind that a trustee is safekeeping assets for others. You are not required to do all of the accounting and investing yourself; you can have professionals help you if you wish.

The following checklists will help give you some direction at a time when you may not know where to begin.

I'M THE SUCCESSOR TRUSTEE. WHAT DO I DO AT THE GRANTOR'S INCAPACITY?

■ Oversee Care of Ill Person.

Make sure this person is receiving quality care in a supportive environment, and that the hospital or nursing home, physician(s) and staff are qualified. Check to make sure the insurance company has been notified.

Make sure the attending physician has a copy of the health care documents (durable power of attorney for health care, health care proxy, living will). If someone has been appointed to make health care decisions (agent), check to make sure he/she has been notified. If not, find the health care documents (they should be with the trust document) and give copies to the doctor and agent.

Offer to help notify this person's employer, friends, and relatives. If the person wrote a letter explaining what you should do at his/her incapacity (as we suggest), it may be very helpful.

■ Find the Trust Document.

Hopefully, you already know where it is. See if you will be able to write checks and sell assets with just your signature or if someone will be a co-trustee with you. If you have a co-trustee, notify him/her as soon as possible.

■ Notify the Attorney.

Notify the attorney who prepared the trust document. He/she should be aware of the incapacity in case you have any questions. You may also want to schedule an appointment to go over the trust and your responsibilities. Remember, you've probably never done this before, so you are bound to have some questions along the way. And it will be comforting for you to know there is someone you can call.

■ Find Out What the Insurance Covers.

Assuming the insurance will cover a certain procedure or facility could be a very costly mistake. Find out the alternatives before a major decision is made. If you need help understanding the coverage, the insurance agent or the person's personnel/benefits department may be able to help you. Most insurance companies also have a toll free telephone number you can call 24 hours a day if you have questions. If the person has long term care insurance, make sure you are familiar with the coverage if it turns out the incapacity will be lengthy.

■ Have Doctor(s) Document the Incapacity.

It may be necessary to have the appropriate physician(s) write a letter documenting the person's condition. Some trust documents will only require a letter from an M.D., some from one or two specialists, others require none. You will probably need to show this letter to the bank and others so you can sign checks and conduct business as trustee.

■ Look After Minors.

If there are any minor children, read the trust document for instructions for their care. If the incapacity is expected to be lengthy, a guardianship hearing will probably be required to officially appoint the guardian. The attorney can help you with this.

■ Become Familiar with the Finances.

You need to know what the assets are, where they are located, and their current values. You also need to know where the income comes from, how much it is, and when it is paid, as well as regular, ongoing expenses. You may need to put together a budget.

Familiarize yourself with any business dealings this person was involved with. If there is real estate, make sure you have keys, take care of utilities, etc. If this person owns a business, you will probably need to make arrangements for its continuation.

Hopefully, the person organized this information as we suggested. But if not, you'll need to start a list of the assets, where they are located, account numbers, current values, phone numbers, and your contact persons. The Organizer in the back of this book will be very helpful in this process.

If you don't know what assets this person has, the accountant, banker, broker, employer, adult children, and close friends may know. Look for bank and brokerage account statements. Is there a safe deposit box or a safe? Last year's income tax return may also be helpful.

If you find any assets that were not transferred to the trust, you can use the durable power of attorney to transfer them into the trust as soon as possible so they will not have to go through probate when this person dies. If you have any problems, contact the attorney who prepared the trust. Usually a phone call from the attorney will be all that is needed. Keep in mind, however, that an asset may have been intentionally left out of the trust. Check with the attorney *before* you transfer the asset.

■ Apply for Benefits.

Apply for any disability benefits through the employer, private insurance, Veteran's benefits, Social Security, etc.

■ Put Together Team of Advisors.

Depending on the values of the assets, and the expected length and severity of the incapacity, you will probably want to put together a team of professional advisors to help you. These will likely include the attorney, accountant, banker and/or trust officer, financial advisor, and insurance advisor. Be sure to talk to them *before* you sell *any* assets. There could be some tax consequences, and they may be able to suggest better alternatives.

■ Notify the Bank, Broker, Etc.

Notify the bank and others that you are now the trustee for this person. They will probably want to see a copy of the doctor's letter, trust document, and your personal identification.

Transact any necessary business for the incapacitated person. You can receive and deposit funds, pay bills (including mortgage and other obligations) and, in general, use the person's assets to take care of him/her until recovery or death. If you have any problems, a quick phone call from the attorney should straighten things out.

■ Take Care of Record Keeping and Accounting.

Keep careful records of medical expenses and file claims promptly. Keep a ledger of the bills you have paid and any income received. An accountant or bookkeeper can show you how to set up these records properly. (The trust document may require you to send accountings to the beneficiaries.)

Don't forget that income tax returns must be filed by April 15 each year. Contact the accountant early to find out what information he/she will need so you will have plenty of time to locate statements, etc. Also, find out when property taxes are due.

If, for whatever reason, these responsibilities prove to be too much, consider having a bookkeeper, accountant, or a corporate trustee help you. A corporate trustee can manage the investments and do the record keeping for you.

If you feel you simply cannot handle any of the responsibilities due to work, family demands, or any other reason, you can resign and let the next successor trustee step in. If no other successor trustee has been named, or none are willing or able to serve, a corporate trustee can usually be named.

I'm The Successor Trustee. What Do I Do at the Grantor's Incapacity?

- ☐ **Oversee Care of Ill Person.**
- ☐ **Find the Trust Document.**
- ☐ **Notify the Attorney.**
- ☐ **Find Out What the Insurance Covers.**
- ☐ **Have Doctor(s) Document the Incapacity.**
- ☐ **Look After Minors.**
- ☐ **Become Familiar with the Finances.**
- ☐ **Apply for Benefits.**
- ☐ **Put Together Team of Advisors.**
- ☐ **Notify the Bank, Broker, Etc.**
- ☐ **Take Care of Record Keeping and Accounting.**

I'M THE SUCCESSOR TRUSTEE. WHAT DO I DO AT THE GRANTOR'S DEATH?

The successor trustee has essentially the same duties as an executor named in a will. But if the titles and beneficiary designations have been changed to the trust, the probate court will not be involved. This means you will be able to act on *your* schedule, instead of the court's.

The trustee is responsible for seeing that everything is done properly and in a timely manner. You may be able to do much of this yourself, but an attorney, corporate trustee, and/or accountant can give you valuable guidance and assistance. The following checklist will give you an overview of what needs to be done.

■ Assist with the Funeral.
Inform the family of your position and assist them as needed with funeral arrangements, flowers, cemetery marker, announcement in paper, special wishes for service, notifying friends, relatives, employer, etc. If the person left instructions, this will be much easier on everyone.

■ Find the Trust Document.
Read it for any specific instructions, and to find out if you will be able to write checks and sell assets with just your signature. If there is a co-trustee, notify him/her as soon as possible.

■ Contact Attorney to Review Trust Document, Process.
Contact an attorney and schedule an appointment to go over the trust document, the assets, and your responsibilities as soon as possible. It will also be comforting for you to know there is someone you can call if you have questions. You do not have to use the attorney who prepared the trust, although he/she will probably be more familiar with the document.

If this person has a surviving spouse and the estate is more than the federal and/or state estate tax exemption or the trust document has an A-B or A-B-C provision, the attorney will need to do additional planning. For information about this process, read about tax planning under "My Spouse Has Died. What Do I Need To Do?"

■ **Keep Beneficiaries Informed.**

Give copies of the trust document to all beneficiaries, and make sure you keep them fully informed throughout the process.

■ **Order Death Certificates.**

Order at least 12 certified death certificates from the funeral home. You will need these to transfer titles, collect benefits, and conduct other business as trustee. Multiple copies will help speed things up, as you won't have to wait to get copies back in order to give one to someone else.

■ **Put Together Team of Advisors.**

Depending on the values of the assets, you may want to put together a team of professionals to advise you and the beneficiaries. These will likely include the attorney, accountant, banker and/or trust officer, financial advisor, and/or insurance advisor. Talk to them before you sell any assets or change any investments, as they will be able to give you valuable guidance and suggestions.

■ **Inventory Assets/Determine Current Values.**

Before you meet with the attorney, it would be a good idea to put together a preliminary list of the assets and their estimated values. Later on, you'll need to determine exact values for accounting and tax purposes.

The attorney, accountant, or trust officer will need this quick estimate to know which tax returns may need to be filed and to be able to advise you properly.

Determining the values of assets is also important because they receive a new basis when the owner dies. If assets have appreciated, this can save a considerable amount in capital gains tax when the assets are eventually sold. (Read "Inventory Assets/Determine Current Values" under "My Spouse Has Died. What Do I Need To Do?")

If the deceased was the second spouse to die, you will also need to know if the assets had been placed in multiple trusts for tax planning or other purposes.

Hopefully, the person organized this information as we suggested. But if not, you'll need to start a list of the assets, where they are located, account numbers, current values, phone numbers, and contact persons. You'll also need the actual title documents. (The Organizer in the back of this book will be helpful in this process.)

If you don't know what the assets are, the advisors, beneficiaries, and close friends of the deceased may be able to help. Look for bank and brokerage account statements. Is there a safe deposit box or a safe? Last year's income tax return may also be helpful.

If there is any real estate, make sure you have keys, the insurance is in force, and the mortgage is paid. Make arrangements to keep the utilities on (or turn them off), etc.

How to Determine Values

It is important that current values are appropriately determined; otherwise, the IRS will not accept them. The IRS has specific rules that must be followed in establishing "fair market value" when an estate tax return is required or when calculating basis for income tax purposes. In other words, a ballpark estimate by a neighbor who happens to be a real estate agent—or your own best guess—usually will not do.

A banker or investment advisor can provide you with the values of accounts on the day the person died. *The Wall Street Journal* for that day can also be a good source for values of stocks and mutual funds. Some items (especially real estate and collectibles) will need to be appraised, and this should be done as soon as possible. The attorney or a trust officer can recommend a reputable appraiser. There are also companies that do estate valuations; the attorney or trust officer will know about them, too.

■ Notify the Bank, Others.

Notify the bank, brokerage firm, and others that you are now the trustee. They will probably want to see a certified death certificate, a copy of the trust document (a certificate of trust may suffice), and your personal identification. Remember, you are conducting business as a trustee now—not as an individual—and you will sign checks and papers as the trustee.

■ Make Partial Distributions if Needed.

If the surviving spouse or other beneficiary needs money to live on, you can make some partial distributions. If the gross value of the estate is more than the federal or state estate tax exemption, check with the attorney before you make any distributions, especially within the first six months after the death. You'll want to make sure you keep enough to pay expenses (including taxes and known creditors). And be sure to have the beneficiary sign a receipt.

■ Collect Benefits.

Notify Social Security, life insurance companies, retirement plans, associations, and any others that will provide a death benefit. Put these in an interest bearing account (titled in the name of the trust) until distributed.

■ Take Care of Record Keeping/Tax Returns.

Keep good records of final medical and funeral expenses. (They may be deductible.) File medical claims promptly. Start a ledger of bills to be paid and income received.

Contact an accountant for preparation of the final income tax return as soon as possible. If the gross value of the estate is more than the federal estate tax exemption in effect at that time, or if portability is desired, a federal estate tax return (IRS Form 706) must be filed within nine months after the death. (An attorney or accountant with experience in federal estate taxes will be very helpful.) A state inheritance tax return may also have to be filed.

■ Pay Bills/Final Accounting.

Verify and pay all bills and taxes. Make a final accounting record of all assets and bills paid. Give a copy to all beneficiaries when assets are distributed.

■ Distribute Assets.

To distribute the assets, you will need to change titles from the trust to the beneficiaries (or to the trustee, if the assets are to stay in trust). Part Six will give you a general idea of how this is done. Basically, the process is reversed—instead of putting assets into the trust, you will be taking them out. Make sure you get a receipt signed by each beneficiary stating that he/she has received the assets.

Distribute the assets in the following order.

1. Assets on special gifts lists, if any.

2. Remaining personal property. Hold estate sale if necessary.

3. If there is a children's trust, transfer assets to the trustee.

4. If the assets are to be fully distributed, divide cash and transfer titles of assets according to trust instructions. Nothing else needs to be done. The trust has been dissolved.

5. If the assets are to stay in the trust and will be distributed to the beneficiaries later (for example, if the beneficiaries will receive their inheritances in installments), the trust will need a new tax identification number and proper bookkeeping and reporting procedures will need to be established. (If separate trusts are to be established, each will need its own tax ID number, and separate bookkeeping and reporting procedures will need to be followed.) Each year, the trust will file IRS Form 1041 and Form K1 to report any income earned.

It is very important that the bookkeeping be set up properly from the beginning, with a complete listing of the assets and their values. The trustee is responsible for accurate accounting. But, remember, that doesn't mean you have to do it all yourself. A bookkeeper, accountant, or corporate trustee can help. (A corporate trustee can invest the trust assets *and* do the accounting.)

If you feel you simply cannot handle these responsibilities due to work, family demands, or any other reason, you can resign and let the next successor trustee step in. If no other successor trustee has been named, or none are willing or able to serve, a corporate trustee can usually be named.

I'm The Successor Trustee.
What Do I Do at the Grantor's Death?

☐ **Assist with the Funeral.**

☐ **Find the Trust Document.**

☐ **Contact Attorney to Review Trust Document, Process.**

☐ **Keep Beneficiaries Informed.**

☐ **Order Death Certificates.**

☐ **Put Together Team of Advisors.**

☐ **Inventory Assets/Determine Current Values.**

☐ **Notify the Bank, Others.**

☐ **Make Partial Distributions if Needed.**

☐ **Collect Benefits.**

☐ **Take Care of Record Keeping/Tax Returns.**

☐ **Pay Bills/Final Accounting.**

☐ **Distribute Assets.**

Summary

We know that was a lot of information, but it should be very helpful to your family and/or successor trustee when something happens to you. And we hope the checklists have enlightened you and will help motivate you to continue putting things in order.

Remember, if your trust has been properly prepared and funded, it will work even if you don't do any of the things we have suggested in this section. However, if you take the time now to:

■ organize your financial information as we suggest,

■ make sure your spouse and/or successor trustee(s) know where this information and these checklists are, and

■ review your trust and information each year and keep it current, then you will be able to relax and get on with living, knowing you have done the best you can for the people you care about. And that will give you the best benefit of all—tremendous peace of mind.

Part Eight—

Income tax issues after you die

As we have explained, your living trust has no effect on your income taxes while you are living. You continue to report your income and pay taxes as you always have. As long as you are a trustee, you file your regular 1040, using your social security number.

But what happens *after* you die? Income that is earned on your assets from the time you die until the assets are distributed to your beneficiaries is still subject to income taxes. (This should come as no surprise. *Any* time income is earned, it is subject to taxes.) However, different tax rules apply during this time.

In the past, there were even different rules depending on whether the income was earned by assets in a trust or by assets in a probate estate. Most of these differences had little, if any, impact on most families. Even so, pro-trust attorneys pushed for several years to make the taxation of trusts and probate estates equal. Finally, in *The Taxpayer Relief Act of 1997*, the last remaining differences were all but eliminated.

In this section, we explain how income earned on your assets after you die will be taxed, how the rules were different, and how they are now virtually the same. If you plan to keep assets (and income) in your trust for some time after you die, you may want to read this section now. If not, you can probably skip over it for now and come back later if you want to. At least you know where to find the information if you need it.

INCOME TAX RATES FOR TRUSTS AND PROBATE ESTATES

At one time, the income received by some trusts and probate estates was taxed at a lower rate than income received by individuals. As a result, some people set up trusts specifically to save income taxes. Instead of the beneficiaries reporting the income and paying taxes at their higher rates, the trust reported the income and paid taxes at its lower rate. Naturally, Congress caught on and passed laws that increased the tax rates for trusts and probate estates.

So, now, the income received by many trusts (those in which the trustee can decide whether or not to distribute the income or to keep it in the trust) and the income received by *all* probate estates is taxed at a *higher* rate than the income received by most individuals.

In 2019, if one of these trusts, or a probate estate, has income over $9,300, the income will be taxed at a rate of 35%. If the income is over $12,750, the tax rate is 37%. To put this in perspective, the following chart shows the level of income when these rates apply for trusts and estates as compared to married taxpayers filing jointly and to single individual taxpayers.

Taxable Income Comparison (2019 Tax Rates)

Tax Rate	Level of Taxable Income Probate Estates & Trusts	Level of Taxable Income Married, Filing Jointly	Level of Taxable Income Single Individual
10%	$0 to $2,600	$0 to $19,400	$0 to $9,700
12%	N/A	$19,401 to $78,950	$9,701 to $39,475
22%	N/A	$78,951 to $168,400	$39,476 to $84,200
24%	$2,601 to $9,300	$168,401 to $321,450	$84,201 to $160,725
32%	N/A	$321,451 to $408,200	$160,726 to $204,100
35%	$9,301 to $12,750	$408,201 to $612,350	$204,101 to $510,300
37%	$12,751+	$612,351+	$510,301+

Because the tax rates apply to lower levels of their income, probate estates and trusts pay more in taxes than individuals on the income they receive after you die. As a result, most trustees will distribute the income to the beneficiaries or invest in assets that produce little, if any, income.

Now, remember, *these higher rates do not apply to your living trust while you are living*. They only apply *after* you die, *if* your assets are earning income and *if* the income stays in the trust.

In many cases, these higher tax rates will not apply after you die because the income will be distributed to the surviving spouse (for example, if you have a B Trust or C Trust) or to other beneficiaries. This is one reason why it is important to give the trustee some flexibility in how to distribute the income.

If, for some reason, you did not want the income distributed—for example, a beneficiary is a minor, is irresponsible, or has special needs—the trustee can avoid the higher tax rates by investing in tax-exempt investments or in assets that will appreciate in value but produce little, if any, income. This is why you want to give your trustee flexibility in how to invest the trust's assets.

These tax rates do not apply to your living trust while you are living

PREVIOUS INCOME TAX DIFFERENCES BETWEEN TRUSTS AND PROBATE ESTATES

Even though the tax *rates* are the same for trusts and probate estates, as we mentioned earlier there used to be some different rules for how the taxes were determined. Most families were not affected by these differences. Even so, in *The Taxpayer Relief Act of 1997*, the laws were changed to all but eliminate these differences and put trusts and probate estates on more equal footing.

Here is a brief summary of these issues—how they were different and, now, how they are virtually the same.

Living Trust Can Be Treated The Same As Probate Estate

One of the provisions in *The Taxpayer Relief Act of 1997* states that if the trustee of a revocable living trust decides it would be advantageous to have the trust treated as a probate estate for income tax purposes, the trustee (along with the executor, if any, of the probate estate) can choose to do so by making a one-time, irrevocable election.

If a probate is opened after you die (for example, if an asset was inadvertently left out of your trust or if a shorter creditor claims period is desired, as explained in Part Two), the election can be made during this proceeding.

If there is no need for a probate (for example, if no assets were left out of your trust or if a shorter creditor claims period is not needed), the general consensus is that the trustee should be able to make this election without having to open a probate.

Here's what you get if the trustee decides to have the trust treated as a probate estate for income tax purposes.

■ Calendar Year vs. Fiscal Year

With few exceptions, a trust has been required to report income on a calendar year basis (January 1 through December 31) just like most beneficiaries. A probate estate, however, can elect to report income on a calendar year *or fiscal* year basis. In other words, its year can be any 12-month period, as long as it ends at the end of a month. This often results in a short first year.

For example, let's say Grandpa dies on March 1, 2019. A fiscal year ending January 31 is chosen. So the first fiscal year will begin March 1, 2019 and end on January 31, 2020. The second year (and subsequent years, if his estate continues in probate) will be February 1-January 31.

In most cases, any income you receive in a calendar year must be reported on that year's tax return. But if an heir receives income from a probate estate that has elected a fiscal year, the heir may not have to report the income until the *following* year's tax return is filed.

In the example given above, the income the heirs receive between Grandpa's death and December 31, 2019 will not be reported by the heirs on their 2019 tax returns. That's because the estate does not report the income as having been distributed until the end of *its fiscal year*, which is January 31, 2020. The heirs, then, report the income they received from Grandpa's estate from March 1, 2019 through January 31, 2020 on their income tax returns for 2020—which are due the following April. So the heirs will not pay taxes on income they receive from the estate in 2020 until they file their tax returns in April, 2021.

The ability to choose a fiscal year over a calendar year sometimes gave a probate estate a slight advantage. However, in most cases, the ability to delay taxes on income for one year hardly justified having to go through probate.

Also, if the heirs were required to file quarterly income tax payments, they probably did not see much of a benefit because the estimated taxes had to be paid in the year the income was received.

Now, however, the trustee of a living trust can also have the option to elect a fiscal year.

■ Annual Personal Exemptions

A probate estate is entitled to a $600 annual exemption from income taxes—in other words, each year $600 of income produced by the assets in a probate estate are exempt from income taxes.

Generally speaking, if a trust is required to distribute all the income each year, it is allowed a $300 annual exemption. If the trust is not required to distribute all the income each year, it is allowed a $100 annual exemption. If the trust distributes any principal (regardless of whether it is required to distribute the income), it is only allowed a $100 annual exemption for that year.

Many trusts these days distribute the income, so you are only looking at a $300 difference in the amount of the exemption (when principal is not distributed). Even in a 37% tax bracket, that produces a tax savings of about $111 a year—a very insignificant savings compared to the expenses of probate.

Now, however, a living trust can be entitled to a $600 exemption if the trustee elects for the trust to be treated as a probate estate for income tax purposes.

■ Amounts "Set Aside" for Charity

In both a will and a trust, you can specify that a certain asset is to be given to a charity. Sometimes, the distribution may not occur immediately after you die, and the asset is "set aside" during the administration process (the time from the date you die until your assets are distributed).

Any income that is generated by the asset before it is distributed to the charity is not included in the taxable income of either the probate estate or the trust. However, if the asset is sold before it is transferred to the charity, the tax on the gain is handled differently for probate estates and trusts.

A probate estate can keep the gain in the estate until the administration is complete and the full proceeds from the sale are distributed to the charity. A trust, however, must distribute the gain to the charity in the year the asset is sold; otherwise, the trust will have to pay a capital gains tax on the gain.

The trustee of a living trust can now elect the same treatment as a probate estate.

■ Passive Losses on Rental Real Estate

While you are living, if your adjusted gross income (as defined on IRS Form 1040) is less than $150,000 and you actively participate in the management of rental real estate (approve repairs and new tenants, write checks, make management decisions, etc.), you can deduct up to $25,000 ($12,500 if married filing separately) in net losses each year from your ordinary income. (If your AGI is more than $100,000, the $25,000 is gradually phased out so that, by the time the AGI is $150,000, the amount of passive net losses that can be deducted from ordinary income is reduced to "0.")

A probate estate can continue to deduct these losses (up to $25,000 per year) for up to two tax years. If the surviving spouse also has rental real estate (separate property or property that was jointly owned), the $25,000 maximum will be reduced by the amount the spouse uses within the estate's tax year.

The trustee of your trust can now elect the same treatment as a probate estate. However, if the election is not made and the trustee actively participates in the management of the property as you did, it may still be possible for your trust to deduct from ordinary trust income the net losses that occur between the date of your death and when the property is transferred to your beneficiary(ies).

If that is not possible, the deductions still will not be lost—your beneficiary(ies) will be able to use them later. The net losses that occur between the time you die and when the property is distributed will be added to the cost basis of the property when it is distributed to your beneficiary(ies). So, when the property is sold, the cost basis will be higher. This means your beneficiary(ies) will have less profit (as far as the IRS is concerned) and will pay less in capital gains tax.

Other Differences Eliminated

Here are other differences that have been eliminated.

■ Sixty-Five Day Rule

This is a tax-planning opportunity that previously was available only to certain trusts—those that let the trustee decide whether to pay income to the beneficiaries or to keep the income in the trust. Basically, it gives the trustee 65 extra days in which to decide if it is better for the trust or for the beneficiaries to pay the income tax.

If the trustee realizes after the end of the year that the trust has too much income, the trustee has 65 days in the new year (until around March 5) to distribute income to the beneficiaries—and the income will be considered as having been distributed in the previous year.

Here's an example. In February 2020, while reviewing the 2019 year-end accounting for a trust, the trustee realizes that the trust has more than $12,750 in income and would have to pay income taxes at the highest tax rate (currently 37%). The beneficiaries, however, are in a lower tax bracket, so they would pay less in taxes if they had received the income. On February 28, 2020, the trustee distributes the income to the beneficiaries. As far as the IRS is concerned, the income was distributed to the beneficiaries on December 31, 2019. So the beneficiaries include this income on their 2019 tax returns.

This option is also available now to probate estates.

■ Throwback Rule Repealed

When trusts had a lower tax rate than individuals, it sometimes made sense to accumulate income in the trust from one year to the next, with the trust paying the income tax each year at its lower tax rate.

Of course, Uncle Sam wanted to make sure he received as much tax as possible. So, the purpose of the Throwback Rule was to make sure that when the income was eventually distributed, it would be "thrown back" and taxed as if the beneficiary had received it in the year it was earned. If it turned out that the trust had already paid *more* in income taxes than the beneficiary would have paid, Uncle Sam would not issue a refund.

This law applied only to trusts and not to probate estates. However, because the tax rates on trusts are now higher than those that apply to most individuals, there is no longer an advantage to accumulating income in a trust. In most cases, it made more sense to pay the income to the beneficiary in the year it was generated and have the beneficiary pay the tax—and not even deal with the Throwback Rule.

Congress agreed. This law was repealed for domestic trusts (except for certain trusts created before March 1, 1984) in *The Taxpayer Relief Act of 1997*.

■ Recognition of Losses

In the past, probate estates and trusts have handled losses on assets differently. For example, let's say you leave $25,000 to a beneficiary. Your trust says the beneficiary can receive this amount in cash or in assets of the same value. (This is called an "in kind" distribution.) The beneficiary decides on some stock that was valued at $30,000 when you died, but is now worth $25,000.

When the stock is distributed to the beneficiary, your trust cannot claim the $5,000 loss on its income tax return. But the deduction is not lost—the beneficiary will use it later. The $5,000 loss is added to the cost basis of the asset when it is distributed to the beneficiary. So instead of having a $25,000 cost basis, the cost basis is now $30,000.

If the beneficiary later sells the asset for, let's say, $40,000, the taxable gain will be $10,000 ($40,000 sales price less $30,000 cost basis equals $10,000 taxable gain). If the asset is sold at a loss, say $20,000, the beneficiary will be able to report the $10,000 capital loss on his/her income tax returns. (Up to $3,000 capital loss is allowed per year; the rest can be carried forward.)

By contrast, in a probate estate, when the stock was distributed the estate could take the $5,000 loss on its income tax return—or, in the final year of the probate, the loss could be distributed to the heirs so they could take it on their income tax returns.

The difference was that the probate estate could deduct the loss when the stock was distributed. But this meant all the heirs would share the loss (even though, in the example above, only one received the asset). With a trust, the beneficiary who receives the asset gets the full benefit of the loss (when it is added to the cost basis), but only *sees* the benefit when the asset is sold.

In *The Taxpayer Relief Act of 1997*, this law was changed so that probate estates now handle losses the same way as trusts—but *only* if the heir is to receive a *percentage* of assets (say, 10% of your stock portfolio). If the heir is to receive a *specific dollar amount* of assets, as in the example above, the old rules (as explained above) still apply. (This is called *tax simplification?!*)

Note that the law only changed how *losses in a probate estate* are handled. There was *no change* for trusts.

■ Gain on the Sale of Depreciable Assets

If you sell a depreciable asset for a price that is greater than its depreciated cost basis, the difference is a taxable gain.

For example, let's say you buy a car for business use for $30,000. Each year you own it, you depreciate its value on your income tax return by using the five-year double declining balance method (not claiming the Section 179 deduction). In the fifth year, you sell it for $17,500. In the four years you have owned it, you have depreciated $14,457 of its value, so its depreciated cost basis is now $15,543 ($30,000 purchase price less $14,457 in depreciation). You have a taxable gain of $1,957 ($17,500 sales price less $15,543 depreciated cost basis equals $1,957 taxable gain).

If a trustee sells a depreciable asset (or makes an exchange) to a beneficiary, any gain is taxed as ordinary income. If the executor for a probate estate did the same, the gain was taxed as capital gains income. However, if the trustee or the executor elected not to recognize the gain (which either one could do), the beneficiary would recognize the gain later when the asset was sold.

The reason for the different tax treatment was that, as far as the IRS was concerned, a trustee and the beneficiaries of the trust were and are considered "related parties," while a probate estate and the heirs were not.

In *The Taxpayer Relief Act of 1997*, this law was changed so that a probate estate and the heirs are also considered "related parties." So now the gain will be taxed the same way as in a trust (as ordinary income instead of capital gains)—but *only* if the heir is to receive a *percentage* of assets. If the heir is to receive a *specific dollar amount* of assets, as in this example, the old rules (as explained above) still apply.

Note that the law only changed how gains on depreciable assets are handled *in a probate estate*. There was *no change* for trusts.

■ Two-Year Exemption from Estimated Tax Payments

In the past, only a probate estate was allowed this exemption. But now, both probate estates and living trusts are exempt from having to make quarterly estimated tax payments for the first two years.

Summary

Income earned by your assets from the time you die until the assets are transferred to your beneficiaries is subject to income tax. While the tax *rates* are the same for trusts and probate estates, there used to be different rules for how the taxes were determined. Thanks to pro-trust attorneys who pushed for changes in the tax laws, those differences have been virtually eliminated.

Part Nine —

ADDITIONAL PLANNING STRATEGIES

You may be wondering, "Once I have a living trust, have I finished my estate planning?" The answer is, "Not necessarily." A living trust is the perfect foundation for most estate plans. And, packaged with the appropriate support documents (pour over will, durable power of attorney for asset management, and health care documents explained in Part Six), it *will* be all many families need.

However, depending on the size of your estate, the types of assets you own, your family situation, and your income and goals, your attorney may suggest some additional strategies to give you more control, create and preserve your wealth, and save you and your family as much as possible in taxes.

In this section, we provide an introduction to some situations that may warrant additional planning, and some popular and proven strategies that can help. The descriptions are intentionally brief and fairly general in nature. You will, of course, need to learn more about any strategies that interest you and how they would apply in your situation.

Most of these strategies are irrevocable, which means the documents usually cannot be changed after you have signed them. Having a trust protector (see Part Four) is especially important for irrevocable trusts, as this can make it possible to update the documents to accommodate changes in the law, change the trustee, and possibly even change the situs (location) of the trust. Even so, make sure you read the documents carefully and that you completely understand the strategies you are implementing.

With the gift and estate tax exemption at $11.4 million, there has never been a better time to use many of these strategies.

USING LIFE INSURANCE IN YOUR ESTATE PLAN

Part of the estate planning process includes reviewing the amount of life insurance you currently have and determining if more is needed to provide for your family the way you want. Your estate planning attorney and life insurance agent will work with you to help you achieve your goals.

Life insurance can replace an income stream, preserve assets, and/or create wealth for your dependents after you die. For example, life insurance proceeds can be used to:

- Pay final expenses, including medical, funeral, burial/cremation, etc.
- Pay off credit cards and other debts/loans.
- Pay off a mortgage.
- Replace the income you contribute to the household.
- Continue care for those for whom you provide care: your spouse, aging parents, children, pets, siblings, and others who depend on you.
- Pay college expenses for your children or grandchildren.
- Provide funds to replace a stay-at-home parent.
- Provide for a surviving spouse's retirement, medical, and possible long-term care expenses.
- Replace wealth following a sizeable charitable gift during life.
- Provide funds for a private (family) charitable foundation.
- Provide funds for a trust for future generations (dynasty trust).
- For business owners, fund a buy-sell agreement so that when one owner dies or becomes disabled, the other is able to buy the deceased owner's share of the business from his/her family.
- For business owners, create an inheritance for all children, including those not working in the family business.
- For business owners, fund a key man policy, insuring the life of an employee or partner who has a critical role in the business. If this person dies, money would then be available to continue the business while a replacement is found.
- If your estate is sizeable, life insurance can be used in a variety of planning techniques to create cash to pay estate taxes and fund other needs.

How Much Life Insurance Do You Need?

A simple calculation is to take the amount of income you want to replace and multiply it by the number of years you want to replace it. If you will be replacing your income, keep in mind that there will be no personal expenses for you—food, clothing, travel, insurance, taxes on your income—if you are not here. So instead of using the amount you earn, use the amount you actually contribute to your household. If the person to be insured is a stay-at-home parent and does not earn an income, estimate how much will be needed to pay someone to take over those responsibilities. You can use the same general calculation to determine how much insurance you need for other purposes.

Now, how long will you want to replace this income or provide this support? If you have young children, you probably want to provide for your family until they are grown and out of college. You may want your spouse to have enough to last until he/she can collect Social Security and other retirement benefits. You may want to provide for an elderly parent for as long as he or she is expected to live, or replace a key employee for just a couple of years.

As an example, let's say you are 40 and you want life insurance that will provide for your family for 25 years. Take the amount of annual income you want to replace, multiply by 25 (number of years), and multiply again by an assumed rate of inflation—that's how much life insurance you want. This amount, called the face value or death benefit, may be a pretty big number. So, now the issue becomes how much life insurance you can afford, and that will depend, in part, on the kind of life insurance you purchase.

What Kind of Life Insurance Should You Purchase?

Basically, there are two kinds of life insurance: term and permanent. (Permanent can include sub-categories like whole life, universal life, and variable universal life, but we will keep to a basic explanation of term and permanent.)

Term life insurance covers you for a set number of years, or a term. It is pure insurance, and is similar to the insurance you have on your car or home. It can be a good choice if you want coverage for a certain number of years—for example, until your kids are out of college or your mortgage is paid off. It is also generally less expensive than permanent insurance and is least expensive when you are young and healthy. For these reasons, term life insurance is a popular choice for young families.

Life insurance can help you provide for your family the way you want

229

Permanent life insurance, on the other hand, does not expire at the end of a specified term (assuming you continue to pay the premiums, of course). Generally, the coverage stays in effect during your lifetime and the premium, depending upon the type of policy, can either stay the same or fluctuate based upon the financial performance of the policy. Permanent policies also build cash value over time that can be borrowed from the policy (reducing the proceeds paid at your death), used to help pay the premiums, or refunded to you if you cancel the policy.

Depending on your needs and what you can afford, you may decide to go with some combination of the two. In any event, the amount you pay for life insurance must be an expense you can live with. Buying life insurance to provide for your family for 20 or 25 years may be out of the question, even with term insurance. A viable alternative is to cover five to seven years of expenses, which will give your family time to adjust and cope with your absence.

Be a careful consumer when buying insurance. You want to choose a reputable company that will be around when you die and will be able to pay the benefits. Look for a company that has top ratings from ratings companies like A.M. Best, Moody's, and Standard & Poor's.

Remember that illustrations are just that—illustrations. Premiums are based on your age, health, and assumed interest rates. If interest rates fall below a certain level, the insurance company may increase your premium. Check that the interest rates used in the illustrations are realistic. Also, some policies reduce the death benefit if you live beyond a certain age. Make sure you know how much the policy will pay, regardless of your age when you die.

Planning With Life Insurance

Life insurance proceeds are not subject to income taxes and were designed to be paid immediately in cash to the beneficiary upon the death of the insured without having to go through probate. However, as you now know, if the beneficiary designation is not valid or the beneficiary is a minor, incapacitated or deceased at the time, or if the beneficiary is "my estate," the proceeds will have to go through probate court proceedings.

Making your living trust the owner and beneficiary of your policies will give you more control over the proceeds than if they are paid to an individual beneficiary. Also, proceeds that are kept in a trust are protected from a beneficiary's creditors (bankruptcy and divorce proceedings), predators (those with undue influence) and irresponsible spending. But you already knew this, didn't you? See how much you are learning?

As you learned in Part Three, life insurance proceeds are generally included in your estate for estate tax purposes. With the federal estate tax exemption currently at $11.4 million, this is not a concern for most people. But if the amount of your life insurance pushes you beyond the federal estate tax exemption (or beyond your state's exemption), or if you want maximum control over the policy and proceeds, your attorney may recommend that you have an irrevocable life insurance trust for your insurance policies.

An irrevocable life insurance trust gives you more control and, if needed, saves estate taxes

IRREVOCABLE LIFE INSURANCE TRUST

An irrevocable life insurance trust gives you maximum control over the policies and their proceeds and, if needed, can save estate taxes so more of your estate can go to your loved ones. Here's how it works.

The trustee you select (it must be someone other than you) purchases an insurance policy with you as the insured and the trust as owner and beneficiary. The trustee makes sure the trust is administered correctly and that the premiums are paid on time. After you die, the trustee collects the proceeds, makes them available to pay expenses, and distributes them to the trust's beneficiaries as your trust document directs.

For example, you could allow the trustee to make the funds available to provide a loan to, or purchase assets from, your living trust so that cash is available to pay expenses without having to liquidate other assets. Expenses could include debts, legal fees, estate taxes, and income taxes that might be due on IRAs and other retirement benefits. If you provide periodic income to your children or other loved ones—without giving them the full amount—money that remains in the trust would be protected from creditors, predators and irresponsible spending.

The way the trustee purchases a new policy must be done in a special way so you don't incur a gift tax. Each year, you can make an annual tax-free gift (explained next) to each beneficiary of the insurance trust. But instead of giving this money directly to the beneficiaries, you give it to the trustee *for* them.

The trustee then notifies each beneficiary that a gift has been received on his/her behalf and, unless the beneficiary elects to receive the gift now, the trustee will invest the funds—by paying the premium on the insurance policy. Of course, for this to work, the beneficiaries must understand not to take the gift now. (By the way, the written notification to the beneficiaries is known as a "Crummey letter," named after the man who first tested it with the IRS.)

Because a life insurance trust owns your insurance policies *for* you, instead of you personally owning them, the insurance will not be included in your taxable estate. This reduces your taxable estate and any resulting estate taxes. An insurance trust will also let you provide your spouse with lifetime income and keep the proceeds out of *both* of your estates.

Existing policies can also be transferred into an insurance trust. But if you die within three years of making the transfer, the death benefits of the policies will be included in your estate, possibly making them subject to estate taxes. There may also be a gift tax.

Alternatively, another person (like your spouse or an adult child) could own your insurance for you. This would also keep the insurance out of your taxable estate. But you would not have as much control because this person could change the beneficiary, take the cash value, or even cancel the policy.

Gift Tax Planning

Whether you are married or single, you can start giving away some of your assets *now* to the people or organizations who will eventually receive them after you die. This is an excellent way to reduce estate taxes because you are reducing the size of your taxable estate. But often more satisfying is that you can see the results of something that may not have happened without your help. Of course, any gifting program needs to be done with professional assistance. Also, make sure you don't give away too much!

Tax-Free Gifts
Each year, you can make as many tax-free gifts to as many recipients as you wish, as long as the amount does not exceed the limit set by Congress. In 2019 the amount is $15,000. If you are married, you and your spouse can *each* make annual tax-free gifts. For example, in 2019 you and your spouse can each give

$15,000 to your three children and five grandchildren—a total of $240,000 ($15,000 to eight people by two givers). If you want to give noncash assets like stock or real estate, you can gift shares over time to avoid going over the limit. You can also give an *unlimited* amount for tuition and medical expenses if you give directly to the educational organization or health care provider.

As long as the gift is within these limits, you don't have to report it to Uncle Sam. Just the same, it's a good idea to get appraisals (especially for real estate) and document these gifts in case the IRS later tries to challenge the values.

What if you want to give someone *more* than the tax-free amount in one year? You can—it just starts using up your federal estate tax exemption. That's because the federal estate tax exemption is a *combined* gift and estate tax exemption. Under current law, it's the same tax. If you transfer the asset while you are living, it's called a *gift* tax. If the transfer is made after you die, it's called an *estate* tax. So you can either use part or all of the exemption now while you are living, or you can use it later after you die. With the exemption at $11.4 million, many professionals recommend using it to make substantial gifts now.

If your gift exceeds the annual tax-free limit, you need to let Uncle Sam know by filing an informational gift tax return (IRS Form 709) for the year the gift is made. The gift is applied against your federal gift and estate tax exemption, and you only pay a gift tax after you have used up your exemption.

The amount of tax-free gifts has been tied to inflation since January 1, 1999. However, the amount will only increase in increments of $1,000, and it will be rounded *down* instead of up. So, for example, if adjustments for inflation would increase the current amount to $15,999, it would remain at $15,000. This chart shows how the amount for tax-free gifts has increased in recent years.

You can make annual tax-free gifts to as many recipients as you wish

Recent Historical Annual Tax-Free Gifts

Year	Amount
1997-2001	$10,000
2001-2005	$11,000
2006-2008	$12,000
2009-2012	$13,000
2013-2017	$14,000
2018-2019	$15,000

Pay The Tax Now—And Save

After your combined federal gift and estate tax exemption is used up, you will have to pay a gift tax if you make any more taxable gifts (currently, those more than $15,000) while you are living. Or, you could wait and have your estate pay an estate tax after you die. The tax rate is the same, whether you pay it now or after you die. But it costs you less to pay the gift tax now than to pay the estate tax after you die.

As explained in Part Three, after you die, taxable gifts you have made since 1976 are added back into your estate before estate taxes are calculated. The amount you have paid in gift taxes is then subtracted from the estate taxes due. (Think of the gift tax as a prepayment of the estate taxes you will owe.)

The amount you've already paid in gift taxes is not in your taxable estate when you die. You've already paid it to Uncle Sam. Making the gift now lets you forever remove the amount paid in gift tax from your taxable estate.

If you keep the asset in your estate until you die, the amount you would have paid in gift taxes is still in your estate. This makes your taxable estate larger and increases the amount of estate taxes your estate will have to pay. Keeping the asset in your estate until after you die forces you to pay estate taxes on the amount you would have paid in gift tax. In effect, you're paying a tax on the tax.

This is best explained with an example. Let's assume you have used up your federal gift and estate tax exemption through prior gifts and, as a result, your estate is now subject to the 40% gift and estate tax.

If you give your children $1 million as a gift (while you are living), the gift tax will be $400,000 ($1 million times .40 = $400,000). You, the donor, pay the gift tax. Your children would receive the full $1 million, and an additional $400,000 would be removed from your taxable estate to pay the gift tax. So, it would cost you $400,000 to give your children $1 million.

But if you wait until after you die, it would take $1,666,667 to leave them $1 million. That's $266,667 more than if you gave them the $1 million while you were living. (To determine the amount needed after death, divide the gift amount by the inverse of the tax rate: $1 million divided by .6 = $1,666,667.)

There is an exception of which you need to be aware. Any gifts you make within three years of your death will be included in your estate—and so will any gift tax you pay on them. This is to prevent you from making enormous gifts from your deathbed so you can get the gift tax out of your estate. (Yes, Uncle Sam already figured out that one.)

Appreciating assets are the best to give

Which Assets Are The Best To Gift?

It can be especially smart to give away assets that are appreciating in value, because any income and appreciation that occur after the gift is made are also removed from your taxable estate.

But you also have to look at the estate tax savings compared to what the recipient may have to pay in capital gains tax if the asset is later sold. Remember, when you give away an appreciated asset, it keeps your original cost basis (plus any gift tax paid). And if the recipient decides to sell it, he/she will have to pay capital gains tax on the difference between the selling price and what you paid for it.

If you don't give it away and it stays in your estate, the asset will receive a full step up in basis as of the date of your death (saving capital gains tax). But, depending on the size of your estate when you die, there may be estate taxes. So it's a trade off.

Currently, the federal long-term capital gains rate (for assets held longer than 12 months) is 20%, while the estate tax rate is 40%. (The Medicare surtax on investment income, explained next, can increase the top capital gains rate to 23.8% if it applies.) But it isn't always better to give away an asset and let the recipient pay the lower capital gains tax. Among other things, consider what you paid for the asset, what it's worth now, what you think it will be worth when you die, and if the recipient plans to sell or keep it.

Making Gifts From Your Living Trust

You may have heard that you should remove an asset from your living trust *before* making the gift. For example, if you wanted to give your son a $5,000 gift in cash and your checking account is titled in the name of your trust, you would make the check payable to yourself, cash it, then make the gift in cash or use a cashier's check.

That's because, in the past, if the grantor died within three years of making a gift directly from his/her living trust, the IRS tried to include the gift—even annual tax-free gifts—in the grantor's taxable estate.

You don't have to do this anymore. *The Taxpayer Relief Act of 1997* says that gifts made directly from a revocable living trust are considered the same as if they were made directly from you, even if they are made within three years of your death.

INCOME TAX PLANNING

The Tax Cuts and Jobs Act of 2017 (TCJA), which President Trump signed into law December 22, 2017, significantly changes the federal estate/gift tax exemptions. TCJA also significantly changed income rates and, in many cases, lowered deductions for high income taxpayers and trusts. In addition, the Medicare surtaxes of *The Affordable Care Act of 2010*, which went into effect in 2013, remain. As a result, you now likely need *income* tax planning as much as, or more than, *estate* tax planning!

Here is a brief summary of what you need to know. It is important to realize that, while you may usually have an average income, a one-time event like the sale of a business, farm, or investment property could push you into the highest tax rates and deduction limitations.

■ Federal taxation continues to be based on adjusted gross income (AGI), rather than *taxable* income which is lowered by deductions. AGI is the last line on page one of your Form 1040 or 1041 tax return. It includes wages and salaries, capital gains, income from business entities as reported on Schedule C, and income reported on K-1s and 1099s.

■ The top federal income tax rate is 37%. In 2019, it applies to married taxpayers filing jointly with AGI above $612,350; $510,300 for single taxpayers; and $12,750 for trusts and estates. These "threshold amounts" are indexed for inflation. (There are different thresholds for heads of household and married filing separately.)

■ State and local income taxes can push rates higher. For example, in Cali-

You may now need income tax planning more than estate tax planning

fornia the top combined income tax rate is nearly 54%. In New York City, the combined top rate for federal, state and city income tax is nearly 56%.

■ Capital gains and dividends are taxed at 20% if, when added to other taxable income, they push you beyond these AGI thresholds. If you are subject to the 3.8% Medicare surtax on investment income (explained below), the capital gain rate increases to 23.8%.

■ The standard deduction increases in 2019 to $24,400 for married couples filing jointly. Therefore, far fewer Americans will benefit from itemized deductions (including mortgage interest and charitable deductions). For those who do itemize, the so-called "SALT" (state and local tax) deduction, which includes state taxes, local taxes and real estate taxes paid, is capped at $10,000 for both single and married filing jointly filers. This will have a significant impact on the deductions of those living in high state income tax or real estate tax states. However, the use of certain types of trusts may allow you to double, triple or even quadruple the $10,000 SALT limitation.

■ Miscellaneous itemized deductions in excess of 2% of AGI, and the casualty/theft loss deduction (except for President-declared disasters) are also eliminated.

■ In 2019, the medical expense deduction floor returned to 10% of AGI from 7.5% of AGI for all taxpayers This means a family with $100,000 AGI will now have to have more than $10,000 in medical expenses, instead of $7,500, before they can take any as itemized deductions.

Medicare Surtaxes on Earned Income and Investment Income

These are part of *The Affordable Care Act of 2010* and both went into effect in 2013. The .09% surtax on earned income applies to wages and self-employment income above modified adjusted gross income that exceeds $250,000 for married taxpayers filing jointly and $200,000 for single filers. (There are different thresholds for heads of household and married filing separately.)

The 3.8% surtax on investment income applies to the *lesser* of total net investment income and a modified AGI over these same thresholds. It also applies to trusts and estates if the net investment income is more than $12,500 and is not paid out to the beneficiaries. (Net investment income is total investment

Traditional income tax planning may not work now

income less allocable expenses. Modified AGI is adjusted gross income plus the net foreign income exclusion amount.)

To see if this applies to you, first look at your modified AGI.

- If your modified AGI is *less than or equal to* your threshold amount for this tax (above, based on your filing status), no surtax will be due, regardless of the amount of your investment income.

- If your modified AGI is *more than* your threshold amount, the 3.8% surtax will be due on 1) the amount of adjusted gross income over the threshold amount *or* 2) net investment income, *whichever is less.*

Here are some examples, which may help to clarify it a bit more:

- A married couple filing jointly has $270,000 in salaries and $50,000 in net investment income, resulting in adjusted gross income of $320,000 — $70,000 over their threshold amount. Because their net investment income is less than the amount over their threshold, they will pay $1,900 in surtax on the $50,000 of investment income (3.8% of $50,000 = $1,900).

- A trust has net investment income of $200,000 but it distributes all of the income to the beneficiaries. The trust will not pay a surtax, and each trust beneficiary will count the income distribution toward his or her own surtax calculation.

Planning Opportunities

Given these changes, traditional income tax planning strategies may not work as well as they have in the past. For example, it may be better to pay income taxes now and invest in a Roth IRA instead of delaying taxes on earned income through 401(k)s and IRAs. The creation of an entity like a family limited liability company (explained later in this section) may help shift income to family members in a lower tax bracket and allow for the deduction of medical expenses and insurance that are no longer deductible on a personal return. An installment sale of a business or real estate may also make sense.

Your CPA and your attorney can work together to find the best solutions for you. Fortunately, many estate planning professionals have also become highly proficient in income tax planning. And, as you will see, many of the planning strategies in this section can help save both income and estate taxes.

CHARITABLE REMAINDER TRUST

You might be interested in a charitable remainder trust if you own investment assets that have appreciated significantly since you purchased them and you would like to enjoy the profits—but you have been hesitant to sell the assets because you would have to pay capital gains tax.

When you set up a charitable remainder trust, you transfer the appreciated asset to an irrevocable trust. You receive a charitable income tax deduction, reducing your current income taxes. The asset is also removed from your estate, so estate taxes (if applicable) are reduced when you die.

The trustee then sells the asset at full market value—paying no capital gains tax—and reinvests in income-producing assets. Typically, for the rest of your life, the trust pays you an income. Alternatively, the trust can be set up to exist for a set number of years, up to 20. When you die, the remaining trust assets will go to one or more charities you have chosen. That's why it's called a charitable *remainder* trust.

Of course, this means that your children or other beneficiaries will not receive this asset when you die. If you are concerned about this, you can use the income tax savings and part of the income you receive from the charitable remainder trust to fund an irrevocable life insurance trust. The trustee can then purchase enough life insurance to replace the full value of the gifted asset.

CHARITABLE LEAD TRUST

A charitable lead trust is, in some ways, similar to a charitable remainder trust. But with a charitable lead trust, the charity receives the income and your beneficiaries will eventually receive the principal. And because the beneficiaries must wait a while before they can receive the asset, its value is reduced for gift tax purposes. So you will pay substantially less in gift tax than if you left the asset to them outright. Also, when you transfer the asset to the trust, it is removed from your taxable estate, potentially saving estate taxes.

A charitable lead trust would be appealing if you currently do not need the income, or if you have current charitable commitments you would like to continue in the future, and you want someone other than the charity (perhaps your spouse, children or grandchildren) to eventually have the assets.

Jacqueline Kennedy Onassis included a charitable lead trust provision in her estate plan. The assets in the trust would benefit charities for 24 years, then go to her grandchildren. Unfortunately (for the charity), the trust was optional, and no assets were transferred into it. However, had her beneficiaries utilized this strategy, it would have eliminated her estate tax completely. (This strategy uses a formula to eliminate the estate tax so it works for estates of any size.)

PRIVATE CHARITABLE FOUNDATION

Instead of giving your tax money to Uncle Sam and letting Congress decide how to spend it, you can set up your own charitable foundation, donate your assets to it, and keep some control over how the money is spent. (The IRS does have restrictions on how the money is used.) You can also fund it with a life insurance policy on your life.

You can set up the foundation while you are living, or it can be established after you die. To qualify, a small percentage of the trust assets must be distributed to charity each year. But you can name whomever you wish to run the foundation—including your children—and the foundation can pay them a reasonable salary. You can be very specific about which charities you want to support, or you can leave that up to the trustees of the foundation to decide (within the IRS guidelines, of course).

The tax benefits of setting up your own foundation can be substantial—you can save estate, capital gains, and ordinary income taxes:

- The assets you give to the foundation will be removed from your taxable estate. So, for example, if you give your entire estate to the foundation (or the entire amount over the estate tax exemption), your estate will pay no estate taxes.
- There will be no capital gains tax when the assets are sold by the foundation, so it's great for appreciated assets.
- If you donate publicly traded securities to a private foundation, you can receive a charitable income tax deduction for their full fair market value—up to 30% of your adjusted gross income. (The deduction is less than the

50% limit for standard charitable contributions because this is a *private* charitable foundation.)

Other Forms of Charitable Giving

Charitable giving has benefits for you and the charity

Here are some other ways to make charitable gifts that may appeal to you.

Donor Advised Fund

These are quickly becoming a favorite among charitable donors, and it's easy to understand why. A donor advised fund is established through a public charity. It's like having your own charitable bank account. You open an account in the fund, make contributions to it, and receive an immediate charitable income tax deduction. Your contributions are invested and grow tax free. Then, over time, you recommend that grants be made from your account to qualified charities.

The gifts you make to the donor advised fund are irrevocable, and once made, the fund owns the assets. (That's why you recommend the grants instead of making them yourself, although typically the fund honors your request.) If you give appreciated assets, there will be no capital gains tax when the assets are sold, so the fund receives the full value of your gift.

You can make contributions as often as you wish, and you can recommend grants to as many charities as you wish, often with the ability to remain anonymous if you prefer. There is professional asset management for your account and you can direct how its assets are invested. You can also name successors to continue family involvement. Usually the sponsoring charitable organization prepares the paperwork, providing both cost savings and convenience.

Pooled Income Fund

You may be interested in a pooled income fund if you do not have sufficient assets to contribute to a charitable remainder or lead trust, or if you would prefer to make smaller contributions over a period of time. You make these contributions directly to the charity and the charity will "pool" your contributions with others and invest them together. Your contributions then become shares of the fund (similar to a mutual fund). You or a designated beneficiary will receive a lifetime income from the fund. When the last beneficiary dies, your shares will transfer to the charity. Your gifts can be made in cash, stock, or bonds, and you will receive an income tax deduction in each year you make a contribution.

Gift Annuity

With a gift annuity, you (or whomever you name as beneficiary) will receive a guaranteed income for life in exchange for making a direct gift to a charity. The gift can be in cash, real estate, or another asset. The income will be paid in the form of an annuity, which means each payment you receive will be for the same dollar amount. Part of each payment is a return to you of your gift (the principal), so only a portion is taxable as ordinary income.

You can begin receiving the income immediately when the gift is made or the income can be delayed until a later date (usually at retirement, when your income and income tax bracket are lower). If the income is delayed, this is called a deferred gift annuity. Under this option, the income will be higher because the original investment will have time to grow. Regardless of when the income begins, you can take a charitable income tax deduction in the year you make the gift. Upon your death or the death of the last beneficiary, the charity will keep the remaining principal and any undistributed income.

Life Estate

This is an arrangement through which you can give a portion or all of your home, vacation home, or farm to the charity of your choice while you are living. Until your death, you continue to enjoy the property as if you still own it—you can live on it, take care of it, and keep any income it may generate. You would consider this option if you were planning to give the property to the charity after your death, but wanted to take the charitable income tax deduction while you are alive. You may also save on estate taxes by removing the property from the value of your estate.

Conservation, Mineral, And/Or Use Rights

You can give a charity the right to use property for a certain number of years as a public park, a wildlife refuge, an historic landmark, etc. Or you could give away just the mineral rights to a parcel of real estate and keep the land in your family. The tax advantages of this type of gift are generally less than others mentioned here.

Personal Property

You may have certain investments or valuables (for example, artwork, musical instruments, books) that you want to give to a charity—not to have them sold and the proceeds re-invested, but to have them be enjoyed as you have enjoyed them. For you to receive a charitable income tax deduction, the gift must be related to the charity's tax-exempt purpose—for example, giving artwork, antiques, or jewelry to a museum; books to a university or library; musical instruments to a symphony; and so on.

Insurance

This is often an overlooked gift. You can give an old policy to a charity, making it both the owner and beneficiary. Or you can work with a charity and have it purchase a new policy on your life (the charity should be the applicant, owner, and beneficiary). In either case, you can receive a charitable income tax deduction.

Qualifying The Charity/Finalizing The Gift

You will want to make sure the organization meets the IRS guidelines as a "qualified" charity. Otherwise, you could lose the tax advantages. The IRS publishes a list of qualified charities and their tax status, which determines the amount of the income tax deduction. The charity will also have a *determination letter* from the IRS which verifies its tax status.

You may want to research an organization before finalizing your gift. One source of information is www.CharityNavigator.org. Another is the National Charities Information Bureau. Both evaluate many local and national not-for-profit organizations.

Your attorney can help you evaluate which charitable options would be best for you and make sure the documentation is prepared properly. Check that the document contains the correct legal name and specific location of the organization that will receive the gift.

It is also a good idea to discuss a potential gift with the charitable organization while you are in the planning stages; they will be able to give you and your attorney some insight and suggestions on how a gift may be most useful to them. You may also want to designate a successor charitable beneficiary in case your first choice ceases to exist.

You may want to research charities before making a gift

LIMITED LIABILITY COMPANY (LLC) FAMILY LIMITED PARTNERSHIP (FLP)

Both a limited liability company and a family limited partnership let you remove assets (like a family business, farm, stocks, real estate, or insurance) and any future appreciation on these assets from your taxable estate *without* giving up control. These entities can be especially useful when real estate or a family business might otherwise have to be liquidated to pay estate taxes or you want to protect the assets from future lawsuits and creditors. (They are often used in asset protection planning, as explained later in this section.)

When you establish the LLC or FLP, you transfer assets into it in exchange for ownership shares. Though you have a fiduciary obligation to the other owners, you keep control of the limited liability company (as the manager) or the family limited partnership (as the general partner). You determine how the assets are managed, when income is distributed, and how the entity is run.

Over time, you can give ownership interests to your children and other family members, which removes value from your estate. These ownership interests cannot be sold or transferred without your approval, and because there is no market for these shares, their value is highly discounted. (What would someone pay for minority shares in assets over which they would have no control?) This allows you to transfer these assets to your children, removing them from your taxable estate, at a discounted value—without losing control.

If you gift shares in increments equal to the amount of annual tax-free gifts, there is no gift tax. Larger gifts can be applied to your federal estate tax exemption. Because you are making gifts based on current value—not the appreciated value when you die—this lets you, in effect, freeze the value of these assets at the time the gifts are made.

Both an LLC and an FLP give you more control than a corporation, in which even minority stockholders (either your children or their creditors) can have substantial voting rights and can force sales, distributions, or even liquidations. If a creditor is allowed to place a lien on a member's interest through a *charging order*, the creditor has no more rights than the debtor-member and will have to wait for any income distributions—which you control.

If you and your attorney are considering an LLC or FLP, be sure to consider where you establish it, as some states have more favorable laws than others. For example, Wyoming (which invented the LLC) has enacted what it considers to be the country's strongest protections against creditor claims for multi-member LLCs and single-member LLCs. It also has no state income, inheritance, gift, inventory, use, or intangibles taxes, making it a very friendly business state. Residents of any state can establish a Wyoming LLC—you just need to have a registered agent in the state of Wyoming to represent your LLC. Other popular states include Nevada, Delaware, and South Dakota.

QUALIFIED PERSONAL RESIDENCE TRUST

A qualified personal residence trust lets you continue to live in your home but transfer it to your children now so you will save estate taxes when you die.

When you set up a personal residence trust, you transfer your home or vacation home to an irrevocable trust. For a specified period of time (often 10 to 15 years), you retain the right to use and live in the residence. After that time, the residence transfers to your beneficiaries (usually your children). In effect, you are giving your home to your children today. But because your children will not receive it until sometime in the future, the value of this gift is reduced. This uses less of your federal gift and estate tax exemption than if you had kept the home (and any future appreciation) in your estate.

If you die before the term of the trust is over, there is no penalty—your home will just be included in your taxable estate, which is what would happen anyway without the trust. If you live longer than the duration of the trust and want to keep living there, you will have to pay rent at fair market value. Under this arrangement, the house will not receive a stepped-up basis when you die. So you will want to see whether it's better for your beneficiaries to save the capital gains taxes or to save the estate taxes.

GRANTOR RETAINED ANNUITY TRUST (GRAT)
GRANTOR RETAINED UNITRUST (GRUT)

GRATs and GRUTs are similar to a qualified personal residence trust. The main difference is that a GRAT or GRUT lets you transfer *any* asset—not

245

just your home—out of your taxable estate. And, with a GRAT or GRUT, you receive an income, instead of continuing to live in your home, for a set number of years.

When you set up a GRAT or GRUT, you transfer an income-producing asset (like a family business, stocks or real estate) into an irrevocable trust for a set number of years. During this time, the trust pays you an income.

If the income you receive is a set dollar amount and does not fluctuate each year, the trust is a GRAT (grantor retained *annuity* trust). If the income is a percentage of the trust assets and the amount of income you receive fluctuates each year, the trust is a GRUT (grantor retained unitrust).

At the end of the trust term, the asset will be owned by the beneficiaries of the trust (usually your children) and will not be included in your estate when you die. However, if you die before the trust term is over, the asset will be taxed as part of your estate.

Like the personal residence trust, the beneficiaries will not receive the asset until sometime in the future (when the trust term is over). So the value of the gift you are making (transferring the asset to the trust is considered a gift) is reduced. This uses less of your federal gift and estate tax exemption than if you had kept the asset and any future appreciation in your estate.

Various forms of GRATs and GRUTs are often used in business succession planning as a means to transfer a family business to the next generation and provide the departing owner with retirement income.

BUSINESS SUCCESSION PLANNING

Small businesses, those that have less than 500 employees, are the heart of America. In fact, they comprise over 99% of all American businesses. Some day, all of the owners of these businesses will exit their businesses due to retirement, incapacity, or death. But most owners are so busy working that they don't take the time to think about business succession and estate planning issues. That is the primary reason that only about 30% of all family-owned businesses survive to the next generation; only 12%

make it to the third generation; and a meager 3% are functioning into the fourth generation and beyond.

If you are a business owner, you may wonder if you can ever retire, who could possibly take over your business, if you can receive retirement income without going out of business, and what would happen to your business and your family should you become incapacitated and when you die. But there is much you can do to build your business and prepare for its succession if you start planning now, before something happens to you.

No one professional has all the answers. In business succession planning, you will get the best results (and probably save time and money) by working with a team of advisors who can bring their own areas of expertise. Your team may include your accountant/CPA, financial planner, insurance advisors, investment advisor, business attorney, estate planning attorney, valuation specialist, and a business broker if an imminent sale of the business is desired.

Your team will help you determine and work toward your long-term goals. These may include building and preserving the value of the business; exchanging that value for cash with the least amount in taxes; leaving a legacy or making a charitable donation; shifting wealth to your children; rewarding key employees; selling the business at your exit or keeping it in the family.

Most owners have no idea what their business is worth, so a professional valuation is usually the first step. This will help with projecting cash flow, estate and gift tax planning, determining how much insurance may be needed for various purposes, retirement planning, and so on. This also helps you and your advisors monitor progress as you work toward your objectives.

Growing your business and protecting its value will maximize the amount you will be able to receive from it. It can take seven to ten years of proactive planning to successfully prepare a business for sale to an outside party. It can also take years to select and groom an internal successor, whether a family member or a key employee.

During this time, your advisors may suggest that you increase cash flow, develop operating systems, improve company performance, and pay down debt. You may need to restructure the organization, diversify your customer base,

All business owners will eventually leave due to retirement, incapacity, or death

create and protect proprietary technology or trademarks, build a management team, and prepare your successor.

Depending on your situation, other specific recommendations may include:
- Asset protection planning (see below).
- Creating a buy/sell agreement with other owners, funded with life insurance. When one owner dies, the remaining owners are able to use the proceeds to buy the deceased owner's share of the business from the family.
- Purchasing life insurance on the life of an employee who has a critical role in the business. If this person dies, money would be available to continue the business while a replacement is found.
- Using life insurance to provide an inheritance for your children who are not interested in continuing in the business.

Remember, you are preparing for the time when you will not be running the business. You want it to be able to survive without you—whether it continues in your family or with a new outside owner. By starting to plan now, your advisors can help you shift your focus from how much you are making today to the future rewards you can build for your family and your retirement.

ASSET PROTECTION PLANNING

Asset protection planning has proved especially valuable for those who are in professions in which they are likely to be sued. These include health care professionals, physicians, dentists, lawyers, accountants, and sometimes those involved with business enterprises that pertain to health care, such as skilled nursing facilities and assisted living facilities. Entrepreneurs and those in construction (builders, developers, architects) may also be concerned about protecting their assets from lawsuits.

But it is important to realize that all of us are exposed to potential lawsuits that can result from car accidents, accidents in the home, and our children's behavior. Most of us know someone who had a problem and lost everything. Asset protection planning is also important to prevent the loss of family assets due to divorce.

Asset protection planning is not about hiding assets. It is about using existing laws appropriately to obtain the best possible protection for assets. The best time to plan is before a claim arises, as it is highly important to avoid fraudulent transfers. But even with an existing claim, some planning options may still be available.

Asset protection planning can potentially save money by reducing the need for large amounts of insurance, and eliminating your insurance "deep pockets" can go a long way toward discouraging lawsuits.

All of us are exposed to potential lawsuits

Strategies In Asset Protection Planning

Malpractice insurance is always the first line of defense for professionals. For the rest of us, having personal liability insurance (an umbrella policy) is a good first step. Then, depending on your situation, your attorney may recommend a combination of strategies. Here is a brief introduction to some of them, going from simplest to most advanced.

- Use exemptions. Certain assets are automatically protected by state and federal exemptions. State exemptions will vary, but may include personal property, life insurance, annuities, IRAs, homestead, and forms of joint ownership. Federal exemptions include ERISA, which covers 401(k)s, pension, and profit sharing plans.

  Sometimes it is possible to convert a non-exempt asset to an exempt asset. For example, if your state has a large homestead exemption, you could use cash (a non-exempt asset) to pay down your mortgage and increase the equity in your home. Another possibility is moving an IRA that is not well-protected under state law into an ERISA-qualified retirement plan that is protected under federal law.

- Convert some jointly owned property into separate property for the spouse not at risk. However, once transferred, it stays separate property. Depending on the length and strength of your marriage, this could be riskier than a potential lawsuit.

- Form a professional limited liability company (PLLC) or leasing LLC. LLCs can be created to own specialized or valuable equipment and/or real estate to remove these assets from a professional practice. "Lease back" agreements can then be created between the professional practice and the

**Be sure to use
an experienced
attorney**

leasing LLCs. A family limited partnership or a family LLC can also own non-practice assets like personal use real estate, investment accounts, cash or bank accounts, and investment real estate.

■   Create a domestic asset protection trust. These are U.S. based trusts that, depending on the state in which they are created, can provide extra layers of protection, especially if LLC interests are transferred to them. Currently, Alaska, Delaware, Nevada, and Wyoming have the most favorable laws.

■   Create an offshore asset protection trust. These are created under the laws of a foreign country that does not enforce the judgments of other countries. (Bermuda, Bahamas, Isle of Man, Cayman Islands, and the Cook Islands are popular choices.) If you are sued in this country and a judgment is awarded, it has no effect in the country where title of your assets is held (in your foreign trust). The case would have to be retried in the foreign country, but first a local attorney must be hired and the witnesses would have to go there to convince the court to even accept jurisdiction over the case. Be aware, however, that if the U.S. court orders you to repatriate the assets and you refuse, you could be cited for contempt and even jailed! It is absolutely imperative that you use an attorney who is experienced with these trusts to design the offshore structure properly.

LAND TRUST

A land trust, or a title holding trust, is sometimes used for real estate when the true owner desires privacy.

The concept is simple. You transfer title of the property to a corporate trustee or corporation, yet you keep full control over how the property is managed. However, since the title is in the name of the corporate trustee or corporation, no one will ever know that it is yours. In all financial transactions and dealings, your personal name never comes up.

Land trusts are valid in many states and the cost to have an outside trustee administer them is very low. However, it is becoming more difficult to find a corporate trustee who is willing to act as trustee because of the liabilities associated with contaminated property.

Planning for the GENERATION-SKIPPING TRANSFER TAX

If some or all of your estate bypasses your children and goes directly to a grandchild, there could be another tax called the generation-skipping transfer tax (GSTT). This can happen intentionally, if you "skip" the living parent (your child) and leave an inheritance directly to your grandchildren.

It can also happen unintentionally. For example, if the inheritance is in a trust for your child, he or she dies after you but before receiving the full amount and, under the terms of the trust, your grandchildren will receive their parent's remaining inheritance, it could then be subject to the GST tax.

Why do we have this tax? Well, in the past, generation skipping trusts were common, especially among the wealthy. The grandfather would set up a trust that distributed only income (no principal) to his children. The trust principal would be distributed later to his grandchildren and future generations.

This allowed the trust assets to grow tax-free and appreciate in value. And it avoided the heavy taxation that would have occurred if each generation had been taxed on the full inheritance. The Rockefellers are one family who used this concept to great advantage, building and retaining considerable wealth for several generations.

Eventually, of course, Uncle Sam decided he wanted his share of taxes, just as if each generation had received its inheritance and paid taxes on it. So, now, if you leave substantial assets to your grandchildren and future generations—bypassing your children's generation—these assets may be subject to the generation skipping transfer tax. (This tax also applies if you leave assets to a non-relative who is more than 37 1/2 years younger than you.)

The bad news is that this is an expensive tax. It is equal to the highest federal estate tax rate in effect at the time. (Currently, that rate is 40%.) *And* the GST tax is *in addition to* the federal estate tax.

The good news, however, is that most people won't be affected by the GST tax because everyone has an exemption. Under current law, the GSTT exemption is equal to the federal estate tax exemption, and is also tied to inflation.

This means, in 2019, you can leave up $11.4 million to your grandchildren and future generations without having to pay the generation-skipping transfer tax. If you are married, you and your spouse can leave them up to $22.8 million. To fully appreciate this, just look at what the GSTT exemption and tax rate have been in recent years. This is an excellent time to transfer wealth to future generations!

Just like the federal estate tax exemption, you have to plan ahead so you don't waste one of these exemptions. One way is with the A-B-C living trust (as explained in Part Three). When one spouse dies, the estate can be divided in half. The deceased spouse's GST tax exemption can be applied to his/her half (Trust B + Trust C). And when the surviving spouse dies, his/her GST tax exemption can be applied to Trust A. This makes full use of both exemptions. Your attorney, of course, may suggest other planning options.

Recent Historical GSTT Exemption and Tax Rate

Year of Death	Exemption	Tax Rate
1997	$1,000,000	55%
1998	$1,000,000	55%
1999	$1,010,000	55%
2000	$1,030,000	55%
2001	$1,060,000	55%
2002	$1,100,000	50%
2003	$1,120,000	49%
2004	$1,500,000	48%
2005	$1,500,000	47%
2006	$2,000,000	46%
2007 and 2008	$2,000,000	45%
2009	$3,500,000	45%
2010	N/A (repealed)	0%
2011	$5,000,000	35%
2012	$5,120,000	35%
2013	$5,250,000	40%
2014	$5,340,000	40%
2015	$5,430,000	40%
2016	$5,450,000	40%
2017	$5,490,000	40%
2018	$11,200,000	40%
2019	$11,400,000	40%

Dynasty Trust

It is an excellent time to transfer wealth to future generations

Most parents leave their assets to their children who, in turn, leave their assets to *their* children, and so on down the line. This causes the assets to be subject to taxes at every generation, making it difficult for most families to build up any kind of wealth from one generation to the next. But anyone can create and build their own family dynasty just like wealthy families have done for years, by setting up a dynasty trust. This is a trust that is specifically designed to benefit descendants of multiple generations.

You can fund a dynasty trust with any assets, although appreciating assets are usually best. Life insurance can also be used, which makes a dynasty trust attainable for less wealthy families. Consider purchasing a life insurance policy on your child's life instead of yours; the younger age lets you buy substantially more insurance.

With appropriate allocation of your GST exemption, the assets in a dynasty trust can be protected from estate and GST taxes for the life of the trust. In 2019, you can contribute up to $11.4 million to a dynasty trust; up to $22.8 million if you are married.

You will want as much of the trust assets to remain in the trust as possible so the trust principal can grow. But you can give the trustee discretion over when to distribute income and principal to your children, grandchildren, and future generations as they may need it for education, to start a business, buy a home, or to pay for medical expenses. Think of it as your own family bank.

Where a dynasty trust is set up makes a big difference. Until recently, states were bound by the *rule against perpetuities,* which says that the longest a trust may exist is 21 years after the death of the youngest beneficiary who was living at the time the trust was established (about 90 years). At that time, the trust assets must be distributed and taxed, which often causes family holdings to be sold.

The Boston Globe is a good example of this. The Taylor family had owned and operated the newspaper since 1873, but the approaching expiration of two family trusts prompted its sale in 1991 to *The New York Times*. It was recently purchased by John Henry, the owner of The Boston Red Sox.

About half of the states now allow dynasty trusts to last longer. For example, trusts established in South Dakota, Idaho, Ohio, Delaware, Wisconsin, Maryland, and Alaska can continue in perpetuity (forever). Wyoming and Utah allow a trust to continue for 1,000 years; Tennessee and Nevada, 365 years; Florida, 360 years. The longer the trust can last, of course, the larger it can grow.

You do not have to live in one of these states to establish a trust there, although you typically do need to have a local trustee. Because the trust will last for generations, a corporate trustee is your best choice. (It should come as no surprise that corporate trustees, who stand to make substantial fees on these trusts, have played a large role in convincing their state legislatures to change their laws.)

State laws vary on these trusts, and you and your attorney will want to shop around and compare. For example, some have a state income tax and others do not; some provide better creditor protection for the assets in the trust; ease of administration varies; and so on. Also, consider whether you really want to provide for potentially hundreds of descendants you will not know.

QUALIFIED DOMESTIC TRUST

Using a qualified domestic trust is the only way your estate will be allowed to use the marital deduction if your spouse is not a U.S. citizen. That's because Uncle Sam doesn't want noncitizen spouses to inherit sizeable estates and then return to their homelands without paying any estate taxes.

Remember, the marital deduction lets you leave your spouse an unlimited amount of assets with no estate taxes when you die. Uncle Sam plans to collect the taxes when your surviving spouse dies. But if your spouse takes the assets and leaves the country, Uncle Sam is left empty handed. So, in 1988, Congress decided to eliminate the unlimited marital deduction for noncitizen spouses.

This means that, when you die, everything in your estate over the federal estate tax exemption will be taxed—unless your living trust plan includes a qualified domestic trust (QDOT or QDT).

The QDOT works a little like Trust C, which we explained in Part Three. The assets that are transferred to this trust (probably all of your assets over the federal estate tax exemption) are not taxed when you die, so the entire estate is available to provide for your surviving spouse. The trust (not your spouse) owns the assets, but your spouse can receive income from the trust and, with the trustee's approval, may also receive principal.

To make sure estate taxes are paid when your spouse dies, at least one trustee of the QDOT must be a U.S. citizen or U.S. corporation. (Sometimes a surviving spouse wants to return to his/her homeland and finds it would be easier to have the trust administered there. But some countries do not authorize trusts or allow trusts to have U.S. trustees. For these situations, Congress passed legislation that will allow the requirement for a U.S. trustee to be waived and will allow a similar legal arrangement to be used instead of a trust.)

The income your spouse receives from the QDOT is taxed as ordinary income in the year it is received. But any principal your spouse receives (unless the distribution is due to "hardship" as defined by the IRS), plus assets remaining in the QDOT when your spouse dies, will be taxed as if they were part of your estate when you died (at your highest estate tax rate).

Without a QDOT, these estate taxes would have to be paid when you die. But *with* a QDOT (just like a C Trust), the taxes are delayed until your surviving spouse dies. So more is available to provide for your spouse. Of course, if your spouse becomes a U.S. citizen before the assets are transferred to the QDOT, you would not need one.

The gift tax rules are also different for those who are not residents of the U.S. so it's important to speak to an attorney knowledgeable in this area before making gifts greater than $15,000.

Summary

These are just a few of the many planning strategies available. There are some brilliant minds in estate planning, and they are constantly thinking of new and better ways to accomplish their clients' goals.

If some of these strategies sound interesting to you, ask your attorney if they would be helpful in your situation. Remember, these strategies are *in addition to* your living trust, and most are irrevocable. So, you'll want to do your homework and make sure this is what you want *before* you put one in place.

Many of these can be complicated, and it could cost you (or your family) a bundle if they are not correctly prepared and implemented. You simply cannot afford to use an inexperienced attorney. Make sure you find someone who is well qualified, has experience with the strategy(ies) that interest you, and knows what he/she is doing. (If you're not sure where to begin, see "How To Find The Right Attorney" in Part Five.)

Also, be aware that some of these strategies may not be around for much longer. Congress continues to discuss limitations on several advanced planning strategies as a way to close loopholes for the wealthy and generate more tax revenue.

Finally, as mentioned earlier, you will usually have the best results if you work with a team of advisors. Depending on the strategies used, your team may include your attorney, CPA, financial advisor, insurance advisor, retirement plan administrator, charitable planned giving representative, and others. They will bring their own areas of expertise as they consider your objectives, weigh various legal and financial options, and determine the best solution(s) for your needs.

Part Ten—

THE PERSONAL AND FINANCIAL ORGANIZER

INSTRUCTIONS FOR COMPLETING THE PERSONAL AND FINANCIAL ORGANIZER

To set up your living trust, your attorney will need to know some basic information about you and your family, your assets, and your decisions about your trust—whom you want to be your trustee, successor trustee(s), and your beneficiaries, and how you want your beneficiaries to inherit from you.

Our Personal and Financial Organizer gives you one place to write down all this information as you prepare to meet with your attorney. Being organized will undoubtedly save you time and money. And actually writing down this information will help you to think seriously about your plan.

In this section, we'll help you complete the Organizer with the following step-by-step instructions.

General Instructions

1. Print or write *legibly*. Using a pencil is a good idea, since you will probably make some changes. (It's okay to make a few copies of the Organizer for your own personal use. However, because it is copyrighted, professionals must call us for approval before making copies.)

2. We suggest that you complete the Organizer as much as possible *before* you meet with your attorney. Of course, we realize that you will

probably have some questions you will want to ask him/her before actually making some decisions. Just make notes in the appropriate sections or write your questions down in Section 7 so you won't forget about them.

3.   If you don't have enough room on the Organizer to put all of the information requested, use a separate sheet of paper and attach it to that page. If a question doesn't apply to you, mark "N/A" for "not applicable" rather than leaving it blank—this way your attorney will know that you did not overlook the question or forget to answer it.

4.   *Take your time* completing this Organizer; these are *serious* decisions. You may want to re-read sections of the book that apply to each decision, so we've included page numbers whenever appropriate.

5.   And, finally, be thorough. Remember, your attorney can only plan with the information you provide. If you withhold information about your assets or personal situation, your plan may not work the way you want.

Now, let's complete the organizer.

SECTION 1 GENERAL INFORMATION

Be sure to date the Organizer and mark your marital status. If you are single, you only need to complete the sections that apply to you. If you are married, you and your spouse need to complete this entire section.

The information in the box on the right will help your attorney plan for some special circumstances. For example, if your spouse is not a U.S. citizen, your attorney may need to include an additional provision (QDOT) in your trust document. Your attorney also needs to know (for tax planning purposes) if you expect to receive money or other assets from an outside source.

If you have a previous will or trust that this living trust will replace, make sure you take a copy with you when you meet with your attorney.

2 ABOUT YOUR CHILDREN

This section requests some basic information that will help introduce your family situation to your attorney—how many children, stepchildren, or grandchildren you have, their ages, where they live, if they are dependent on you, and if any of them require special care.

3 FINANCIAL INFORMATION

This section requests information about the current values of what you own and what you owe. Remember, your attorney is not being nosy. He/she needs this information to know if you will need tax planning in your living trust.

Your attorney also needs to know about your assets so he/she can advise you about transferring them into your trust. This section will be a good check list for you, too, when making sure all appropriate titles and beneficiary designations are changed.

You'll notice we have included space for you to write down in whose name each asset is titled. This information is important for both tax planning and funding purposes. For example, if you are married but you and your spouse own substantial assets separately, your attorney may recommend that you have separate living trusts in addition to, or instead of, one living trust.

Questions 1, 5, and 7 have a place for you to list the purchase price of these assets; remember, this is your cost basis. Depending on what you paid for these assets and what the current values are, your attorney may recommend some additional tax planning options for you to consider. (Some of these are explained in Part Nine.)

You'll also notice on Questions 1 and 2 that we've included a formula to help you determine the net value/equity in these assets. (As explained in Part Three, if the net value of your estate is more than the federal estate tax exemption in effect when you die, federal estate taxes will have to be paid. Also, your estate may be exempt from federal tax but not from state tax.) You will list the current market value of each asset and subtract from that the remaining mortgage or loan value. This will give you the net value/equity of each asset.

You may need to have some current appraisals done if some assets have not been appraised recently. For these purposes, a formal appraisal of your home is not necessary. It's okay to have a real estate agent give you a general idea of its value, based on recent sales of comparable homes in your area.

If you have any guns, be sure to list them in Question #10. Because guns need special planning, your attorney will need to know if you have them.

It is very important that you fully complete this section. Remember, your attorney can only plan with the information you provide. If you omit assets or undervalue them, you could end up paying too much in taxes. If you need more room to answer any of the questions in Section 3, list them on a separate sheet of paper and attach it to these pages.

SECTION
4 TRUST DECISIONS: YOUR LIVING TRUST TEAM

Okay, so far this has been pretty straightforward. Beginning in this section, you will need to start making some decisions about your living trust.

1. Trustee(s)
See pages 101-111 for more information.
The trustee is responsible for management of your trust now. You can be your own trustee. If you are married, you and your spouse can be co-trustees. You can also name someone else as your trustee or co-trustee—an adult son or daughter, another relative, or a corporate trustee. You should probably consider naming someone else as your trustee or co-trustee if you don't have the time, ability, or desire to manage your own affairs anymore or if you and/or your spouse are ill. (Remember, until you become incapacitated or die, you can always change your trustee.)

2. Successor Trustee(s)

See pages 102-111 for more information.

Your successor trustee will step in and take control for you if you become physically or mentally incapacitated and are no longer able to handle your own affairs. When you die, your successor acts just like an executor named in a will—pays your final bills, has tax returns prepared, and distributes your assets according to the instructions in your trust—but without court supervision. If you have a co-trustee (perhaps your spouse), he/she will assume these responsibilities until his/her own incapacity or death, at which time your successor trustee will take over.

You will probably want to name two or three successor trustees if, for some reason, the first is not available. They should be people you know and trust, whose judgment you respect, and who will also respect your wishes. They do not have to live in the same state as you do, although it would be helpful if they live close to you. If you have adult children, they can be named as successor trustees.

If you wish, you can name two or more successor trustees to jointly share the responsibilities (for instance, you may want two of your adult children to act together). You may also want to consider naming a third impartial co-successor trustee (like a corporate trustee) to prevent deadlocks or major disagreements. If you do want to name two or more to act together, just cross out "1st choice," "2nd choice," and "3rd choice" and write in "co-trustees."

If you don't feel you have good candidates for your successor trustee—your family lives too far away, they're too busy, or aren't responsible enough, or if you feel you have no one you can trust—you should definitely consider a corporate trustee.

Note: If you name a corporate trustee as a trustee or to act alone as your successor trustee, you do not need to name any other successor trustees.

3. Guardians For Minor Children

See page 113 for more information.

If you have minor children, you will need to select a guardian for them. This is a very important decision. The person you name will be *responsible for raising* your children if both parents become incapacitated or die. Guardians must be adults. You will, of course, want to choose someone who respects your values and religious beliefs, and will raise your children the way you would want.

Remember, the court must still approve your selection. If you are a single parent with custody and really don't want your "ex" to be guardian, go ahead and name your preference anyway. While the other natural parent is almost always the court's preferred choice, your choice will probably receive careful consideration. It's possible that the other parent may not be able to take the responsibility (or won't want it), or the court could agree with you that he/ she is not a suitable choice. In these situations, the judge would want to know your preference.

4. Trustees For Minor Children
See page 113 for more information.
Remember, the guardian is only responsible for *raising* your children and does not control the inheritance. You also need to name a trustee for your children's trust—someone who will be responsible for the safekeeping of their inheritance, and will provide the money for education, medical care, maintenance, and other needs from the assets in the children's trust.

You can name the same person as trustee and guardian, making it convenient for one person to take care of your children. However, remember that the person you want to raise your children may not be your best choice to manage the money—and vice versa. The trustee can be a different individual, a corporate trustee or, if you wish, you can name two as co-trustees.

Grandparents and others who leave assets for minor children: You will also need to name a trustee to manage the inheritance in the children's trust.

SECTION

5 BENEFICIARIES

Your beneficiaries are the persons and/or organizations who will receive your assets when you die. Most people prefer to pass their assets down to family members, but you can leave them to any person or organization you wish. If you are married and you want to make sure the beneficiaries you have named cannot be changed if you die first, ask your attorney about including an A-B provision in your living trust. (See Part Three for more information.)

1. Special Gifts To Organizations

See pages 112 and 129 for more information.

This is an excellent time to think about giving to a charity or organization that has special meaning to you. There are many excellent ones and they are all in need of funding to continue their work. In addition to the tax benefits of charitable donations, you will have the satisfaction of knowing that your contribution will make a difference. Your gift can be as specific or as general, as large or as small, as you want to make it. The charity or foundation of your choice will be glad to make suggestions.

2. Special Gifts To Individuals

See page 112 for more information.

You probably will want to leave specific items to certain individuals—a favorite piece of jewelry or antique that you want a special friend or relative to have. Remember, in most states, you just need to make a list of these special gifts on a separate sheet of paper, have it notarized, and keep it with your living trust document. If you change your mind, you can usually just make a new list and have it notarized. You may want to make a separate list for each of your children or grandchildren.

Use the space on this organizer to start getting your special gifts lists organized. This way, if you have any questions, you will be prepared when you meet with your attorney. (Be sure to let your attorney know if you have any guns.)

3. Beneficiaries

See page 111-125 for more information.

Whom do you want to receive the rest of your assets after your special gifts have been distributed? For most people, this will probably be the bulk of your estate—your home, other real estate, investments, etc.—everything that you did not list as a special gift. Because values can fluctuate, it's usually better to specify a percentage instead of a dollar amount.

4. Inheriting Instructions

See page 117-125 for more information.

When do you want your beneficiaries to inherit? If your beneficiaries are younger, you may want to keep strings on their inheritances until each one reaches an age at which you feel he/she will be mature enough to have outright control, such as age 21, 25, 35. Some parents specify a certain amount at certain ages (some at 21, some at 25, etc.) or at certain intervals (some every three to five years). You may want to keep the assets in trust indefinitely. It's completely up to you. You just need to specify how long you want the trustee(s) to keep control.

5. Dependents Who Require Special Care

See pages 121-124 for more information.

If you have a spouse, parent, child, or another loved one who requires special care, your attorney will need to know this. Under "Explanation," briefly explain the situation. Include whether the person is currently receiving government benefits or may need to qualify for them in the future. If you have pets, write down a brief explanation, who will care for them if they outlive you, and if you want to provide any funds to cover the expense. (See page 128 for more information about pets.)

6. Alternate Beneficiaries

See page 125-130 for more information.

Whom do you want to have your assets if all of your beneficiaries die before you? Many people specify their place of worship or a favorite charity.

7. Disinheriting

See page 124 for more information.

Are there any persons that you specifically want to exclude? Make sure you consider this very carefully as disinheriting someone is a serious action with far-reaching consequences.

SECTION

6 SPECIAL INSTRUCTIONS AT INCAPACITY

This is a very appropriate time to think about what you would want to happen to you and your assets if you were to become physically or mentally incapacitated and unable to handle your own affairs. You may have some specific requests and/or instructions if this should happen to you—and your co-trustee or successor trustee(s), family members, and physicians should know your wishes.

1. Keeping/Selling Assets

If you become incapacitated, it may become necessary to sell some of your assets to pay for your care. Do you have a preference for which ones are sold first? Are there others you don't want sold unless absolutely necessary? Do you have any special instructions you want followed? Are there any potential buyers you would want contacted? You may also want some special gifts distributed at this time.

2. Medical Care

You may have specific requests regarding your medical care. For example, you may want to be cared for in a specific hospital or nursing home. Or maybe there's one you *don't* want to be in. You may also have some definite ideas about the type or extent of care you receive at this time—life support, blood transfusions, organ transplants, etc.

3. Living Will

See page 148 for more information.

A living will is a document that lets you express your wishes about life support in terminal situations.

4. Durable Power of Attorney for Health Care

See page 149 for more information.

A durable power of attorney for health care (also called a health care proxy or medical power of attorney) is a document that lets you appoint someone to make *any* health care decisions for you if you are unable to make them yourself. This keeps these personal decisions out of the courts. You can choose your spouse, another relative, or a trusted friend as your agent. You should list at least two choices, in case your first is unavailable.

5. HIPAA Release Authorizations

See page 150 for more information.

Unless you have provided a signed HIPAA release form, medical professionals are not allowed to discuss any aspect of your health information or care with others, even family members. Start a list here of the people you want to be informed about your care.

SECTION

7 QUESTIONS TO ASK YOUR ATTORNEY ABOUT YOUR LIVING TRUST

Use this space to start a list of your questions so you won't forget to ask your attorney.

SUMMARY

There! You've got your information all organized. That was a big step. Now it's time to see a qualified estate planning attorney who can answer your questions and prepare your documents for you. (Remember to take this book and your completed Personal and Financial Organizer with you.) We suggest that you re-read Part Five if you don't yet have an attorney selected.

Good for you for taking care of this now!

PERSONAL AND FINANCIAL ORGANIZER FOR YOUR LIVING TRUST

1 GENERAL INFORMATION

Home Phone _____ Date _____

Email Address _____

Marital Status: ☐ Married ☐ Single ☐ Divorced ☐ Widowed

Your Legal Name _____

Spouse's Legal Name _____

Street Address _____

City _____ State _____ ZIP _____

Mailing Address (if different) _____

Your Employer _____

Address _____

Your Occupation _____ Work Phone _____

Spouse's Employer _____

Address _____

Spouse's Occupation _____ Work Phone _____

	You	Your Spouse
Social Security #		
Date of Birth		
U.S. citizen?	Yes No	Yes No
Currently have Will or Trust? If so, give year & state in which prepared.	Yes No Yr. _____ State _____	Yes No Yr. _____ State _____
Expect to receive money or other assets from (circle all that apply):	Gift Inheritance Lawsuit Other	Gift Inheritance Lawsuit Other
If so, approximately how much?	$	$

2 ABOUT YOUR CHILDREN

1. _____

Legal Name _____ Date of Birth _____

Goes By _____ Soc. Sec. # _____

Street Address _____

City _____ State _____ ZIP _____ Phone _____

☐ Natural ☐ Legally Adopted ☐ Foster
☐ Married ☐ Needs Special Care ☐ Dependent
Related To:
☐ You Only ☐ Spouse Only ☐ Both

2. _____

Legal Name _____ Date of Birth _____

Goes By _____ Soc. Sec. # _____

Street Address _____

City _____ State _____ ZIP _____ Phone _____

☐ Natural ☐ Legally Adopted ☐ Foster
☐ Married ☐ Needs Special Care ☐ Dependent
Related To:
☐ You Only ☐ Spouse Only ☐ Both

3. _____

Legal Name _____ Date of Birth _____

Goes By _____ Soc. Sec. # _____

Street Address _____

City _____ State _____ ZIP _____ Phone _____

☐ Natural ☐ Legally Adopted ☐ Foster
☐ Married ☐ Needs Special Care ☐ Dependent
Related To:
☐ You Only ☐ Spouse Only ☐ Both

How many grandchildren do you have? _____ Yours Only _____ Your Spouse's Only _____ Both

FINANCIAL INFORMATION

1. Do you own a **home** or any **other real estate**?

Description and Location	Titled in whose name	Purchase Price	Current Value	(-) Mortgage	(=) Equity
					Total Net Value =

2. Do you own any **other titled property** such as a car, boat, etc.?

Description	Titled in whose name	Current Value	(-) Loan	(=) Equity
				Total Net Value =

3. Do you have any **checking accounts**?

Name of Institution	Account Number	Titled in whose name	Approx. Balance
			Total Value =

4. Do you have any **interest bearing accounts** (savings, money market) and/or **CDs**?

Name of Institution	Account Number	Titled in whose name	Approx. Balance
			Total Value =

5. Do you own any **stocks, bonds or mutual funds** (including company stock)?

# of Shares	Description	Account Number	Titled in whose name	Purchase Price	Current Value
					Total Value =

6. Do you have any **profit sharing, IRAs or pension plans**?

Description/Location	Beneficiary	Current Value
	Total Value =	

7. Do you or your spouse own a **business** or have any **partnership interests**?

Description	Type of Ownership	Purchase Price	Current Value
		Total Value=	

8. Do you have any **life insurance** policies and/or **annuities**?

Name of Company	Policy Owner	1st Beneficiary	2nd Beneficiary	Death Benefit
			Total Value =	

9. Does anyone owe you money?

Description	Approx. Value
	Total Value =

10. Do you have any **guns or special items of value** such as coin collections, antiques, jewelry, etc.?

Description	Approx. Value
	Total Value =

11. What is the approximate total value of all your remaining **personal property**—whatever you own that has not been included above? (clothes, furniture, etc.) Just estimate........................$ _____

12. Do you have any **debts** other than mortgage(s) and loans listed above (credit cards, personal loans, etc.)?

	Amount owed
	Total Debt =

13. Total value of everything you (and your spouse) own (add totals of lines 1 thru 11 above) $ _____

14. Total amount you (and your spouse) owe (total of line 12 above)................................... _____

15. Subtract line 14 from line 13.   NET ESTATE = $ _____

16. Do you have a **safe deposit box**?

Location	Titled in whose name

TRUST DECISIONS: YOUR LIVING TRUST TEAM

1. Trustee(s)—Manages your trust now; usually you (and your spouse) and/or a corporate trustee.

2. Successor Trustee(s)—Steps in at your incapacity or death. Can be adult children, trusted friend, and/or a corporate trustee.

#1 Choice: Name _____ Phone _____
Address _____

#2 Choice: Name _____ Phone _____
Address _____

#3 Choice: Name _____ Phone _____
Address _____

3. Guardian For Minor Children—Responsible adult who will raise your minor children if something happens to you.

#1 Choice: Name _____ Phone _____
Address _____

#2 Choice: Name _____ Phone _____
Address _____

4. Trustees For Minor Children— Manages inheritance. Can be same person as guardian, another adult and/or a corporate trustee.

#1 Choice: Name _____ Phone _____
Address _____

#2 Choice: Name _____ Phone _____
Address _____

BENEFICIARIES

1. Special Gifts To Organizations

Do you want to make a gift (cash or a specific item) to a charity, foundation, religious or fraternal organization?

Name of Organization	Address	Description of Gift

2. Special Gifts To Individuals

Do you want to give any specific items to a family member or other individual? (For example: wedding ring to your daughter, gun collection to a son or nephew, etc.)

Name of Person	Address	Description of Gift

3. Beneficiaries

Whom do you want to receive the rest of your estate after these special gifts have been distributed? You can designate a dollar amount or a percentage.

Name of Person/Organization	Address	Amount/Percentage

4. Inheriting Instructions

When do you want your beneficiaries to inherit: in installments, at certain ages, all at once, or keep in trust?

_____

_____

_____

_____

_____

5. Do you provide for someone who requires special care?

Do any of your dependents (aging parents, disabled child) require special care? Are they currently receiving government benefits? Is there someone you want to provide for who is not related to you (significant other, friend, pet)?

Name	Age	Relationship	Explanation

6. Alternate Beneficiaries

Whom do you want to receive your estate if you (and your spouse) outlive the beneficiaries you've named above?

Name of Person/Organization	Address	Amount/Percentage

7. Disinheriting

Are there any relatives that you specifically do not want to receive anything from you?

_____

_____

SPECIAL INSTRUCTIONS AT INCAPACITY

1. Keeping/Selling Assets:

If it becomes necessary to sell assets to pay for your or your spouse's care, are there certain ones you prefer to be sold first? Are there potential buyers you want contacted? Are there certain assets you prefer not be sold unless absolutely necessary?

_____

_____

_____

2. Medical Care:

Do you prefer (or want to avoid) a certain hospital/nursing home? Do you have strong feelings about blood transfusions, life support, etc.?

You _____   **Your Spouse** _____

_____   _____

_____   _____

	You	Your Spouse
3. Do you want a **Living Will**? This lets others know how you feel about life support treatment if you become terminally ill	Yes No	Yes No
4. Do you want a **Durable Power of Attorney for Health Care**?	Yes No	Yes No

3. Do you want a **Living Will**? This lets others know how you feel about life support treatment if you become terminally ill ....

4. Do you want a **Durable Power of Attorney for Health Care**? ....
This document lets you choose the person you want to make any health care decisions (including life support) for you if you are unable to make them for yourself, keeping these personal decisions out of the courts. You can choose anyone you trust: your spouse, friend or other relative, etc. List your choices below:

You

#1 Choice: Name _____

Address _____

_____

Phone _____

#2 Choice: Name _____

Address _____

_____

Phone _____

Your Spouse

#1 Choice: Name _____

Address _____

_____

Phone _____

#2 Choice: Name _____

Address _____

_____

Phone _____

5. HIPAA Release Authorizations. Start a list here of people you want kept informed about your medical situation:

_____

_____

QUESTIONS TO ASK YOUR ATTORNEY

_____

_____

_____

_____

_____

IN CONCLUSION

Our goal in writing this book has been to give you accurate and understandable information about living trusts and estate planning.

It's now up to you to use this knowledge and turn it into wisdom.

When is the best time to set up your living trust? *Right now*—while you are healthy and you don't think you need one.

If you think a living trust would probably be a good idea, but you just haven't gotten around to it yet, here are some things to keep in mind:

■ You write a check every year for car insurance and for homeowner's insurance to protect you against a loss that, odds are, won't even occur. The cost to set up a living trust is a one-time cost. It protects *all* your assets—not just one or two. And, unless you know something that we don't, dying is something that *will* happen to all of us some day!

■ Perfection is impossible. Don't postpone getting your trust because you are trying to come up with the perfect plan that covers every conceivable possibility.

■ Your trust is a snapshot of you, your family and your assets *right now*—not one year, five years, or twenty years from now. No one can predict what your personal, family, or financial future will be. Go ahead and set up your trust now—then change it as your situation changes.

■ None of us likes to think about our own mortality—which is why so many families are caught off guard and unprepared when incapacity or death strikes. But remember, a living trust is *not* about dying. It's about doing what's best for you and your family, so *you* can enjoy peace of mind *now—while you're living.*

Please—act now.

DEFINITIONS

We may have introduced some legal terms that are new to you, so we've put together this handy reference. There are also some legal terms that we have purposely *not* used in this book because we wanted to keep it easy to understand. But, you will probably feel more comfortable dealing with an attorney if you know some of their "legalese," so we've included some here.

A Trust—Surviving spouse's portion of an A-B trust. Also called marital trust or survivor's trust.

A-B Trust—A provision added to your living trust that lets you provide for your surviving spouse and keep control over who will receive your assets after your spouse dies. It also lets both spouses use their federal estate tax exemptions. This can save a substantial amount in estate taxes and leave more money for your beneficiaries.

Administration—The court-supervised distribution of an estate during probate. Also used to describe the same process for a trust after the grantor dies.

Administrator—Person named by the court to represent a probate estate when there is no will or the will did not name an executor. Female is administratix. Also called personal representative.

Alternate Beneficiary—Person or organization named to receive your assets if the primary beneficiaries named in your trust die before you do.

Ancillary Administration—An additional probate in another state. Typically required when you own real estate in another state that is not titled in the name of your trust.

Annual Exclusion—Amount you can give someone each year without having to file a gift tax return or pay a gift tax. It is currently $15,000 per recipient ($30,000 if married). This amount is tied to inflation and may increase from time to time.

Assets—Basically, anything you own, including your home and other real estate, bank accounts, life insurance, investments, furniture, jewelry, art, clothing, and collectibles.

Assignment—A short document that transfers your interest in assets from your name to another. Often used when transferring assets to a trust.

B Trust—Deceased spouse's portion of an A-B trust. Also called credit shelter or bypass trust.

Basis—What you paid for an asset. The value that is used to determine gain or loss for income tax purposes.

Beneficiaries—In a living trust, the persons and/or organizations who receive the trust assets (or benefit from the trust assets) after the death of the trust grantor.

By-Pass Trust—Another name for the "B" part of an A-B living trust because the assets in this trust bypass federal estate taxes.

C Trust—See "QTIP."

Certificate of Trust—A shortened version of a trust that verifies the trust's existence, explains the powers given to the trustee, and identifies the successor trustee(s). Does not reveal any information about the trust assets, beneficiaries, or their inheritances.

Children's Trust—A trust included in your living trust. If, when you die, a beneficiary is not of legal age, the child's inheritance will go into this trust. The inheritance will be managed by the trustee you have named until the child reaches the age at which you want him/her to inherit.

Codicil—A written change or amendment to a will.

Co-Grantors—Two or more persons who establish one living trust together.

Co-Trustees—Two or more individuals who have been named to act together in managing a trust's assets. A corporate trustee can also be a co-trustee.

Common Trust—One living trust established by two or more individuals (usually a married couple).

Community Property—Assets a husband and wife acquire by joint effort during marriage if they live in one of the states that allow community property ownership. Each spouse owns half of the assets in the event of divorce or death.

Conservator—One who is legally responsible for the care and well-being of another person. If appointed by a court, the conservator is under the court's supervision. May also be called a guardian. (Duties and titles can vary by state. For example, in Missouri, there is a guardian of the person and a conservator of the estate.)

Conservatorship—A court-controlled program for persons who are unable to manage their own affairs due to mental or physical incapacity. May also be called a guardianship.

Contest—To dispute or challenge the terms of a will or trust.

Corporate Trustee—An institution, generally a bank or trust company, that specializes in managing trusts.

Credit Shelter Trust—Another name for Trust B in an A-B living trust because this trust "shelters" or preserves the federal estate tax "credit" of the deceased spouse.

Creditor—Person or institution to whom money is owed.

Custodian—Person named to manage assets left to a minor under the Uniform Transfer to Minors Act. In most states, the minor receives the assets at legal age.

Deceased—One who has died.

Deed—A document that lets you transfer title of your real estate to another person(s). Also see warranty deed and quitclaim deed.

Disclaim—To refuse to accept a gift or inheritance so it can go to the recipient who is next in line. A legal "no thank you."

Discretion—The full or partial power to make a decision or judgment.

Disinherit—To prevent someone from inheriting from you.

Distribution—Payment in cash or asset(s) to one who is entitled to receive it.

Durable Power of Attorney for Asset Management—A legal document that gives another person full or limited legal authority to sign your name on your behalf in your absence. Valid through incapacity. Ends at death.

Durable Power of Attorney for Health Care—A legal document that lets you give someone else the authority to make health care decisions for you in the event you are unable to make them for yourself. Also called a health care proxy or medical power of attorney.

Equity—The current market value of an asset less any loan or liability.

Estate—Assets and debts left by an individual at death.

Estate Taxes—Federal or state taxes on the value of assets left at death. Also called inheritance taxes or death taxes.

Executor—Person or institution named in a will to carry out its instructions. Female is executrix. Also called a personal representative.

Federal Estate Tax Exemption—Amount of an individual's estate that is exempt from federal estate taxes.

Fiduciary—Person having the legal duty to act primarily for another's benefit. Implies great confidence and trust, and a high degree of good faith. Usually associated with a trustee.

Funding—The process of transferring assets to your living trust.

Gain—The difference between what you receive for an asset when it is sold and what you paid for it. Used to determine the amount of capital gains tax due.

Generation-Skipping Transfer Tax—A steep tax on assets that "skip" a generation and are left directly to grandchildren and younger generations. This tax is in addition to the federal estate tax. Currently, the generation-skipping transfer tax exemption is equal to the federal estate tax exemption. The GST tax on amounts over the exemption is currently 40%.

Gift—A transfer from one individual to another without fair compensation.

Gift Tax—A federal tax on gifts made while you are living. Currently $15,000 per person per year is exempt from gift tax. Also see "Annual Exclusion."

Grantor—The person who sets up or creates the trust. The person whose trust it is. Also called creator, settlor, trustor, trustmaker, or donor.

Gross Estate—The value of an estate before debts are paid.

Guardianship—See "Conservatorship."

Health Care Proxy—See "Durable Power of Attorney for Health Care."

Heir—One who is entitled by law to receive part of your estate.

Holographic Will—A handwritten will.

Homestead Exemption—Portion of your residence (dwelling and surrounding land) that cannot be sold to satisfy a creditor's claim while you are living.

Incapacitated/Incompetent—Unable to manage one's own affairs, either temporarily or permanently. Lack of legal power.

Independent Administration—A form of probate available in many states. Intended to simplify the probate process by requiring fewer court appearances and less court supervision.

Inheritance—The assets received from someone who has died.

Inter vivos—Latin term that means "between the living." An inter vivos trust is created while you are living instead of after you die. A revocable living trust is an inter vivos trust.

Irrevocable Trust—A trust that cannot be changed (revoked) or cancelled once it is set up. Opposite of revocable trust.

Intestate—Without a will.

Joint Ownership—A form of ownership in which two or more persons own the same asset together. Types of joint ownership include joint tenants with right of survivorship, tenants in common, and tenants by the entirety.

Joint Tenants with Right of Survivorship—A form of joint ownership in which the deceased owner's share automatically and immediately transfers to the surviving joint tenant(s).

Land Trust—Often used for privacy. Title is transferred to a corporate trustee or corporation, but you keep control over how the property is managed. Because the title is in the name of the corporate trustee or corporation, no one knows the property belongs to you. In all financial transactions and dealings, your personal name never comes up. Also called a title-holding trust.

Liquid Assets—Cash and other assets (like stocks) that can easily be converted into cash.

Living Probate—The court-supervised process of managing the assets of one who is incapacitated.

Living Trust—A written legal document that creates an entity to which you transfer ownership of your assets. Contains your instructions for managing your assets during your lifetime and for their distribution upon your incapacity or death. Avoids probate at death and court control of assets at incapacity. Also called a revocable inter vivos trust. A trust created during one's lifetime.

Living Will—A written document that states you do not wish to be kept alive by artificial means when the illness or injury is terminal.

Marital Deduction—A deduction on the federal estate tax return that lets the first spouse to die leave an unlimited amount of assets to the surviving spouse free of estate taxes. (Surviving spouse must be a U.S. citizen.) However, if no other tax planning is used, and the surviving spouse's estate is more than the amount of the federal estate tax exemption in effect at the time of his/her death, estate taxes will be due at that time.

Marital Trust—See "A Trust."

Medicaid—A federally-funded health care program for the poor and minor children.

Medicare—A federally-funded health care program, primarily for Americans over age 65 who are covered by Social Security or Railroad Retirement benefits.

Minor—One who is under the legal age for an adult. Varies by state, but usually age 18 or 21.

Net Estate—The value of an estate after all debts have been paid. (Federal estate taxes are based on the net value of an estate.)

Net Value—The current market value of an asset less any loan or debt.

Payable-on-Death Account—See "Totten Trust."

Per Capita—A way of distributing your estate so that your surviving descendents will share equally, regardless of their generation.

Per Stirpes—A way of distributing your estate so that your surviving descendents will receive only what their immediate ancestor would have received if he/she had been living at your death.

Personal Property—Movable property. Includes furniture, automobiles, equipment, cash and stocks. Opposite of real property that is permanent (like land).

Personal Representative—Another name for an executor or administrator.

Portability—A relatively new provision in the law that allows a surviving spouse to use the deceased spouse's unused federal estate tax exemption. This is not automatic. An estate tax return must be filed within nine months of the death of the first spouse, unless an extension is granted.

Pour Over Will—A short will often used with a living trust. It states that any assets left out of your living trust will become part of (*pour over* into) your living trust upon your death.

Power of Attorney—Legal document giving someone legal authority to sign your name on your behalf in your absence. Ends at incapacity (unless it is a *durable* power of attorney) or death.

Probate—Legal process of validating a will, paying debts, and distributing assets after death.

Probate Estate—The assets that go through probate after you die. Usually this includes assets you own in your name and those paid to your estate. Usually does not include assets owned jointly, payable-on-death accounts, insurance, and other assets with beneficiary designations. Assets in a trust also do not go through probate.

Probate Fees—Legal, executor, and appraisal fees plus court costs that are incurred when an estate goes through probate. Probate fees are paid from assets in the estate before the assets are fully distributed to the heirs.

Qualified Domestic Trust (QDOT)—Allows a non-citizen spouse to qualify for the marital deduction.

Qualified Terminable Interest Property (QTIP) Trust—A trust that delays estate taxes until your surviving spouse dies so more income will be available to provide for your spouse during his/her lifetime. You can keep control over who will receive these assets after your spouse dies.

Qualifying Subchapter S Trust (QSST)—Trust that meets certain IRS qualifications and is allowed to own subchapter S stock.

Quitclaim Deed—Document that allows you to transfer title to real estate. With a quitclaim deed, the person transferring the title makes no guarantees, but transfers all of his/her interest in the property.

Real Property—Land and property that is permanently attached to land (like a building or a house).

Recorded Deed—A deed that has been filed with the county land records. This creates a public record of all changes in ownership of property in the state.

Revocable Trust—A trust in which the person setting it up retains the power to change (revoke) or cancel the trust during his/her lifetime. Opposite of irrevocable trust.

Required Beginning Date (RBD)—The date you must begin taking required minimum distributions from your tax-deferred plans. Usually, it is April 1 of the calendar year following the calendar year in which you turn age 70 1/2. If your money is in an employer plan, you may be able to delay your RBD beyond this date if you continue working, providing you are not a 5% (or greater) owner of the company.

Required Minimum Distribution (RMD)—The amount you are required to withdraw each year from your tax-deferred plan after you reach your Required Beginning Date. This amount is determined by dividing the year-end value of your tax-deferred account by a life expectancy divisor provided by the IRS.

Separate Property—Generally, all assets you acquire prior to marriage and assets acquired by gift or inheritance during marriage.

Separate Trust—A trust established by one person. A married couple has separate trusts if each spouse has his/her own trust with its own assets. In contrast, see "Common Trust."

Settle an Estate—The process of handling the final affairs (valuation of assets, payment of debts and taxes, distribution of assets to beneficiaries) after someone dies.

Settlor—See "Grantor."

Special Gifts—A separate listing of special assets that will go to specific individuals or organizations after your incapacity or death. Also called special bequests.

Special Needs Trust—Allows you to provide for a loved one with special needs without interfering with government benefits.

Spendthrift Clause—Protects assets in a trust from a beneficiary's creditors.

Spouse—Husband or wife.

Stepped-up Basis—Assets are given a new basis when transferred by inheritance (through a will or trust) and are re-valued as of the date of the owner's death. If an asset has appreciated above its basis (what the owner paid for it), the new basis is called a stepped-up basis. A stepped-up basis can save a considerable amount in capital gains tax when an asset is later sold by the new owner. Also see "Basis."

Subchapter S Corporation Stock—Stock in a corporation which has chosen to be subject to the rules of subchapter S of the Internal Revenue Code.

Surviving Spouse—The spouse who is living after one spouse has died.

Survivor's Trust—See "A Trust."

Successor Trustee—Person or institution named in the trust document who will take over should the first trustee die, resign, or otherwise become unable to act.

Tax-Deferred Plan—A retirement savings plan (like an IRA, 401(k), pension, profit sharing, or Keogh) that qualifies for special income tax treatment. The contributions made to the plan and subsequent appreciation of the assets are not taxed until they are withdrawn at a later time—ideally, at retirement, when your income and tax rate are lower.

Taxable Gift—Generally, a gift of more than $15,000 in one year to someone other than your spouse. (This amount is tied to inflation and may increase from time to time.) Under current law, the value of the gift is applied to your federal gift/estate tax exemption, and no gift tax is required to be paid until the exemption has been exhausted.

Tenants-in-Common—A form of joint ownership in which two or more persons own the same property. At the death of a tenant-in-common, his/her share transfers to his/her heirs.

Tenants-by-the Entirety—A form of joint ownership in some states between husband and wife. When one spouse dies, his/her share of the asset automatically transfers to the surviving spouse.

Testamentary Trust—A trust in a will. Can only go into effect at death. Does not avoid probate.

Testate—One who dies with a valid will.

Title—Document proving ownership of an asset.

Transfer Tax—Tax on assets when they are transferred to another. The estate tax, gift tax, and generation-skipping transfer tax are all transfer taxes.

Trust—An entity that holds assets for the benefit of certain other persons or entities.

Trust Company—Institution that specializes in managing trusts. Also called corporate trustee.

Trustee—Person or institution who manages and distributes another's assets according to the instructions in the trust document.

Trustor—See "Grantor."

Totten Trust—A "pay-on-death" account. A bank account that will transfer to the beneficiary who was named when the account was established. The terms transfer on death (TOD), in trust for (ITF), as Trustee for (ATF), and pay on death (POD) often appear in the title.

Unified Credit—The amount each person is allowed to deduct from federal estate taxes that would be due if there were no estate tax exemption. For example, in 2019, the credit is $4,560,000 and is equal to a 40% tax on the first $11,400,000 of a taxable estate.

Uniform Transfer to Minors Act (UTMA)—Law enacted in many states that lets you leave assets to a minor by appointing a custodian. In most states, the minor receives the assets at legal age.

Unfunded—Your living trust is unfunded if you have not transferred assets into it.

Warranty Deed—Document that allows you to transfer title to real estate. With a warranty deed, the person guarantees that the title being transferred is clear (free of any encumbrances). If the title is defective, the person making the transfer is liable. Compare to quitclaim deed.

Will—A written document with instructions for disposing of assets after death. A will can only be enforced through the probate court.

INDEX

Here's how you can order additional copies of *Understanding Living Trusts*® at special savings...

...and share with your friends and loved ones the peace of mind and financial security a living trust offers.

1 If you received *Understanding Living Trusts*® from a professional, ask how you can get additional copies.

2 Check with your local bookstore. (They can order additional copies if they are sold out.)

3 Order directly from us by using the "Special Savings Certificate" below. (Please order single copies from Amazon or your local bookstore and help us build visibility. Reviews, especially positive ones, are greatly appreciated!)

- -

Special Savings Certificate

☑ **YES**, I want to purchase additional copies of *Understanding Living Trusts*® and share with my friends and loved ones the peace of mind and financial security a living trust offers. *30-day Money-Back Guarantee.*

SAVE $7.00 EACH

QTY	Price per book	Shipping/Handling	Total (circle)
2	$24.95	$4.00	$53.90
3	$22.95	$5.00	$73.85
4	$22.95	$6.00	$97.80
CA residents add 8.00% sales tax			.
Total of payment enclosed			$.

SHIP TO:

Please print clearly. No P.O. Boxes.

Mr./Mrs./Ms. _____

Company _____

Address _____ Apt./Suite _____

City   State   Zip

Telephone/Email _____

METHOD OF PAYMENT: ☐ Check enclosed

☐ Mastercard *MasterCard*   ☐ Discover *DISCOVER*

☐ VISA *VISA*   ☐ American Express *AMERICAN EXPRESS*

Account # _____ Exp. Date _____

Signature _____ Billing Zip Code _____

MAIL THIS CERTIFICATE AND PAYMENT TO:

Schumacher Publishing, LLC
P. O. Box 2065
Costa Mesa, CA 92628-2065

OR FAX TO: 714-908-0330
OR CALL TOLL-FREE

1-800-827-7941 ext.11

(M-F, 7 am-5 pm, Pacific Time)

Please allow 2-3 weeks for delivery. Larger quantity discounts are available. Call or email info@SchumacherPublishing.com for information.

ULT 2019

Was *Understanding Living Trusts*® helpful for you and your family?

Help us reach others by writing a review on Amazon.com!

It's actually very easy to do:

1 ❯ **Go to** SchumacherPublishing.com/Consumers

2 ❯ **Click** on the "Purchase Book at Amazon.com" button.

3 ❯ **Scroll** down to where the reviews are listed (toward the bottom).

4 ❯ **Click** on the button to write a review.

5 ❯ **Select** a star rating.

6 ❯ **Write** your review, then press the "Submit" button.

Understanding Living Trusts: How You Can Avoid Probate, Save Taxes and Enjoy Peace of Mind
Vickie Schumacher

⭐⭐⭐⭐⭐   ✓ Posted publicly as Amazon Customer | Clear

Insert product link   What's this? ▼

Best Book I've ever bought!

Made in the USA
Middletown, DE
07 July 2019